Move Beyond 1

TEACHER'S EDITION PACK

macmillan education

Anna Cole
David Corp
Alexandra Hearn

ENGLISH CLASS

Grammar (2): *This/that/these/those*, plurals, object pronouns

Vocabulary (2): Classroom things, colors, the alphabet
PRONOUNCE the /i/ sound

LISTENING & VOCABULARY	GRAMMAR (2)	LANGUAGE & BEYOND	SPEAKING	WRITING
Meet my family ***Listen for the main ideas*** **Vocabulary (2):** Family	*Have* ***Talk about relationships and possessions***	Communicate & cooperate ***Understand different ways to say "hello"***	How do I get there? ***Ask for and give directions***	Hello from Cartagena (e-postcard) ***Use correct punctuation***
Let me show you around ***Use sounds to help you understand*** **Vocabulary (2):** Furniture and other things in the home	Simple present with adverbs of frequency ***Talk about how often you do things***	Get organized ***Organize your things***	When's the next one? ***Ask for and tell the time when you travel***	My favorite room (description) ***Use also and too***
Dress code ***Listen for specific information*** **Vocabulary (2):** Clothes and accessories PRONOUNCE The /oʊ/ sound	Possessive *'s*, *whose*, and possessive pronouns ***Talk about possessions and relationships***	Know yourself ***Understand your learning style***	What are they like? ***Describe people***	Things we do and like (questionnaire) ***Use and, or, and but***
Soundscape ***Identify the type of audio*** **Vocabulary (2):** Places in public buildings	Present progressive and simple present ***Talk about how often you do things***	Get thinking ***Find ideas and information***	At the tourist information office ***Ask for information***	School concert (flier) ***Use headings***
Food for the brain ***Identify the speaker*** **Vocabulary (2):** Lifestyle adjectives	*Like + -ing* ***Talk about your likes and dislikes***	Respect others ***Follow the rules in electronic communication***	I don't believe it! ***React to news***	My favorite meal (description) ***Use because***

IRREGULAR VERBS page 74

EXTRAS pages 75–76

CONTENTS

WELCOME TO THE *MOVE BEYOND* TEACHER'S EDITION

Move Beyond is an exciting eight-level course for teenagers, covering CEFR levels from A1+ to B2. Its scope and sequence is meticulously mapped to the CEFR and international exams. The course offers comprehensive coverage of the four language skills through the incremental and cumulative development of subskills. It equips students with transferable linguistic strategies to use in the English classroom and beyond. The inclusion of age-appropriate 21st-century skills adds an inspiring new dimension to language teaching. The life skills lessons create a learning environment that's relevant and accessible to teenagers.

The course is flexible and works in a number of teaching contexts. Lessons are clearly labeled so that you can choose to prioritize material that's relevant in your teaching contexts. The extensive online materials present you with a variety of teaching and practice alternatives to enrich the learning experience.

With eight levels, your school's needs can be met with one single course – be it for streaming, multilevel entry or a program that takes your students from A1+ all the way up to B2.

The material has a creative and dynamic approach to topics that motivates students and makes language learning more meaningful and successful. Units provide constant opportunities for students to express themselves, while the pages are brought to life through a series of specially produced videos. Throughout the course, language is recycled and reviewed, allowing students to assess and consolidate their progress.

The course's combination of language skills, life skills, and motivating material prepares students for success in and beyond the classroom.

A message from the authors

"Secondary teaching is a rewarding but demanding profession. With this course we have tried to make your role as a teacher as easy as possible. The material is clearly organized and can be taught with little or no preparation time. We have also provided resources to help you test and evaluate progress, review material, and work with mixed-ability classes.

Having enthusiastic and interested students also makes the teaching role easier, so throughout the creation of this series we have considered the teenagers' perspective on learning and come up with materials that teach them about the world and allow them to express their view of the world.

When producing the course, we used the following key principles to guide our writing."

10 KEY PRINCIPLES OF *MOVE BEYOND*

1 Subskills: learning how to read, listen, speak, and write

All reading, listening, speaking, and writing lessons have an integrated subskills focus that teaches students linguistic strategies to maximize their learning. This comprehensive subskills syllabus is a key part of the literacy development objective of *Move Beyond*.

2 Life skills: learning for life

To be successful in school and in life, students need to learn skills that go beyond pure academic knowledge. In order to thrive in today's global market, they need to become aware of and acquire a range of life skills, such as learning to deal with stress, communicating effectively, and understanding different cultures. One lesson in every unit is dedicated to developing a life skill under one of five umbrella headings: Get organized, Get thinking, Respect others, Know yourself, and Communicate & cooperate.

3 Original content and striking images

The cross-curricular focus of *Move Beyond* helps students learn about the world around them, and the original material sustains students' interest. The striking images create a strong visual impact and engage students with the content.

4 Varied and adaptable approach

Move Beyond provides adaptations for students' differing learning styles and levels. There are ideas and prompts for students who need more help and a varied approach to dealing with topics and language. To help with differentiation in the classroom, the Teacher's Edition suggests alternative procedures for stronger or weaker students and for fast finishers.

5 Clear and easy to use

All lessons in *Move Beyond* are easy to teach directly from the page. Goals and stages are clearly marked so that teachers can quickly see the objectives and structure of each lesson.

6 Opportunities for personalization

Throughout the course, students are encouraged to relate what they have learned to their own experiences. This personal investment in the course is motivating and rewarding, and makes the learning process more memorable and the content more relevant.

7 Strong communication focus

In *Move Beyond*, the pairwork discussions, functional speaking tasks, presentations, and variety of writing tasks all encourage students to engage in meaningful and real communication.

8 Language in context

All new language in *Move Beyond* is contextualized so that students can see its function and form in realistic situations before studying the rules.

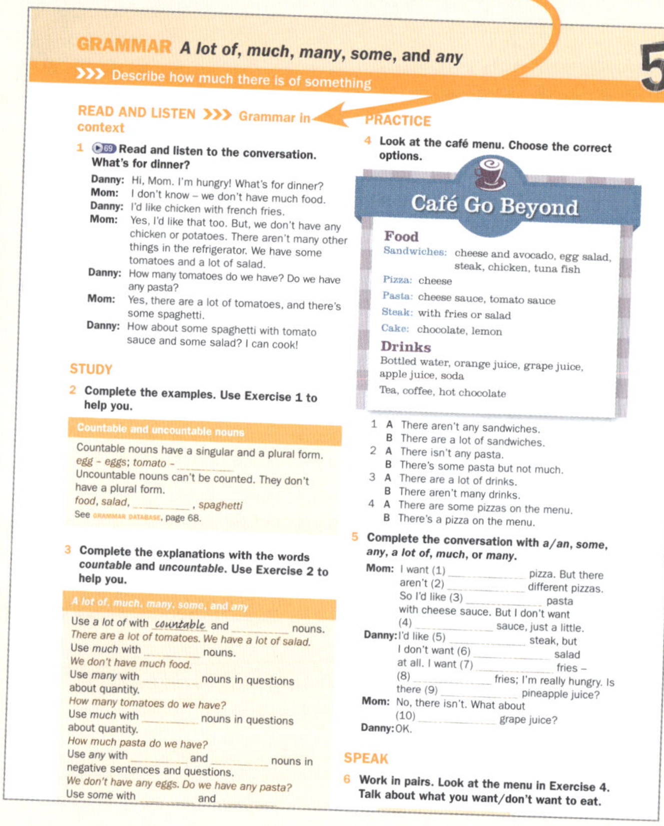

GRAMMAR *A lot of, much, many, some, and any* **5**

>>> Describe how much there is of something

READ AND LISTEN >>> Grammar in context

1 (69) **Read and listen to the conversation. What's for dinner?**

Danny: Hi, Mom. I'm hungry! What's for dinner?
Mom: I don't know – we don't have much food.
Danny: I'd like chicken with french fries.
Mom: Yes, I'd like that too. But, we don't have any chicken or potatoes. There aren't many other things in the refrigerator. We have some tomatoes and a lot of salad.
Danny: How many tomatoes do we have? Do we have any pasta?
Mom: Yes, there are a lot of tomatoes, and there's some spaghetti.
Danny: How about some spaghetti with tomato sauce and some salad? I can cook!

STUDY

2 **Complete the examples. Use Exercise 1 to help you.**

Countable and uncountable nouns

Countable nouns have a singular and a plural form.
egg – eggs; tomato – ________
Uncountable nouns can't be counted. They don't have a plural form.
food, salad, ________, spaghetti
See GRAMMAR DATABASE, page 68.

3 **Complete the explanations with the words *countable* and *uncountable*. Use Exercise 2 to help you.**

A lot of, much, many, some, and any

Use *a lot of* with countable and ________ nouns.
There are a lot of tomatoes. We have a lot of salad.
Use *much* with ________ nouns.
We don't have much food.
Use *many* with ________ nouns in questions about quantity.
How many tomatoes do we have?
Use *much* with ________ nouns in questions about quantity.
How much pasta do we have?
Use *any* with ________ and ________ nouns in negative sentences and questions.
We don't have any eggs. Do we have any pasta?
Use *some* with ________ and ________

PRACTICE

4 **Look at the café menu. Choose the correct options.**

Café Go Beyond

Food
Sandwiches: cheese and avocado, egg salad, steak, chicken, tuna fish
Pizza: cheese
Pasta: cheese sauce, tomato sauce
Steak: with fries or salad
Cake: chocolate, lemon

Drinks
Bottled water, orange juice, grape juice, apple juice, soda
Tea, coffee, hot chocolate

1 A There aren't any sandwiches.
B There are a lot of sandwiches.
2 A There isn't any pasta.
B There's some pasta but not much.
3 A There are a lot of drinks.
B There aren't many drinks.
4 A There are some pizzas on the menu.
B There's a pizza on the menu.

5 **Complete the conversation with *a/an, some, any, a lot of, much,* or *many*.**

Mom: I want (1) ________ pizza. But there aren't (2) ________ different pizzas. So I'd like (3) ________ pasta with cheese sauce. But I don't want (4) ________ sauce, just a little.
Danny: I'd like (5) ________ steak, but I don't want (6) ________ salad at all. I want (7) ________ fries – (8) ________ fries; I'm really hungry. Is there (9) ________ pineapple juice?
Mom: No, there isn't. What about (10) ________ grape juice?
Danny: OK.

SPEAK

6 **Work in pairs. Look at the menu in Exercise 4. Talk about what you want/don't want to eat.**

9 Learner autonomy

Students are encouraged to work independently in a variety of ways, from a carefully guided inductive approach to grammar to self-study worksheets in the Student's Resource Center. This approach makes learning more memorable and supports learner autonomy.

10 Flexible multimedia material

Move Beyond can be used by teachers with limited or no access to technology. But for those wanting to use technology, both inside and outside the classroom, the course includes a projectable digital version of the Student's Book as well as a large bank of additional materials and tests in the Online Teacher's Resource Center. Every *Move Beyond* unit contains an original video to supplement the opening lesson.

"We hope you enjoy teaching with *Move Beyond* and that your students enjoy learning with it. We wish you a successful and productive academic year.

The Move Beyond Team"

Lesson 1 – In the picture

> The first two pages are a single **vocabulary** lesson that serves as an introduction to the unit and its central theme.

Unit themes appeal to teenagers and provide interesting, unusual, and informative material.

1 The lesson starts with a Recall exercise that activates prior knowledge of vocabulary. Recall words are listed in the Words & Beyond section at the back of the book, where students learn and practice a related Vocabulary Tip.

2 New vocabulary is clearly visible in a word box and is presented and practiced with the support of the images on the pages. Lexical sets are recorded for ease of presentation. Once introduced, vocabulary is recycled throughout the unit and reviewed in the Unit Review and every two units in a Progress Check.

UNIT 5 IT'S GOOD FOR YOU!

IN THE PICTURE Food and drink

>>> Talk about food and drink

WORK WITH WORDS Food and drink

1 RECALL **Work in pairs. Look at the words and cross out the wrong word in each group. Can you say why it's different? You have one minute.**

1 bottled water, ~~fish~~, juice, coffee
The other words are drinks.
2 banana, egg, apple, orange
3 pizza, salad, bread, sandwich
4 milk, rice, cheese, ice cream
5 steak, pasta, burger, chicken

2 a **Work in pairs. Look at the pictures (1–14) on Dan's blog. Write the names of the food and drinks in the box under Dan's picture.**

beef butter cake candy carrot chips chocolate french fries onion potato soda soup tomato yogurt

b 64 **Dan is showing his blog to his new friend Myra. Listen and complete or check your answers from Exercise 2a.**

c 65 **Listen and repeat the food and drink words.**

3 a 66 PRONOUNCE **Listen to the words.**

1 How many syllables are there?
2 Underline the stress. Which words have the same stress?

potato tomato banana fantastic seventeen

b 67 **Listen again and repeat.**

4 **Look at the words in Exercise 2a. Find …**

1 something red ....
2 two vegetables ....
3 something with eggs in it ....
4 two white foods ....
5 a drink ....
6 something you put on bread ....
7 something you can eat or drink ....
8 something children (and some adults!) like ....

5 **Work in pairs. Describe what the boy is doing and eating in each picture. Are the food and activities healthy or unhealthy?**

6 THE MOVING PICTURE **Watch the video. What food do you see?**

SEARCH

#lifestyle
#food
#greenliving
#health
#recipes

1 ....
2 ....
3 ....
4 ....
5 ....
6 ....
7 ....
8 ....
9 ....
10 ....
11 ....
12 ....
13 ....
14 ....

PHRASE BYTES

In picture 1 he's eating / having …

It's healthy / unhealthy to …

It's OK to eat … sometimes, but …

52

Teen Blog #food

LOGIN SIGN UP

5

The unit opener is supported by a video that brings the pages to life. Audio and video are located in the Presentation Kit for ease of access in the classroom and easily available for students on the DVD-ROM.

3 The Moving Picture feature on the opening pages brings a dynamic element to the spread by introducing a video and an accompanying task connected to the lesson.

SPEAK

7 a **Work in pairs. Take the survey. Ask your partner the questions and write his/her answers.**

HEALTHY AND HAPPY SURVEY

1 How do you get to school?
A I walk or ride my bike. ◯ B I take the bus. ◯ C My parents take me in the car. ◯

2 How often do you play sports?
A often ◯ B sometimes ◯ C never ◯

3 How often do you eat chips or candy?
A not very often ◯ B sometimes ◯ C most days ◯

b **Check your partner's answers on page 76. Read out loud what the survey says. Does your partner agree?**

MOVE BEYOND
Do the Words & Beyond exercise on page 73.

Workbook, page 132

53

4 The Move Beyond extras provide material for fast finishers, homework, or additional class activities. The boxes refer students to the additional exercises on the Words & Beyond pages at the end of the Student's Book section.

5 The final exercises consolidate language with communicative activities in a personalized context.

Lesson 2 – Reading

> After the double-page opening spread, each individual page is one complete lesson. The **reading** and **listening** lessons include an integrated but explicit subskills focus, designed to teach students how to read and listen successfully to a variety of text types over the course of a level.

1 The first exercise gives students the opportunity to say what they know or think about the topic of the lesson. This increases confidence and helps students focus on the lesson.

2 Students read a variety of text types and learn the subskills they need to deal successfully with each genre. Reading texts include unusual and original perspectives on familiar topics.

3 The HOW TO box provides tips for applying the subskill. Students read the tips, carry out a related task, and then reflect on which tips they used to complete the task.

4 The React exercises encourage students to share opinions on the text and relate to it in a personal way.

5 The Move Beyond task provides a further activity related to the content of the reading text.

Subskills are clearly identified.

All texts are recorded to provide extra classroom and self-study opportunities.

Reading texts contain contextualized examples of the grammar point of the next lesson.

There are links to the corresponding Workbook pages (that can be found at the end of the Student's Book) at the bottom of each page.

READING What's for lunch?

>>> Identify who a text is for

SPEAK AND READ

1 a **Work in pairs. Look at the photos of school lunch in different countries. Describe what you can see in each photo.**

b **Which lunch would you like to eat? Why?**

2 a **Read the tips in the HOW TO box.**

b 68 **Read the text and identify who the text is for.**

A parents B students C teachers D school cooks

PHRASE BYTES

There's … there …
Th… a kind of veg…
I think that's …
I don't know what that is.

HOW TO

identify who a text is for

- Identify the type of text (see page 10).
- Read the first few lines and underline important words.
- Decide who the readers are (teenagers/adults/experts).

Park School Blog

Lunch around the world

Our class is doing a project about kids' lunches around the world. Read other students' descriptions and add a description of your typical lunch. Don't forget to send a photo!

Mikkel, Denmark
All students here take a packed lunch to school. I usually have brown bread with cheese and salad and an apple. We can't take any unhealthy food like chips, candy, or soda.

Jalissa, USA
We eat lunch at school. We usually have things like tacos, pizza, or burgers. We always get milk or juice and some vegetables or fruit.

Dae-Ho, Korea
I like the food at my school, but we don't get many different things. We usually have soup, some vegetables with rice, and a lot of salad. We don't eat much meat.

Mathilde, France
At my school, we have salad or a vegetable dish, and then meat with sauce and potatoes or fish with lemon. My favorite is mussels with fries. Then we have yogurt or some cheese, and after that we have dessert.

Camila, Ecuador
We don't eat lunch at school, so I have lunch at home with my family after school. We usually have soup and then rice with vegetables and chicken, beef, or fish.

3 **Which tips in the HOW TO box did you use for help with Exercise 2b? Check (✓) them.**

4 **Read the descriptions again. Which lunches have no meat or not much meat? Which lunch has dessert?**

REACT

5 **Work in pairs. Tell your partner about your typical lunch. Then describe your dream lunch.**

MOVE BEYOND

Write a school lunch menu for two days.

54

Workbook, page 133

> The target **grammar** is always presented in context, and students are encouraged to figure out rules from examples.

GRAMMAR *A lot of, much, many, some,* and *any* 5

>>> Describe how much there is of something

READ AND LISTEN >>> Grammar in context

1 69 **Read and listen to the conversation. What's for dinner?**

Danny: Hi, Mom. I'm hungry! What's for dinner?
Mom: I don't know – we don't have much food.
Danny: I'd like chicken with french fries.
Mom: Yes, I'd like that too. But, we don't have any chicken or potatoes. There aren't many other things in the refrigerator. We have some tomatoes and a lot of salad.
Danny: How many tomatoes do we have? Do we have any pasta?
Mom: Yes, there are a lot of tomatoes, and there's some spaghetti.
Danny: How about some spaghetti with tomato sauce and some salad? I can cook!

STUDY

2 Complete the examples. Use Exercise 1 to help you.

Countable and uncountable nouns

Countable nouns have a singular and a plural form.
egg – eggs; tomato – ________
Uncountable nouns can't be counted. They don't have a plural form.
food, salad, ________ *, spaghetti*
See GRAMMAR DATABASE, page 68.

3 Complete the explanations with the words *countable* and *uncountable*. Use Exercise 2 to help you.

A lot of, much, many, some,* and *any

Use *a lot of* with *countable* and ________ nouns.
There are a lot of tomatoes. We have a lot of salad.
Use *much* with ________ nouns.
We don't have much food.
Use *many* with ________ nouns in questions about quantity.
How many tomatoes do we have?
Use *much* with ________ nouns in questions about quantity.
How much pasta do we have?
Use *any* with ________ and ________ nouns in negative sentences and questions.
We don't have any eggs. Do we have any pasta?
Use *some* with ________ and ________ nouns in affirmative sentences, questions, and suggestions.
We have some tomatoes. What about some spaghetti?
See GRAMMAR DATABASE, page 68.

PRACTICE

4 Look at the café menu. Choose the correct options.

Café Go Beyond

Food
Sandwiches: cheese and avocado, egg salad, steak, chicken, tuna fish
Pizza: cheese
Pasta: cheese sauce, tomato sauce
Steak: with fries or salad
Cake: chocolate, lemon

Drinks
Bottled water, orange juice, grape juice, apple juice, soda
Tea, coffee, hot chocolate

1 A There aren't any sandwiches.
B There are a lot of sandwiches.
2 A There isn't any pasta.
B There's some pasta but not much.
3 A There are a lot of drinks.
B There aren't many drinks.
4 A There are some pizzas on the menu.
B There's a pizza on the menu.

5 Complete the conversation with *a/an, some, any, a lot of, much,* or *many*.

Mom: I want (1) ________ pizza. But there aren't (2) ________ different pizzas. So I'd like (3) ________ pasta with cheese sauce. But I don't want (4) ________ sauce, just a little.
Danny: I'd like (5) ________ steak, but I don't want (6) ________ salad at all. I want (7) ________ fries – (8) ________ fries; I'm really hungry. Is there (9) ________ pineapple juice?
Mom: No, there isn't. What about (10) ________ grape juice?
Danny: OK.

SPEAK

6 Work in pairs. Look at the menu in Exercise 4. Talk about what you want/don't want to eat.

I want a chicken sandwich.
There isn't any salad, so I'd like a cheese and avocado sandwich.
I don't want any fries.
There aren't many kinds of cake.
I'd like some chocolate cake.

>>> Workbook, pages 134–135

55

1 Target grammar is always presented in context. Students either read or read and listen to a conversation or short text that expands on the theme of the unit.

2 In the Study section, students are guided to notice grammar structures from the text and then to complete explanations or examples in the Study box.

3 The target grammar is practiced in a controlled but meaningful context that often also provides opportunities for personalization.

4 Practice exercises start with more controlled task types and then become progressively freer, preparing students to talk about their own lives and experiences in the Speak or Write and Speak exercise at the end of the lesson.

5 The final tasks focus on speaking and/or writing for accuracy of the target structure within a communicative context.

Lesson 4 – Listening and Vocabulary

> **Listening comprehension tasks are designed to support understanding and not to test. They progress from a focus on global understanding to an understanding of specific details. The exercises are designed to give practice in a specific listening subskill. Students are always asked to react personally to what they hear.**

1 As on the Reading page, the first exercise ensures that students access their relevant knowledge and experiences before they listen.

2 The HOW TO box provides tips that help students focus on the subskill.

3 Listening texts contain contextualized examples of the grammar point of the next lesson, allowing students to hear the language in context before looking at it in depth.

4 The React exercise encourages students to give their personal opinions about the listening text.

5 In the Work with Words section, students focus on the second lexical set of the unit. In some units the Work with Words section comes before the listening section in order to introduce new target vocabulary first.

6 The Move Beyond task allows students to do a further task related to the new vocabulary set.

LISTENING AND VOCABULARY Food for the brain

>>> Identify the speaker

SPEAK AND LISTEN

1 **Take a class survey about how many hours you sleep.**

- One person asks: *Who sleeps for six hours? Who sleeps for seven hours?*, and so on.
- Raise your hand.
- One person writes the results on the board: *six hours: five people ...*

2 a **Read the tips in the HOW TO box.**

b **70 Listen to four speakers in a radio report about sleep. Who are they?**

I think Speaker 1 is a teacher ...

HOW TO
identify the speaker
- ☐ Listen to the voice. Is the speaker young or old?
- ☐ Listen for the general topic.
- ☐ Listen carefully for the names of people and places.

3 **Which tips in the HOW TO box did you use for help with Exercise 2b? Check (✓) them.**

4 **70 Listen again. There's one question for each speaker. Choose A, B, or C.**

1 How do the students look in class?

A B C

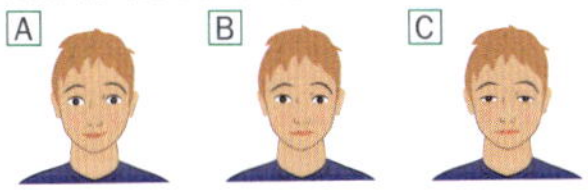

2 What time does the speaker get up?

A B C

3 How do teens feel when they don't sleep enough?

A B C

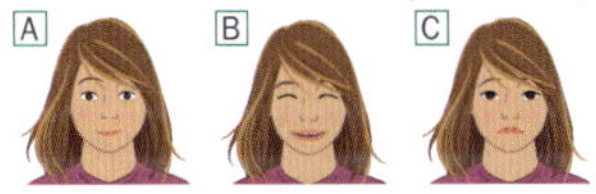

4 How many hours of sleep does a teenager need?

A $8–8\frac{1}{2}$ B $8\frac{1}{2}–9$ C $9–9\frac{1}{2}$

REACT

5 **Work in pairs. Answer the questions.**

1 Do you sleep enough? 2 Look at your class sleep times on the board. Does everybody sleep enough?

WORK WITH WORDS Lifestyle adjectives

6 a **71 Match the words (a–j) to the quotes (1–10). Then listen and check.**

1 "I have a lot of energy and interests."
2 "My body's healthy, and I get a lot of exercise."
3 "I need to sleep now."
4 "I have a lot of things to do."
5 "Good things always happen to me."
6 "I don't feel happy."
7 "I feel bad because I have a lot of things to do."
8 "I feel good."
9 "I have a health problem."
10 "I never want to do anything."

a tired
b lucky
c busy
d active
e healthy
f sick
g lazy
h stressed
i unhappy
j well

b **72 Listen again and repeat.**

7 **Work in pairs. Answer the questions.**

1 Do you feel healthy and well?
2 Are you often tired? Why?
3 Are you stressed? Why?

MOVE BEYOND
Do the Words & Beyond exercise on page 73.

56

Workbook, pages 134–135

> The second grammar lesson follows the same structure as the first grammar lesson of the unit – see page 13.

GRAMMAR *Like + -ing* 5

>>> Talk about your likes and dislikes

READ >>> Grammar in context

1 Read Marc's likes and dislikes. Do you like and dislike these things?

WHAT DO YOU LIKE DOING OR HATE DOING, AND WHY?
WRITE YOUR TOP 3!

MY TOP 3 LIKES
I love being with friends.
I enjoy riding my bike.
I like running, swimming, and other sports.

MY TOP 3 DISLIKES
I hate studying for tests.
I dislike cleaning my room.
I don't like physics
(because I'm bad at it).

STUDY

2 Complete the examples. Use Exercise 1 to help you.

Like + verb + *-ing*

Use the verb *like* to talk about your likes and dislikes.

Verbs to talk about your likes are ________, *enjoy*, *love*.

Verbs to talk about your dislikes are ________, *dislike*, *hate*.

Use verbs for likes and dislikes with a noun.
I like sports. I ________ *physics.*

Use verbs for likes and dislikes with a verb + *-ing*.
I ________ *running. I dislike* ________ *my room.*

See GRAMMAR DATABASE, page 68.

3 Write the correct spelling of the *-ing* form. Look at Exercise 1.

1 be ________ 4 write ________
2 study ________ 5 run ________
3 ride ________ 6 swim ________

>>> Workbook, page 136

PRACTICE

4 a Complete Susie13's reply on the forum Use the *-ing* form of the verbs.

MY TOP 3 LIKES
I enjoy (1) ________ (play) online video games with my friends.
I like (2) ________ (travel) and (3) ________ (visit) new places.
I love (4) ________ (dance) and other activities.

MY TOP 3 DISLIKES
I don't like (5) ________ (get) up early.
I hate (6) ________ (wait) for things.
I don't like (7) ________ (keep) my room neat or (8) ________ (make) my bed.

b What do Susie13 and Marc both like? What do they both dislike?

5 Complete the sentences with your top three likes and dislikes.

1 I like ________.
2 I enjoy ________.
3 I love ________.

4 I don't like ________.
5 I dislike ________.
6 I hate ________.

6 a Write the questions.

1 you / like / go / to school?
Do you like going to school?
2 you / enjoy / speak / English?
3 you / like / use social networking sites?
4 you enjoy / meet / new people?
5 you / like / cook?
6 you / like / shop for clothes?

b Write one more question for a partner.

SPEAK

7 Work in pairs. Ask your partner a question from Exercise 6. Then ask *Why?* or *Why not?*

Do you like going to school?
Yes, I do.
Why?
I see my friends there.

57

> Target vocabulary is recycled throughout the unit.

> When applicable, a pronunciation section focuses on misunderstandings that commonly occur when English is used between speakers of different first languages. Pronunciation sections can appear in any lesson, depending on the content, and focus on key sounds and stress patterns in words and sentences.

> Students are given frequent opportunities to talk about themselves and to express their views.

> The Grammar Database is a useful reference section where all the grammar points of the level are covered in further detail. You can find additional tips and suggestions for using the Grammar Database in the Teacher's Resource Center.

Lesson 6 – Language & Beyond

> The **Language & Beyond** page is the life skills lesson. The goal of these lessons is to equip students with the necessary transferable skills for life beyond the classroom, especially in college and in the workplace. The life skills lessons are grouped under five umbrella headings: Know yourself, Get organized, Get thinking, Respect others, and Communicate & cooperate.

1 A wide range of texts and images is used to raise students' awareness of a particular issue or challenge in their everyday lives. In the first stage, they read or read and listen to texts or conversations about situations that are common to teenagers everywhere.

2 Students are then directed to carry out a practical task in the Do stage. Often working in small groups, they put themselves in the situation described and think about what they would do.

3 The Reflection Point feature encourages students to pause and think about what they've just done and guides them toward drawing their own conclusions.

4 The life skills in *Move Beyond* are transferable to other situations and contexts. The exercises in the Extend section enable students to apply the skills they have learned to a realistic situation, in this way building a bridge from the classroom to real life.

»» Follow the rules in electronic communication

RESPECT OTHERS

SPEAK AND READ

1 **Work in pairs. How often do you do the ... Tell a partner.**

- send text messages on my phon...
- write instant messages (IMs) to my frie...
- send emails
- write comments on an internet forum
- write comments on social networking sites

Working with other students is a key part of the life skills lesson.

2 **Read the situations (1–3). How do you feel if they happen to you? Tell a partner.**

DO

3 **Match four rules to the situations in Exercise 2. Which one is a good rule for all the situations?**

a Everything you write on the internet stays on the internet. ____
b Can't say it face-to-face? Don't write it. ____
c Ask before you share information or photos of other people. ____
d Don't write things when you're tired or stressed. ____
e Think before you send a message or put something on the internet. ____

REFLECT

4 **Talk about the questions. Then read the REFLECTION POINT.**

1 You want to say something important to a friend. Is it a good idea to say it ...
face-to-face / by phone / by text message / on the internet? Why?
2 How often do you or your friends have problems like the situations in Exercise 2?
3 What can you do if others send you hate messages?

EXTEND

5 **Work in small groups. Write two or three more rules for electronic communication.**

How do you feel?

1 You get a text message on your phone from a friend. It starts *"Hi, Joe. Jim is so lazy! I hate lazy people! ..."* But Jim is your name – Joe is another friend. You get the message by mistake.

2 You write ... on your ... next day ... still on th... search.

3 You put ... of a frien... networking page. Th...ext day your friend calls – ...d your friend doesn't th...k it's funny.

Useful phrases help students discuss issues and carry out tasks in English.

PHRASE BYTES

I feel angry / sad / silly.
I feel bad / awful because I ...
I think it's rude / a bad idea to ...

REFLECTION POINT

Be polite on the internet and in text messages. Think before you send a message or put something on the internet. Remember: always tell the website or your parents about hate messages or problems.

58

»» Workbook, page 141

USING THE *MOVE BEYOND* STUDENT'S BOOK

Lesson 7 – Speaking

> Using real-life scenarios, the **Speaking** page provides students with the language they need to communicate effectively in a range of everyday situations. Each speaking lesson helps students develop a specific speaking subskill. Every Speaking page features an audio track of teens using the new language in context.

SPEAKING I don't believe it! 5

>>> React to news

SPEAK

1 **Work in pairs. Look at the photos. Who do you think is receiving …**

- good news?
- bad news?
- surprising news?

1

LISTEN

2 73 **Listen to the conversations. Check your answers from Exercise 1. What's the news?**

1
Beth: No more fries from fast food places for me!
Kevin: Really? I don't (1) __________ it!
Beth: Do you know that they put sugar on fries?
Kevin: Seriously?! That's (2) __________ !

2
Elaine: My grandma's in the hospital.
Paula: Oh, I'm (3) __________ , Elaine. That's terrible.
Elaine: Yeah, she's really sick.
Paula: That's so (4) __________ !

3
Sam: Guess what! Tomorrow we have two extra PE classes. No math test!
Liz: Really? Wow! (5) __________ !
Sam: I know – no math test!
Liz: That's (6) __________ !

2

3
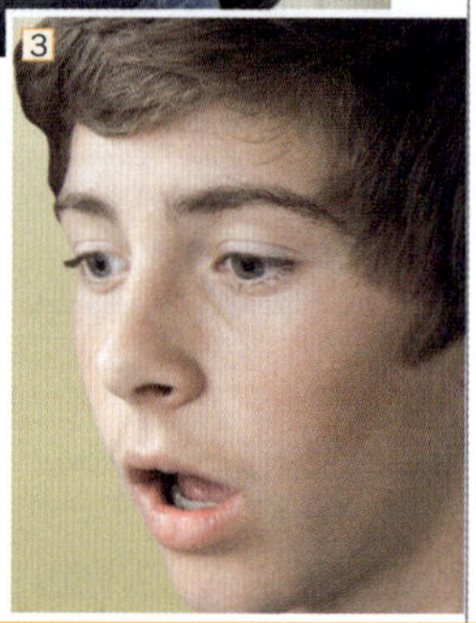

3 a 73 **Listen again. Complete the conversations with the words in the box.**

amazing believe fantastic great sad sorry

b 74 **Listen to the phrases and check.**

4 75 **Listen and repeat all the phrases in the PHRASEBOOK.**

ACT

5 a **Work in pairs and take turns reacting.**

- Choose a situation from the box.
- Give the news to your partner.
- Your partner reacts.
- Choose another situation and repeat.

You're moving to a different town.
You have a new baby brother.
You don't want to eat candy anymore.
You're in a new TV show.
Your school is closing.
Your dog is sick.

b **Think of two new situations. Give your partner the news. React to your partner's news.**

PHRASEBOOK 76

React to good news
Great!
That's fantastic!
Wow!

React to bad news
I'm sorry.
That's so sad.
That's terrible.

React to surprising news
Really? Seriously?
I don't believe it!
That's amazing!

>>> Workbook, page 139

59

1 The lesson starts with listening or speaking exercises, which give students the opportunity to practice functional language.

2 Audio tracks of conversations provide students with the context for key functional language. Students listen to conversations and complete an initial gist exercise before focusing on the speaking function or subskill.

3 A variety of exercise types focuses students' attention on the speaking subskill.

4 Each lesson ends with an Act section in which students prepare a scene of their own to present in groups or to the rest of the class.

5 A PHRASEBOOK with relevant functional phrases is provided for use with the Act section of the lesson. This is part of the audio material provided and also serves as a review of speaking subskills.

Lesson 8 – Writing

> The **writing** lesson in each unit allows students to put everything they've learned in the unit into practice. Each writing lesson also develops a specific writing subskill. Students are systematically guided to plan, write, and check their writing in order to produce a final draft.

1 The lesson opens with a short speaking and reading exercise to introduce the topic. Students read a model text and complete a task to check that they have understood the text.

2 The HOW TO feature focuses on a writing subskill and offers tips on how to structure writing and link ideas more effectively.

3 Students do an exercise to practice the subskill they have learned.

4 After practicing the subskill, students are given a topic for a writing task and instructed to discuss their ideas first to help them prepare for writing.

5 Students follow a three-step writing plan that guides them to organize their ideas, use the grammar from the unit, and follow the tips in the HOW TO box.

6 Students share their work with each other and either write a reply or discuss what they have written.

WRITING My favorite meal

>>> Use *because*

SPEAK AND READ

1 **Work in pairs. Tell your partner your favorite food and drinks. Do you like the same things?**

2 **Read the comment on the *Ask Anything* site. What's Alejandro's favorite meal, dessert, and drink?**

What's your favorite meal?

My favorite meal is tacos with meat, onions, some lettuce, tomatoes, and a lot of cheese. I love tacos because my mom makes them at home. They're fantastic. I like helping her (but I hate cleaning the kitchen after!). My favorite dessert is chocolate ice cream with a lot of chocolate sauce. I always drink water with meals because soda is really bad for your teeth and I don't like it.
Alejandro

new post | reply

3 a **Read the tips in the HOW TO box.**

HOW TO
use because

- Use *because* to give reasons and answer the question *Why?*
- Use *because* + name (*I*, *she*, etc.) + verb.
- Don't use a comma before *because*.

b **Find the answers to these questions in Alejandro's comment.**

1 Why does he like tacos?
2 Why does he drink water with meals?

PRACTICE

4 **Match to make sentences.**

1 I don't like grapes because ____
2 I love vegetables because ____
3 I don't eat steak because ____
4 I drink milk before bed because ____
5 I love chocolate because ____

a I never eat meat.
b I feel happy when I eat it.
c it makes me sleep.
d they're good for you.
e I hate all fruit.

DISCUSS

5 **What is your favorite meal? Talk about what makes the food especially good. What is your favorite dessert and favorite drink? Why?**

WRITE

6 **Write a description of your favorite meal.**

1 Write about the main dish, the dessert, and the drink. Answer these questions in your description: Which foods are in the meal? Why do you like it? Is there a special way you like it prepared? When do you usually eat this meal? What do you like to drink with this meal? Why?
2 Use the correct plural forms of the nouns. Write about quantities of food using *a lot of*, *much*, *many*, and *some*.
3 Use *because* to explain why the meal is your favorite. See the HOW TO box.

SHARE

7 **Take turns reading your descriptions. How many people had the same favorite meal, dessert, or drink? Make a list and decide which meal, dessert, and drink is the most popular in the class.**

60

Workbook, pages 140–141

Lesson 9 – Unit Review

> The **Unit Review** page allows students to check and assess their own progress in vocabulary and grammar.

UNIT REVIEW 5

VOCABULARY Food and drink

1 **Label the food (1–12) with the words in the box.**

butter cake candy carrots chocolate fries onion potatoes soda soup tomatoes yogurt

SCHOOL SUPERMARKET DAY

Buy food on School Supermarket Day from our website. Your family gets good food – and we give your school some of the money to buy books and other things.

1 ____ 2 ____ 3 ____ 4 ____ 5 ____ 6 ____
7 ____ 8 ____ 9 ____ 10 ____

___ /12

Lifestyle adjectives

2 **Complete the adjectives.**

Do you have a (1) b___ ___y and (2) a___ ___ ___ ___e life? Do you feel (3) t___ ___ ___d, (4) s___ ___ ___ ___ ___ ___ ___d, (5) u___ ___ ___ ___ ___y, or (6) s___ ___k? Too (7) l___ ___y to go shopping for healthy food? It's your (8) l___ ___ ___y day – it's School Supermarket Day! Shop online now! Eat our good food and feel (9) h___ ___ ___ ___ ___y and (10) w___ ___l in no time!

___ /10

GRAMMAR *A lot of, much, many, some,* and *any*

3 **Choose the correct words.**

Our meals don't cost (1) *many* / *much* money and you don't need (2) *some* / *any* special ideas. Our tip: buy (3) *a lot of* / *much* vegetables and (4) *a* / *some* rice. You don't need (5) *many* / *much* minutes to make (6) *a* / *some* healthy meal. Do you have (7) *a* / *any* questions? We have (8) *a lot of* / *any* other tips for you. See our FAQ page!

___ /16

Like + -ing

4 **Complete the sentences with *like, enjoy, love, don't like, dislike,* or *hate* with the verb + *-ing*. (Sometimes two answers are possible.)**

WHAT OTHER SUPERMARKET DAY STUDENTS SAY:

"My parents (1) ____ (👍 / help) the school. I (2) ____ (👍 / eat) the food!"

"I usually (3) ____ (👎 / try) different things. But I (4) ____ (👍 / choose) Supermarket Day food."

"I (5) ____ (👎👎 / shop) in the supermarket with Dad. But we (6) ____ (👍👍 / buy) Supermarket Day food online."

___ /12

Your score: ___ /50

SKILLS CHECK

✓✓✓ Yes, I can. No problem!
✓✓ Yes, I can. But I need a little help.
✓ Yes, I can. But I need a lot of help.

I can identify who a text is for. ____
I can identify the speaker. ____
I can follow the rules in electronic communicaton. ____
I can react to news. ____
I can use *because* when I write. ____

Workbook, pages 142–143

61

The exercises in the Unit Review are all set in a single context and reflect the way language is used in real life.

Each exercise has a space for students to record their score.

1 The Unit Review starts with two exercises to test both lexical sets covered in the unit.

2 Two grammar exercises test the two grammar points covered in the unit.

3 After completing all the exercises, students calculate their total score. Each review has the same overall score so that students can assess their progress across units.

4 Students are encouraged to self-assess their progress using CEFR "can do" statements that refer directly back to the objectives of the skills pages.

> After every two units, there is a two-page skills-based **Progress Check** that allows students and teachers to see how well the learning objectives in the preceding two units have been taken on board. Tasks on these pages reflect those that students will see on standardized English exams. The Progress Checks also include tips on how to deal successfully with the various tasks.

1 Progress Check tasks consolidate the language from the preceding two units.

2 The Test-Taking Tips help students prepare for standard test-style tasks.

PROGRESS CHECK

READ

1 Complete the five conversations. For each question, choose A, B, or C.

Example:

0 *What's your favorite food?*
- A *Apple juice.*
- (B) *Pasta with sauce.*
- C *Lunch.*

1 *How many hours do you sleep at night?*
- A *I don't like making my bed.*
- B *I feel healthy.*
- C *Seven.*

2 *Do you like running?*
- A *Yes, he does.*
- B *No, I don't.*
- C *Really?*

3 *My dad has a new job at the hospital.*
- A *That's fantastic.*
- B *That's terrible.*
- C *I'm sorry.*

4 *Are there any cheese sandwiches?*
- A *Yes, please.*
- B *Yes, here you are.*
- C *I don't like chicken.*

5 *Do you like tacos?*
- A *Yes, I do.*
- B *Great!*
- C *I hate all fruit.*

TEST-TAKING TIPS

answer multiple-choice questions

- Look at the example. It shows you what to do.
- Read each question and the three answer choices.
- Decide which choices are definitely wrong.
  - Does the meaning of the answer match the question?
  - Does the grammar in the answer match the question? (Look at pronouns, tenses, and so on.)
- Read the question again and check your answer.

Reading: ______ /10

62

PROGRESS CHECK 5

LISTEN

2 **77 Listen to Angela talking about food and drinks. Which foods or drinks do the people in her family like or make? For questions 1–5, write A–H next to each person. You need only five of the words.**

Example:
0 sister *D*

PEOPLE	FOOD AND DRINKS
	A peanut butter
1 brother	B pizza
2 dad	C chocolate chip cookies
3 mom	D milkshake
4 grandma	E cheese
5 aunt	F pasta
	G cheesecake
	H apple juice

Listening: ______ /10

TEST-TAKING TIPS

match things in two lists

- Read both lists.
- Listen carefully for the words in Column 1. You will hear these in order.
- Listen for the words in Column 2. What do the speakers say about them?

WRITE

3 **Complete the text on Paul's favorite food. For questions 1–10, write one word for each blank.**

Paul likes to (0) *eat* burgers. They are his favorite (1) ______. He likes his burger with French (2) ______. What about (3) ______? What do you like (4) ______ your burger? Do you like pickles? How (5) ______ pickles do you put on your burger? Do you (6) ______ ketchup? (7) ______ about tomatoes or lettauce? Paul likes all (8) ______ these things plus cheese. He thinks cheese burgers (9) ______ fantastic! What is your (10) ______ food?

TEST-TAKING TIPS

complete a text with blanks

- First, read the text quickly.
- Then read each sentence carefully. Look at the words before **and** after each blank.
- Use only one word in the blank.
- Use the correct form of verbs and check your spelling.
- Read the text again: do the words sound right?

Writing: ______ /10

Progress check score ______ /30

63

3 Overall scoring is the same in every Progress Check, so students can monitor both their overall progress and their progress in specific skills.

Other features

At the end of the Student's Book material, you'll find the following resources:

Grammar Database
The Grammar Database provides detailed additional explanations of the grammar points of each unit, as well as grammar tables and common errors to watch out for. It is a valuable reference section for students.

Words & Beyond
These pages contain lists of the main lexical sets from each unit, as well as other important vocabulary from the unit, vocabulary tips, and additional tasks.

Irregular verbs
A list of common irregular verbs is provided for students' reference.

Extras
The material for pairwork activities (with Student A and Student B) from the units is provided here as well as answers to quiz questions.

USING THE *MOVE BEYOND* WORKBOOK

The *Move Beyond* Workbook lessons recontextualize, review, and recycle target items from the corresponding lesson pages of the Student's Book and offer comprehensive practice for homework and class use.

- Two vocabulary pages per unit practice the target vocabulary in new contexts.
- Intuitive instructions make it easier to complete each exercise.
- Puzzles and games add an element of fun and variety.

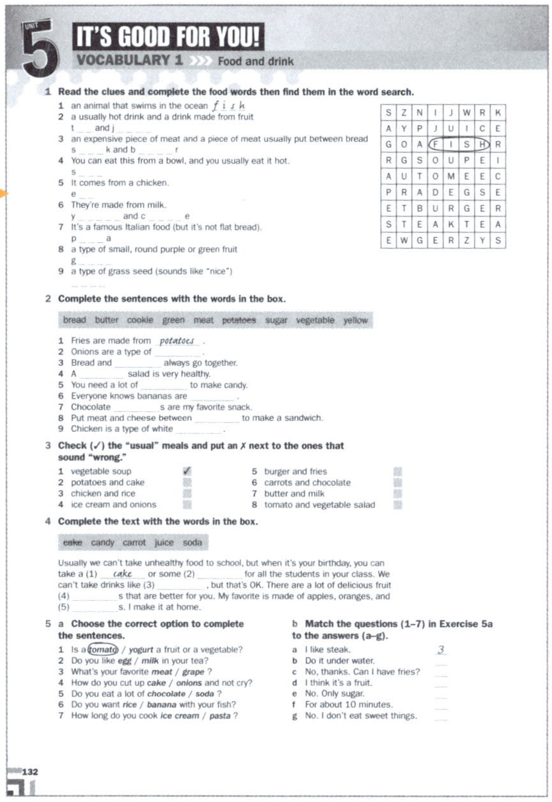

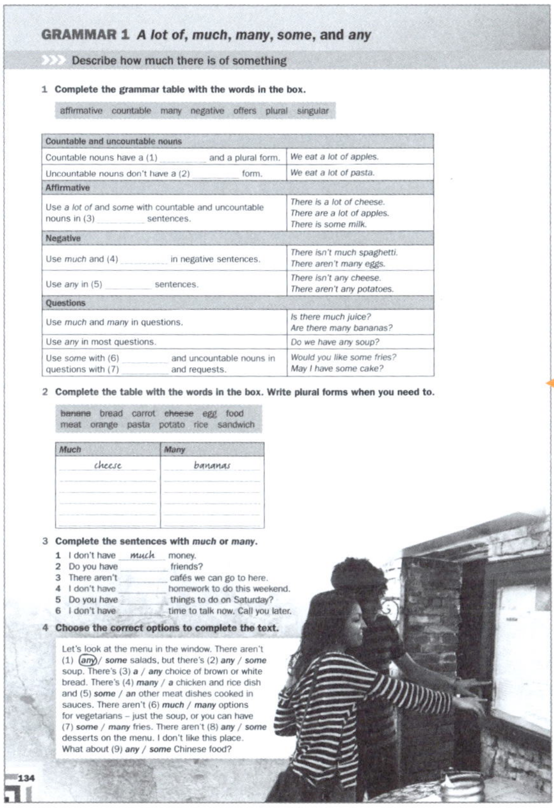

- The Workbook contains three pages per unit for practicing target grammar.
- Grammar Study boxes review the form and use of key grammar.
- Students then practice through contextualized grammar exercises.
- Exercises on the grammar pages are presented in order of difficulty, shown by chevrons (› = easiest, ›› = medium challenge, ››› = most difficult).

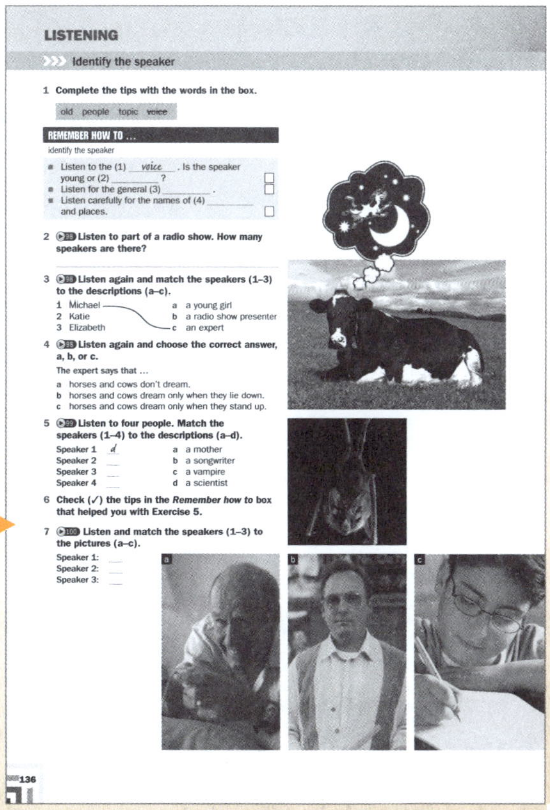

- Key listening subskills from the Student's Book are reintroduced and reexamined.
- Exercises put these skills into practice and review target language.
- Additional listening exercises focus on the theme of the unit, often through test-style tasks related to the subskill in the lesson.

USING THE *MOVE BEYOND* WORKBOOK

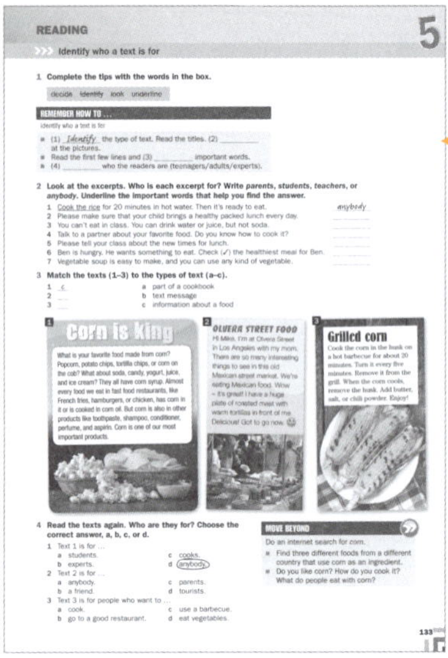

- REMEMBER HOW TO boxes focus on key subskills from the Student's Book lesson.
- Texts build on the themes introduced in the Student's Book.
- Tasks focus on putting reading subskills into practice, recycling key language, and exposing students to test-style tasks.

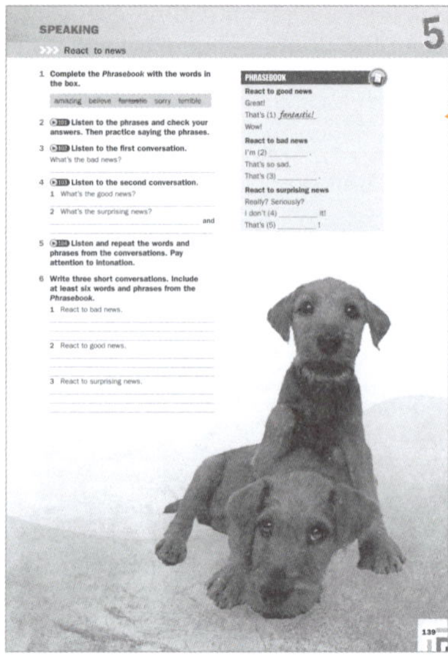

- The speaking lesson focuses on reviewing key lexical items.
- Target items are presented in context, and recordings are frequently used to focus on important aspects of speaking, such as register, stress, and intonation.

- Key writing subskills from the Student's Book are developed in exercises carefully designed to practice the skill.
- Emphasis is put on the planning and structuring of texts, and final productive exercises prepare students with exam-type tasks, giving them guidance on important elements to include.

- The unit life skill is revisited, and students are challenged to apply the skill in a personalized new context.

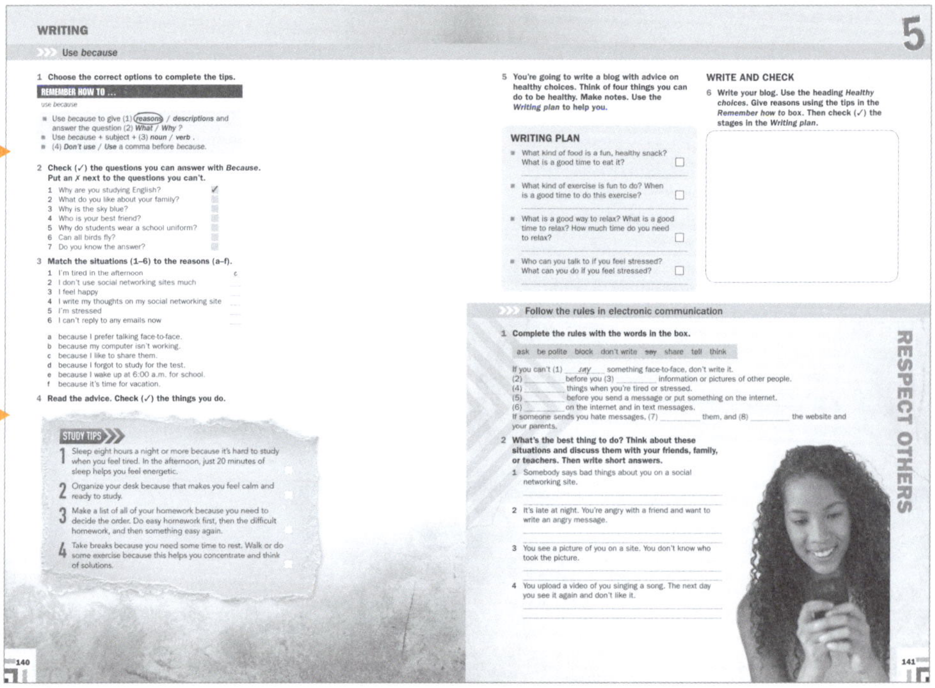

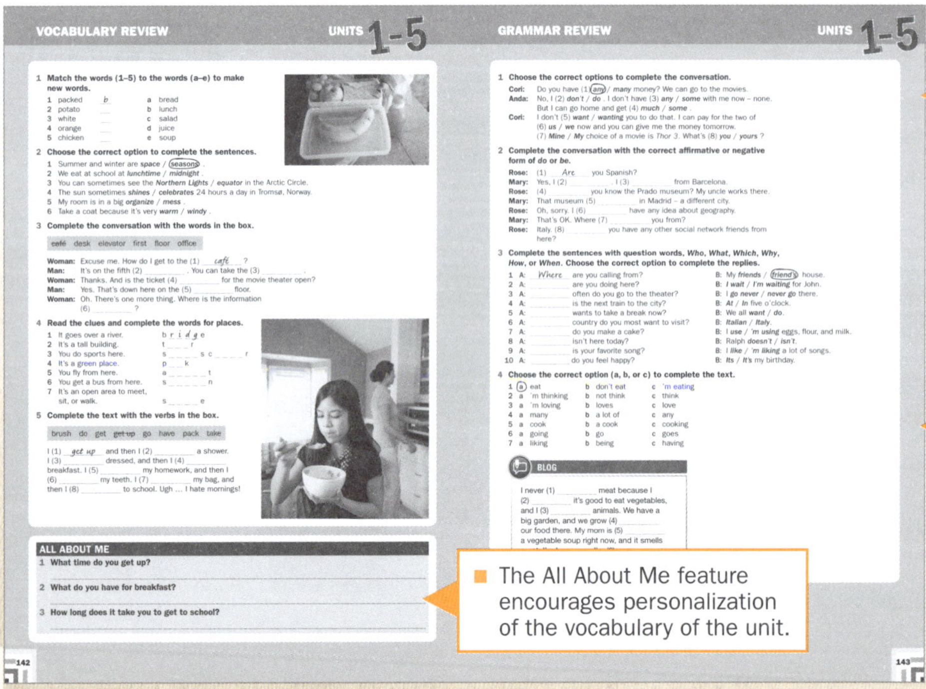

- Target vocabulary and grammar taken from any units of the Student's Book covered to date are recontextualized and reviewed here, allowing students to monitor their own progress.

- The review pages offer cumulative assessment, with exercises combining two or more grammar points or vocabulary sets.

- The All About Me feature encourages personalization of the vocabulary of the unit.

MOVE BEYOND DIGITAL

The digital components of *Move Beyond* are easy to integrate into your regular classroom activities. The range of multimedia resources gives teachers an excellent opportunity to digitize their lessons and present the material in different ways, which varies the pace and dynamics in the classroom. Classwork, homework, and testing are all accommodated in the *Move Beyond* Teacher's Resource Center, where plenty of flexible additional materials for both online and offline use can be found.

Go to mee2.macmillaneducation.com to access:

- *Move Beyond Level 1* Presentation Kit, consisting of a digital Student's Book designed for classroom presentation.
- *Move Beyond Level 1* Teacher's Resource Center, for extra materials, tests, videos, and downloadable audio.

Teacher's Resource Center

The Teacher's Resource Center provides teachers with downloadable extra grammar and vocabulary worksheets, tips, and testing materials to support the course. It contains a whole range of additional *Move Beyond* materials to be used in the classroom or assigned for homework, as well as access to everything in the Student's Resource Center.

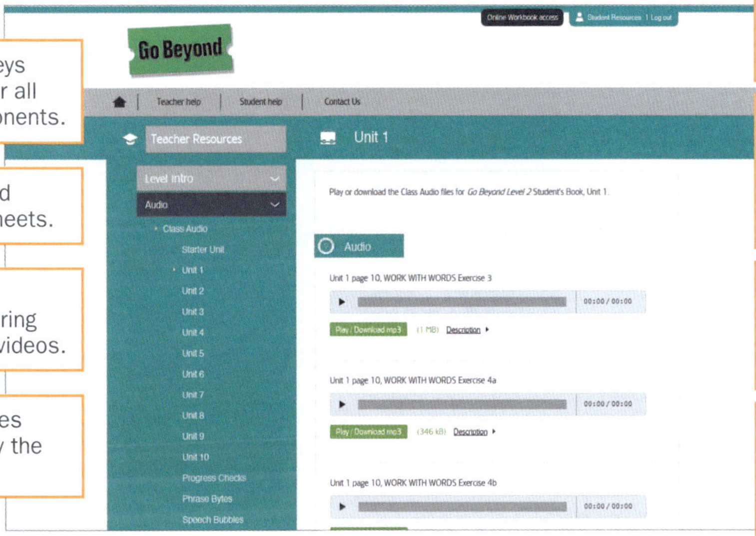

Full answer keys and scripts for all course components.

Extra Grammar and Vocabulary worksheets.

Further ideas and activities for exploring the *Move Beyond* videos.

Teacher's notes to accompany the worksheets.

Tips and model answers to accompany the Student's Book and Workbook writing tasks.

A teacher-delivered speaking section to accompany every Student's Book Progress Check.

Static PDF tests for each unit and for the beginning, middle, and end of each level.

A link to special *Move Beyond* materials on www.onestopenglish.com, as well as access to other useful onestopenglish resources.

Presentation Kit

The Presentation Kit includes a projectable digital version of the *Move Beyond* Student's Book for teachers to use in class to promote "eyes-up" learning and student interaction. Easily downloadable to multiple devices from mee2.macmillaneducation.com, the Presentation Kit can also be used for lesson preparation at home.

Once downloaded, the Presentation Kit can be used offline. Audio recordings, videos, and answer keys are embedded in the pages for easy reference along with optional pop-up audio scripts and video subtitles, which are synched to the content. There are also fully interactive exercises to work through as a class.

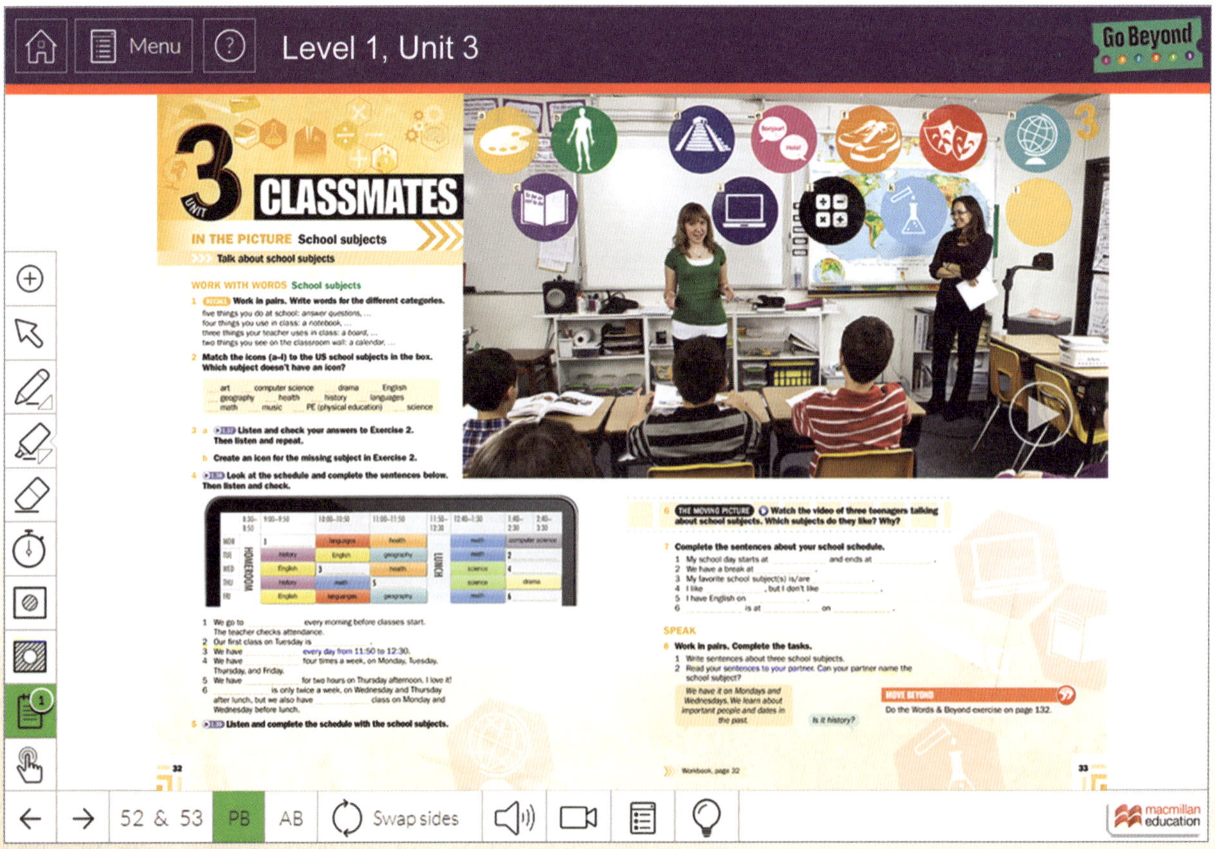

MOVE BEYOND DIGITAL

Move Beyond videos

There is a video for each *Move Beyond* unit, adding richness and variety to the material. The Moving Picture videos from the opening spreads bring global experiences into the classroom. The videos include documentary clips, vox pops, slideshows, digital animation, and YouTube-style videos. These engaging visuals support listening skills and act as conversation starters.

The *Move Beyond* videos are embedded in the Presentation Kit and supplied on a DVD-ROM at the back of the combined Student's Book/Workbook. Teachers can also access them at home via the Teacher's Resource Center.

From the Moving Picture video, Unit 10.

From the Moving Picture video, Unit 3.

Video Tips

You can extend the activities or use the videos separately by using some of these video tips.

Before you watch

Students can predict what they'll see and hear in the video.

- Show students the title of the video or give them the topic and ask them to brainstorm vocabulary they think will come up.
- Show the video using the "Fast forward" option or show one or two stills from the video and ask students to predict what is happening or what people are saying.
- Show the first few seconds of the video and ask students to predict what will happen next.

While you watch

You can ask students to watch the videos normally or use just the picture or audio.

A Picture with no sound

- In pairs, one student watches and describes what he or she sees to a partner, who takes notes. They then watch together and discuss differences.
- Make a worksheet with screen shots from scenes in the video. Students write their own dialog or complete speech bubbles.
- Students write their own scripts for what they see. They then speak over the video, providing the narration or character voices. Finally, they compare their versions to the original.

B Sound with no picture

- Students listen to the sound only and speculate in pairs/groups about what they hear. They then watch to see if they were right.

C Picture and sound

- Students make notes as they watch and then compare notes with a partner or in groups.
- After showing the video a first time, give students cards with key words or phrases from the video. As students watch the video a second time, ask them to hold up their cards each time they hear the key word or phrase from their cards in the video.

After you watch

Use these activities in conjunction with the before/while you watch or as the main activity.

- Students create a fictional story, write a news story, or do a role-play based on the video or part of it.
- Students write an email or a text message to somebody in the video. They can also make a brochure, ad, fact file, or poster related to a topic or place in the video.
- Show students still photos of people from the video and ask them to make a brief biography for that person – name, age, nationality, family, likes and dislikes, hobbies, and favorite food.

To optimize your teaching experience with ***Move Beyond***, we've put together some tips for the following key areas:

- Classroom management
- Teaching skills
- Teaching vocabulary and grammar
- Teaching pronunciation

Classroom management

Managing a classroom of teenagers is not always easy, and good classroom management, including organizing resources, creating an effective learning environment, monitoring student progress, and anticipating potential obstacles to learning, is crucial for keeping students on track. The following tips will help you maximize the time in the classroom and ensure a productive learning environment.

Managing large classes

Teachers of large classes need to make sure students know what is expected of them. At the beginning of the year, set up routines; for example, for how attendance is taken, how teaching materials are distributed and collected, and how homework is dealt with.

Students in large classes may find it difficult to hear instructions. You need to pay special attention to giving all instructions clearly and decisively so that students are in no doubt about what is required of them. Accompany your instructions with hand movements: *Everyone open your books; Stand up, everyone!* etc. Large classes can get noisy and fail to notice when you need their attention. Set up a signal, such as clapping your hands or whistling. One strategy that works well is to raise an arm and put your finger on your lips; students should notice the signal and respond.

Checking answers

Keep students alert and motivated by varying the ways you choose students to answer questions. Alternate between calling on students to give answers and asking for volunteers. Calling on them is good for less confident students as it allows them to answer questions that they are more likely to get right. It is then fun to let the student you called on choose who will answer the next question. Alternatively, if you have closely monitored students while they were doing an activity, "randomly" call on students who have the correct answers. Both of these techniques are good for giving students confidence.

Students appreciate the opportunity to look at a partner's answers to make sure they are not completely off the mark. If students are allowed to compare their answers, they'll have more confidence in them and therefore will be much more likely to volunteer them. It also gives students an opportunity to use English to explain why they chose their answer and helps develop their ability to compare and discuss in English.

Remind students that the most successful learners are usually the ones who are not afraid to experiment and make mistakes.

Correcting errors effectively

It is important not to overcorrect, as this can make students lose confidence. However, undercorrecting leads to students developing bad language habits and decreases their communicative abilities in the long term.

When students are carrying out pair-work activities, the focus is on fluency and it is best not to correct errors. However, monitor students and note important errors and good use of language to go over at the end of the activity in a feedback session. Allot a few minutes of class time to error correction. Write the errors on the board without saying who made the mistake and elicit correct answers from the class.

Open and closed pairs

An open pair is when a pair of students work together with the rest of the class observing. It can help less confident students understand the instructions and highlight the language they will need for an activity. Be sensitive and choose more confident students to demonstrate the activity. Avoid individual error correction at this stage.

Closed pairs means that students are working in pairs all at the same time.

Closed pair work is important because it gives students a chance to explore new language privately; it is also useful for teachers because you can walk around and monitor students and give individual feedback.

Total Physical Response (TPR)

Total Physical Response is a teaching methodology whereby instructors give instructions and students respond with whole-body movements. It was developed by James Asher in the 1960s and is based on the belief that memory is enhanced by associations, particularly through physical movement. TPR activities could be as basic as following instructions such as *sit down*, *stand up*, and *pick up your pen*, and it lends itself well to games such as *Simon Says*.

It can be motivating and fun for students and is especially popular with learners who don't like to be sitting down for too long! Although it may seem unrealistic to sustain a whole lesson by giving commands and repeating them, activities like this can break up the class and reduce stress as students are not under pressure to produce the target language, but rather are responding to it. TPR is especially suited to kinesthetic learners, and activities can be carried out in classes of any size.

Teaching vocabulary and grammar

Test before you teach

Starting a grammar lesson with a test-before-you-teach activity helps you find out how much students already know. If students have problems with form and use at the initial stage, you may need to provide more guidance during the lesson. However, if students are familiar with form and use, you can move more quickly through the lesson.

A2 English plural nouns

In order to change a singular noun to its plural form in English, you usually add s (e.g., *bags*, *days*). These are regular plurals. However, there are many irregular plurals that do not follow this rule:

- Nouns that end in *-ch*, *-x*, *-s*, *-z*, or *-sh* sounds require an *-es* for the plural (e.g., *boxes*, *wishes*, *sandwiches*, *buses*).
- Several nouns have irregular forms (e.g., *women*, *children*, *men*, *people*).
- Nouns that end in a consonant + *-y* drop the *-y* and take *-ies* (e.g., *cities*, *parties*).
- A number of nouns that end in *-o* take *-es* in the plural (e.g., *tomatoes*, *potatoes*).

A2 Subject pronouns and possessive adjectives

A subject pronoun is used as the subject of a sentence (or clause). The subject pronouns are *I*, *you*, *he*, *she*, *it*, *we*, *you*, and *they*. A possessive adjective is used in front of a noun to show ownership or belonging. The possessive adjectives are *my*, *your*, *his*, *her*, *its*, *our*, *your*, and *their*.

A2 Present progressive for future arrangements

Students sometimes struggle to understand the meaning of *arrangements*, so explain that they are plans we make with other people and the type of thing you write in a datebook or on a calendar. You could show students your datebook or calendar on your phone and some examples of events you have coming up (e.g. *mom's birthday dinner*, *important soccer game*), and ask concept-checking questions. (e.g., *When's the dinner/game? Is it in the future? Is it arranged/organized?*) Students don't always assimilate this use easily, so it will probably be necessary to recycle it regularly. Have students practice by talking about real or fictional calendar entries or by asking questions about their plans after class, on the weekend, over the holidays, etc.

A2 Countable and uncountable nouns

Countable nouns (e.g., *potato*, *vegetable*, and *chip*) have singular and plural forms and they can be counted easily. The singular form can take the article *a/an*, and regular plural forms end in *-s/-es*. There are also irregular forms such as *man/men*, *child/children*, and *person/people*. Uncountable nouns (e.g. *pasta*, *spaghetti*, *salad*) have only one form and cannot be counted easily. They are sometimes referred to as mass nouns.

There are several potential problems for learners:

- It is not obvious that the noun is countable, especially in the case of some irregular plurals such as *children*, so students may add an *-s*.
- An uncountable word may be countable in L1. For example, when talking about *news* (uncountable), students may try to use the incorrect singular form *a new*.
- In some cases, students may not use articles for singular nouns, especially if they wouldn't in L1. For example, in some languages, jobs are not preceded by an article; for example, *My father is lawyer*.
- Some nouns can be both countable and uncountable; for example, *I try to eat fruit every day* (uncountable) / *There are some fruits that I don't like, for example, grapefruit* (countable).

You can review countable and uncountable nouns throughout the course. When students have finished reading a text or audio script, have them find as many examples as they can of each type of noun in the text.

A2 Simple past negative

To form the simple past negative, we use the auxiliary verb *didn't (did not)* + verb (base verb), regardless of the subject. It is important to point out to students that it is the auxiliary verb *did* that conjugates in the past and not the main verb:

- *I didn't go to Spain on vacation.* Not ~~*I didn't went to Spain on vacation.*~~
- *You didn't come to my party.*
- *He didn't have breakfast.*
- *She didn't like the movie.*

When we form the simple past negative with *be*, we don't use the auxiliary verb *did*, and *be* conjugates according to the subject:

- *I wasn't at school yesterday.* Not ~~*I didn't was at school yesterday.*~~
- *You weren't hungry.*
- *She wasn't at the movie theater.*

When talking about past ability, we use *could/couldn't* + verb (base verb) regardless of the subject.

- *I couldn't play football when I was a baby.* Not ~~*I couldn't played football when I was a baby.*~~
- *You couldn't come to the movie theater.*
- *He couldn't finish his dinner.*

A2 Word order in questions

Show students an easy way to remember word order in questions. Write *QASB* on the board. Explain that the letters represent the word order we use to form questions:

Q = Question word (e.g., *what*, *where*, *when*)
A = Auxiliary (e.g., *do*, *did*, *is*, *was*)
S = Subject (e.g., *I*, *you*, *he*, *she*, *it*, *we*, *they*)
B = Base verb (e.g., *do*, *play*, *eat*)

Remind students that we don't use question words with *Yes/No* questions but that the rest of the order remains the same. If we want to add any extra information, we put it at the end of the sentence. Give some examples or ask the class to give some examples.

Q	A	S	B	
How	*do*	*you*	*travel*	*to school?*
Who	*did*	*you*	*go*	*on vacation with?*
Where	*was*	*he?*		
	Do	*you*	*play*	*basketball?*

TEACHING TIPS

A2 Comparative adjectives

The rules for forming comparative adjectives are as follows:

Short (one-syllable) adjectives	Add *-er.*	*near – nearer* *fast – faster*
One-syllable adjectives ending consonant-vowel-consonant	Double the final consonant and add *-er.*	*big – bigger* *fat – fatter*
Two-syllable adjectives ending in *-y*	Remove *-y* and add *-ier.*	*happy – happier* *sunny – sunnier*
Long adjectives (two syllables or more)	Use *more* + adjective.	*beautiful – more beautiful* *interesting – more interesting*

The following are some of the most common learner errors that are useful to point out:

Spelling rules: ~~*biger, happyier.*~~

Using *that* rather than *than* in comparative sentences: ~~*He is taller that her.*~~

Overuse of *more* with short adjectives: ~~*He lives more closer to the school than me.*~~

A2 Word lists

When students learn new words, it is important to encourage them to keep a record of them in a separate book or at the back of their notebooks. As they do this, encourage them to group the words into categories as this helps them make further associations and they will be more likely to remember them. Possible categories for making word lists are:

- Positives and negatives: *happy/unhappy*
- Opposites: *cold/hot*
- Topic/theme: *Family – mother, father, aunt, uncle*

A2 Future forms

<u>Future plans</u>

We use *be* + *going to* + base verb to talk about future plans or intentions:

- *He's going to have dinner with his grandparents this Saturday.*
- *I'm going to study chemistry in college.*

<u>Predictions</u>

We can use both *will* + base verb and *be* + *going to* to make predictions about the future.

In many cases, both are possible:

- *He thinks he's going to fail the test.*
- *He thinks he'll fail the test.*

Use *be* + *going to* for predictions based on evidence or things that we see are about to happen:

- *Look at those gray clouds! It's going to rain.*
- *He's driving too fast. He's going to crash!*

Will is often used with phrases like *I think …* and *I don't think …* when we are not sure:

- *I think he'll have a great time on vacation.*

We use *I don't think* + *will*, not ~~*I think* + *won't*~~.

- *I don't think I'll go out tonight.*
- ~~*I think I won't go out tonight.*~~

A2 Adjectives ending in *-ed* and *-ing*

Point out to students that adjectives ending in *-ed* describe how you feel. Adjectives ending in *-ing* usually describe the effect that something has on your ideas and feelings.

Like all adjectives, *-ing* and *-ed* adjectives can be used in front of a noun and can be modified by adverbs such as *very* and *really*. They can also be used in the comparative and superlative forms; for example, *… are always more exciting than other games.*

Teaching skills

Writing

Punctuation

Punctuation is the system of symbols we use to separate sentences and parts of sentences and to make their meaning clear. Punctuation helps the reader understand when to pause between fully formed ideas when speaking, and it helps us organize our thoughts when writing.

A classic way to point out to students the importance of punctuation is to put this sentence on the board and ask them to punctuate it.

- *Let's eat Grandpa*

Check to see who has written the first or the second line!

- *Let's eat Grandpa!*
- *Let's eat, Grandpa.*

Correct punctuation can save lives!

Giving feedback on written work

When students are doing writing tasks in class, it's a good opportunity for you to focus on individual students. Circulate around the class and make sure that students are on task. Give positive feedback and help them with any problems they may have. While you're doing this, note examples of good language and put them on the board at the end of the activity. Then ask students to identify sentences that are correct and ask them to correct any errors. You could have students do this in teams and award points for correct answers.

If the writing is assigned for homework, or if you collect your students' work at the end of a writing activity, you can correct it for students to write down their mistakes or rewrite the text. When marking students' written work, it is important to think about their level and decide which mistakes they can correct themselves. Remember to add a comment at the end to show interest and praise the student if possible. Using a corrections sheet, with symbols and acronyms, to mark students' work can save you time. Give students a copy of the corrections sheet too, to guide them toward correcting their own mistakes. You can also list mistakes that are common to students and some interesting expressions and good use of language to give some general feedback on the written homework at the beginning of the next class.

Speaking

Encouraging extended answers

At this level, students lack confidence in their ability to produce extended answers to questions, often producing one-word answers where possible to avoid making mistakes. It is important to encourage students to extend their answers in speaking activities to help them gain confidence in this area. One way they can do this is to answer the question, add an extra piece of information, and/or give a personal opinion. Another way is to encourage partners to ask *Why?* as this is what they would do in natural conversation in their own language. It is extremely important that you give a model answer to speaking activities to remind students how to give extended answers.

A: *Do you play soccer?*

B: *Yes. I play soccer every weekend with my friends. I love it!*

Checking that you understand

Students often find it embarrassing when they don't understand what someone has said in English and prefer to take a step back from the conversation and not participate rather than have to ask a speaker to clarify what he or she has said. It is important to reassure students that even native speakers have to ask for clarification sometimes. Give them some useful phrases for this:

Showing you don't understand	Asking for clarification
I don't understand.	*What do you mean by … ?*
I'm not sure I understand.	*Do you mean … ?*
Sorry, I didn't quite hear what you said.	*Could you say that again, please?*
Sorry, I didn't get your point.	*Could you repeat that, please?*

Class discussions

When inviting students to share answers and opinions with the whole class, try to ensure that the interaction is not solely student–teacher. Rather than give your opinion, ask other students if they agree and ask them to give their reasons. Develop the conversation by inviting other students to share their opinions. At this level, students may require scaffolding, so you could put some useful expressions on the board (*What do you think? I think, I'm not sure, It depends*, etc.) and encouage students to use them.

Listening

Listening for the main idea

Help your students develop strong listening skills by using a variety of listening activities. Many students experience anxiety and need help to learn to listen effectively. Often students try to listen for everything and they are not in control of the process that leads to comprehension.
One important skill is to learn to identify the gist – the main ideas – of a conversation before breaking down the information and concentrating on the details they need to complete a task. Encourage students to relax and not to worry if they don't understand every word on the first listening. Ask them to focus on picking out words that seem to be "highlighted" with special stress and/or repetition as these will probably signal the main topic of a conversation.

Dictation

Dictation is not only engaging for students, it is also a good way to practice integrated skills (listening, pronunciation, writing) and focus on accuracy. It requires very little preparation and can be used to adapt many exercises.
There are many ways to use dictation, but in its simplest form it consists of you dictating chunks of language for students to write down. As a general rule, say the phrases at normal speed as this should help students notice features of pronunciation such as stressed words and weak forms. However, allow students to listen as many times as they like and to ask questions such as *Can you say that again? What was the second word? How do you spell … ?* etc.

Listening for specific information

Training students to listen closely for the specific information they need to complete a task can be difficult. Students often want to try to understand everything. A key strategy to help students focus on listening for specific information is to encourage them to prepare for the task by looking closely at the questions. They can use the questions to get an idea of the context of the listening and to predict what kind of information they need to listen for in order to complete the task. The words in the task help guide them through the listening and locate where they should concentrate their efforts and listen carefully.

Predicting before listening

Predicting content is something that we all do in our first language before and while we are listening.

- **Predict the topic.** Where possible, draw students' attention to any images on the Student's Book page and ask them what they think the topic will be.
- **Predict the speakers.** Hand out printouts of the audio script for a chosen conversation in the Student's Book. Ask students to cover the speakers' names with a piece of paper, and then ask them to read the conversation and guess the age, gender, and relationship between the speakers. Write their ideas on the board, and after you have listened to the audio, check whether any of their guesses were correct.
- **Predict the word.** While playing the audio track, press the pause button midsentence and ask students if they can predict the next word. Repeat this process throughout the track. At the end of the exercise, ask students if any of their guesses were correct and, if so, why they chose that word. Remember not to comment on the accuracy of their guesses during the exercise – the goal isn't to get everything right, but to concentrate on the language and topic in order to make guessing possible.

Reading

Predicting before reading

The text title and nontextual features like photos or diagrams and even the use of color or fonts can help students make useful predictions about a text before they've read a word. Writers use headings to help the reader understand the main idea of the article. In any reading activity, it can help to explore the nontextual features before reading. When students make connections from their experience to the text, they have a foundation on which they can place new facts, ideas, and concepts.

Reading for specific information

Getting students to think about how they read in their own language can help them transfer reading skills and improve their reading level in English. Ask students if they read in great detail when they do these things in their own language:

- look through a magazine for an article they want to read
- look at a schedule for the time a bus leaves
- read a book to relax
- read a cell phone contract

Point out to students that we often scan texts to find specific information and it is not always important to understand every single word. It is often important to understand practically every word only when we read intensively, such as when reading the detailed information in a contract.

Taking notes

Taking notes is usually not an easy task for students with this level of English as it requires a fairly deep understanding of the text in order to understand what information is important. Students are often tempted to copy sentences as they are unsure what information they will need. Certain strategies can help students take effective notes from a reading text:

- Make sure that students know the purpose for taking notes, such as for a test or important information to tell parents. This will encourage them to think about what they need the notes for in the future and what information they need from the text.
- Have students read the text at least once before they start taking notes so that they become familiar with the text, any unfamiliar language, and the key points.
- Have students read the text and then try to remember the key points and summarize them orally. This will encourage them to pay attention to the text and focus on the main ideas.
- Point out that they need to write only words that carry meaning and do not need to copy full sentences. These words are often names, places, dates, numbers, and possibly adjectives. Give students question prompts to help them: *What? Where? When? Why? How?*

Teaching pronunciation

A2 Long and short vowel sounds

Some languages do not have a distinction between short and long vowels. Students often stretch all vowel sounds and confuse pairs of short and long English vowel sounds like the short vowel sound in *ship* /ɪ/ and the long vowel sound in *sheep* /iː/. The vowel sound /iː/ is a long *ee* (as in *eat*), and you can help students say it by asking them to smile when saying it, as if they are having a picture taken and saying *Cheese!*

A2 Intonation in questions

Intonation is important in questions, especially if we are trying to be polite. As a general rule, information questions or *Wh-* questions have a falling intonation pattern, whereas *Yes/No* questions have rising intonation:

Do you speak English? ↗ *How long are you staying?* ↘

It is a good idea to draw students' attention to these intonation patterns when listening to questions by asking them whether the intonation goes up or down. Choral drills are a good opportunity to have everyone focus on this, and you may want to use gestures, such as sweeping your hand up or down, to indicate that students' voices should go up or down.

A2 Varying drilling techniques

Drilling can be a useful technique if employed in the right way. Make sure you vary the type of drilling you do with your class so that it does not become monotonous and meaningless repetition. Choral drilling (the whole class repeating a word or phrase together after you) works well when students are saying new language for the first time, and you can then move to individuals. Back-chaining (starting at the end of the phrase or word and building up a syllable or chunk at a time) works particularly well with longer sentences. You can alter your delivery (e.g., to a "whisper drill") if your class is becoming too noisy.

A2 Long *o* sound

The alphabet sounds – when the vowel "says its name" – are called "long vowels." We call them "long" because we hold them longer than short sounds, but they are completely different sounds, not a longer version of the same sound.

There are some rules, for example, the silent *e*. When a vowel and consonant are followed by an *e*, the *e* is almost always silent, but it causes the preceding vowel to be long (e.g., *home*). Also, a vowel at the end of a syllable is almost always long (e.g., *photo*). Often the first letter of the vowel combinations (e.g., *oa*) will be long and the second will be silent (e.g., *coat*). (An old rhyme for children says "When two vowels go walking, the first one does the talking.") However, there are many exceptions.

A2 *Can/can't*

The pronunciation of *can* varies depending on how it's used. In terms of production, the most important thing is for students to be using the contracted form *can't* rather than *cannot*. However, on a receptive level, it's useful for students to know the different ways in which *can* is pronounced:

can	I can play badminton. Yes, I can. Can you play badminton?	/kən/ /kæn/ /kæn/
can't	I can't play badminton.	/kænt/

GAMES

Pronunciation Mountain

This is a simple and effective way to drill any list of vocabulary. Students enjoy the competitive nature of it and benefit from repeating each word multiple times. You can play it with words from the vocabulary you have studied in class or at the end of the class with words you have noticed students mispronouncing throughout the class.

- Put a list of about 10 words on the board. Put the word you think is easiest to pronounce at the bottom of the list and the one that is the most difficult at the top.
- Divide the class into teams of four or five.
- Set a time limit of two minutes for the teams to practice saying the words together.
- When you say *Go!* the first team must all say the word at the bottom of the list together. If they pronounce the word correctly, they move up to the next word. They continue moving up the list until the team, or someone on the team, pronounces one of the words wrong.
- Then it is the next team's turn, and they start from the bottom of the list again and keep moving up until they get a word wrong.
- The game continues until one team reaches the top of the list and wins the game.

Pictionary

- Divide the class into two or three teams. Taking turns, each team has one minute to come to the board and draw words for their team to guess.
- The first person from a team comes to the front of the class. Give the student one of the words written on a piece of paper, (e.g., *boat*). The student draws a picture of a boat on the board for the team to guess.
- In order for the team to get the point, they must say a complete sentence, (e.g., *You traveled by boat*).
- When the team has guessed the word, or when the one-minute time limit is up, another member of that team comes to the board and draws another word. Continue until all members of the team have had a turn. Repeat with the other team or teams.
- The team that has guessed the most words at the end of the game wins.

Twenty Questions

This is a good game to practice question formation as well as vocabulary.

- Ask one student to think of an object, person, or place.
- The rest of the class can ask 20 questions, but the student can answer only *yes* or *no*.
- After 20 questions the class has to make a guess at what the object, person, or place is.

Snowman

To elicit a word or phrase or to give extra practice in spelling, write short lines for each letter of a word or phrase on the board and invite students to guess letters. For each incorrect guess, draw a part of a snowman: one circle for the head, one for the body, then two arms, three buttons, a hat, two eyes, and a smile.

Three in a Row

- Divide the class into two teams and draw a 3x3 grid on the board.
- In each cell, write a vocabulary item or a verb in the base form.
- One team chooses a cell and uses the item in it to make a complete sentence. They must use the correct tense in the case of a verb.
- If their sentence is correct, they "take" the cell.
- The teams alternate turns, and the first team to get three cells in a row wins.

Find Someone Who…

This popular and engaging game is good for question practice and for practicing a range of new grammar and vocabulary points.

- Write the following on the board:
  Find someone who …
  … can swim fast.
  … can play the guitar beautifully.
- Elicit more endings from the class and have students copy them down.
- Explain that students have to ask each other questions and find a different person for each ending. Model the task by asking the first question (e.g., *Can you swim fast?*) and writing a name on the board.
- Set a time limit of five minutes and have students mingle and ask questions.
- After five minutes, stop the activity and invite students to say what they have found out.

Running Dictation

This is good integrated skills practice, and the fact that all students have roles means that everyone is engaged and on task. It can be used to present new language in a test-teach-test approach or for reviewing previously studied grammar and vocabulary.

- Prepare a short text of about 50–60 words and stick it to the board. It could include new language, but it shouldn't be too challenging as students are going to have to memorize it.
- Divide students into small teams and assign one student the role of secretary. The other students will be runners.
- When you say *Go!*, one runner from each team runs to the board and reads the first sentence or phrase. They then return to their teams and dictate the sentence for the secretaries to write down.
- The next runners then go to the board, read the next sentence or phrase, and return to the teams, and so on.
- The first team to finish calls you to come and check the text. If it is correctly written down, that team has won and the game is over. If not, the runners have to keep returning to the board until the dictated text is correct.

Vocabulary Tennis

This is a great game to review different sets of vocabulary. You will need a ball for this (or a crumpled-up piece of paper works just as well).

- Divide the class into two teams. Ask them to sit in two lines on either side of the classroom, opposite each other, so that everyone on team A is facing someone on team B.
- Explain that you will give them a category (e.g., *food*). The first person from team A must say a word that belongs to that category and then throw the ball to someone on team B (it doesn't have to be the person opposite).
- The person with the ball now says a word and throws the ball back to someone on team A. This continues until a word is repeated or someone takes longer than five seconds to say a word. In these cases, the points go to the other team and you give them another category.
- Either give one point for each round won or score it like a game of tennis so the first team to reach 40 wins the game.

USING THE *MOVE BEYOND* TEACHER'S EDITION

This Teacher's Edition is a valuable and practical resource. With its clear and comprehensive teaching notes, audio scripts and answer keys, background notes, and extra features, it will help you plan and deliver impactful, well-paced, and memorable lessons.

The topic, content, and lesson objectives of each unit are clearly presented.

The target language, functions, and stages of each lesson are outlined, with suggested timings for each stage shown visually to help you pace your lesson. The darker gray shading shows the part of the lesson already completed and the lighter gray shows the amount of time allocated for each stage.

The Get started feature provides an activity to start the lesson and is an opportunity to recycle language and prepare students for the lesson. These warm-ups do not require additional preparation or materials.

Activities that recycle language are labeled with the recycle icon.

Clear and concise procedural notes maximize the Student's Book material.

UNIT 3 CLASSMATES

IN THE PICTURE School subjects

Talk about school subjects

Pages 30–31

STAGE	TIME	FOCUS
GET STARTED		Sort classroom language into categories and use some of the vocabulary from the lesson.
WORK WITH WORDS		Recycle vocabulary related to the classroom and school subjects. Complete a school schedule. Watch a video of teenagers talking about their favorite school subjects. Complete sentences to describe your schedule.
SPEAK		Use the vocabulary from the lesson to write a definition of three school subjects for a partner to name.

Get started

Recycle classroom language. Write these three categories on the board: *Actions*, *Questions*, *Expressions*.

Ask students to categorize these phrases: *Open your books*; *Time's up!*; *Underline the words in bold*; *How do you pronounce "chemistry"?*; *Good work!*; *How do you spell that?*

Divide the class into pairs and ask them to race against each other to think of more phrases for each category in three minutes. Ask students to stop when the time is up and count how many phrases they have for each category.

Invite students to come to the board and write their phrases in the correct categories. Correct any misspelled words.

Put the title of the unit on the board: *Classmates*. Elicit from students the meaning of the word (*people in your class at school*) and ask them what they think the unit is going to be about (*everything related to school*).

ANSWERS
Actions: Open your books; Underline the words in bold
Questions: How do you pronounce "chemistry"?; How do you spell that?
Expressions: Time's up!; Good work!

WORK WITH WORDS School subjects

1 RECALL

- Focus students' attention on the photo of a classroom in the USA and elicit similarities and differences between it and the classroom they are in now.
- Divide the class into pairs and ask students to write words for the different categories. Draw students' attention to the examples and the photo to help give them ideas.
- Set a time limit of three minutes.
- Choose different students to give their answers.
- Ask students to do the **Work with Words** task on page 71.

2

- Have students match the icons on the photo to the US school subjects.
- Elicit any more school subjects students may know (e.g., *biology*, *chemistry*, *physics*, *social studies*, *French*).
- Point out that we use capital letters when we talk about languages as school subjects, but other subjects don't need a capital letter.
- Find out from students which subject doesn't have an icon (*music*), but don't check answers at this point.

3a 37

- Play the track for students to check their answers to Exercise 2 first.
- Continue the track for students to listen and repeat as the answers are given again.

ANSWERS / AUDIO SCRIPT 37
a art b health c English d history e languages
f PE (physical education) g drama h geography
i computer science j math k science l music

3b

- Ask students to create an icon for the missing subject in Exercise 2 (*music*).
- Have students come to the board and draw their icons.
- Vote on the best icon. Point to each icon and ask students to raise their hands. Ask a volunteer to count the number of votes for each icon and name the winner.

66

CLASSMATES 3

Extra activity
Divide the class into [...] have students act out the school subject[...]

The optional extra activities provide ideas for extending the lesson and offering additional practice.

4 38
- Focus student[...] complete the [...]
- Use this oppo[...] short forms in[...]
- Play the track for students to check their answers.

ANSWERS / AUDIO SCRIPT 38
1 homeroom 2 history 3 lunch 4 math 5 drama
6 Science; health
See Student's Book, page 32, for audio script.

Answer keys and audio scripts are embedded within the teaching notes.

Alternative procedure: less confiden[...]
Recycle saying the time by asking co[...] questions about the schedule to help[...] before they do Exercise 4: *What time do they start school every morning?* (8:30 a.m.); *What time do they have lunch?* (11:50 a.m.–12:30 p.m.); *When do they finish school?* (3:30 p.m.).

5 39
- Play the track for students to listen and complete the schedule with the school subjects.
- Let students compare their answers in pairs before you check them as a class.
- Ask students if they like this school schedule and whether it is similar to or different from their own.

ANSWERS / AUDIO SCRIPT 39
1 English 2 music 3 languages 4 art 5 geography
6 PE
1 Our first class on Monday is English.
2 We have music on Tuesday afternoon.
3 We have languages three times a week from ten o'clock to 10:50. I study French.
4 Our last class on Wednesday is art.
5 Geography is on Tuesday, Thursday, and Friday before lunch.
6 The week ends with two hours of PE.

Extra activity
Ask students to study this audio text in order to reconstruct all the information they remember. Play the track again for students to write down what they hear. Keep playing the track until a student thinks he or she has a perfect version of the text and calls out *Stop!* Divide the class into groups of three or four to compare their sentences. Invite students to come to the board and write their sentences to check. Ask students to underline [...] the prepositions of time to recycle this grammar [...]t.

6 THE MOVING PICTURE
- Explain to students that th[...] teenagers talking about sc[...]
- Play the video and ask stu[...] subjects the students like [...]

Activity suggestions for fast finishers are provided throughout the lessons.

- Let students compare their answers in pairs before you check them as a class.
- You might want to play the video again wi[...] off. Pause after each activity and ask stu[...] remember the exact words of the convers[...] frame.

Complete scripts for the Moving Picture videos are embedded in the lesson notes.

ANSWERS / VIDEO SCRIPT
Charlotte: drama because it's fun to act, sing, a[...]
and she likes being with her friends in drama class
Holly: math because she enjoys algebra, and she l[...] right answer
Aaron: PE because he likes trying new sports and games, and geography because he likes learning about sports in other countries

Robert: Hey, everyone! It's time for *What's Cool in School*. We're [...]king about our favorite school subjects today. I'm [...]bert, and I'm here with three of my classmates. They're [...]ng to tell you about their favorite – and not so favorite – [...]bjects. First, it's Charlotte.
[...] favorite school subject's drama because it's fun to act, sing, and dance. It's very creative. I can be other people or animals or even a machine. I love being with my friends in drama class. We laugh all the time. And Ms. Lowell is the best drama teacher in the world. Hey, Ms. Lowell! Drama class is awesome.
Robert: Next we go to Holly.
Holly: Well, one of my favorite subjects is math because I enjoy algebra. Maybe some people think it's strange, but I like to have one right answer. I don't really like history. There are so many dates and too much information, and then they expect us to remember it all.
Robert: Let's move on to Aaron.
Aaron: My favorite subject is PE. I like to have fun and do different sports. We do a lot of different activities in PE class. I like to try new games. Oh, and I play on the soccer team after school. I like to swim and play basketball and tennis. I also like geography because I like learning about sports that people play in different countries. But I don't like drama or singing. I try not to take those classes.
Robert: Thanks for your thoughts. And that's *What's Cool in School* for today.

7
- Ask students to complete the sentences about their school schedules.
- Have students compare their sentences in pairs and report any differences they found in their school routines and likes and dislikes.

Fast finishers
Ask fast finishers to create an "odd one out" activity (i.e., one item of a group is different and doesn't fit in with the rest of the group) from the vocabulary in this lesson to test the rest of the class. You could write an example on the board; for example, *languages, art, history, science* (*science is the odd one out, as the others are arts and humanities subjects*).

Task-based homework is provided at the end of every lesson and is related to the topic or skill of the lesson.

Other features

The Teacher's Edition also contains:

Procedural notes for the Unit Reviews and Progress Checks
Full and detailed notes are given for the Unit Reviews and Progress Checks in the Student's Book.

Workbook answer keys and audio scripts
At the back of the Teacher's Edition, answer keys and audio scripts are given for the corresponding Workbook.

Teaching Tips
Pages 24–29 of the Teacher's Edition provide useful tips on classroom management, teaching vocabulary; grammar, skills, and pronunciation, as well as using games in the classroom.

Alternative procedures
Alternative procedure suggestions are provided for selected exercises, offering a different approach to teaching the Student's Book content. These alternatives appeal to different learning styles and abilities.

Background information
Useful and interesting background information on specific lesson topics is provided in the Move Beyond for Teachers feature to help with the presentation of the content.

S STARTER ENGLISH 24/7

STAGE	TIME	FOCUS
GET STARTED		Play a word game as an introduction to the topic of meeting people.
THINK AND READ		Talk about activities you can do at a summer camp. Read a story and answer comprehension questions.
RECALL		Recycle vocabulary to talk about dates, nationalities, and how to introduce yourself. Recycle *be* with subject pronouns and possessive adjectives.
THINK AND READ		Complete words about things you do at school. Read a story and identify things people do.
RECALL		Recycle vocabulary to talk about classroom things, colors, the alphabet, and how to say goodbye. Recycle plurals; object pronouns; and *this*, *that*, *these*, and *those*.

Get started

Play a game to learn names and introduce the topic of the lesson. Give one student a soft ball; he or she throws it to another student while calling out the other student's name. That student then throws the ball to another student and calls out his or her name. Continue around the class.

Remind students to throw the ball to classmates who are not sitting directly beside them to include an element of surprise in the game. (See Teaching Tips, *Managing large classes*, page 24.)

SUMMER CAMP *Pages 4–5*

THINK AND READ

1

- Ask if any students know what a summer camp is. If so, invite them to explain what it is in English (*a place where children go to stay during summer vacation and do different activities*). Have students think of three activities they can do at a summer camp.
- Encourage students to call out their answers for you to write them on the board.

Fast finishers
Ask fast finishers to think of three more activities they can do at a summer camp to share with the rest of the class at the end of the activity.

2 01

- Focus students' attention on the story. The story is recorded, so if your students are less confident, you could play the audio as they read.
- Ask students which things in Exercise 1 Marta does on her first day at summer camp.
- Invite a volunteer to say why today is a special day for Marta.
- Ask some simple comprehension questions to check that students have understood the story; for example, *What day is it?* (Monday); *What date is it?* (July 16); *Where does Marta go first at the summer camp?* (to the office for registration); *Does she meet a new friend?* (yes).

ANSWERS / AUDIO SCRIPT 01

She meets new friends and speaks in English. Today's special because it's Marta's birthday.

See Student's Book, pages 4–5, for audio script.

3

- Ask students to read and/or listen to the story again.

RECALL

1a DATES 02

- Ask students to write the dates from the calendar. Ask them to find and circle the day in the calendar for each date listed and then write it out in full, as in the example. Play the track for students to check their answers.
- Play the track again for students to listen and repeat. (See Teaching Tips, *Varying drilling techniques*, page 28.)

ANSWERS / AUDIO SCRIPT 02

1 It's Tuesday, July third.
2 It's Thursday, July twelfth.
3 It's Friday, July twentieth.
4 It's Wednesday, July twenty-fifth.
5 It's Saturday, July twenty-first.
6 It's Monday, July second.

Fast finishers
Have fast finishers write a list of all the ordinal numbers from 1 to 20 (i.e., *first*, *second*, *third*, ...). At the end of the activity, ask them to read the cardinal numbers aloud (i.e., *one*, *two*, *three*, ...) for the rest of the class to respond with the corresponding ordinal numbers.

1b

- Ask students to write the names of the other months.
- Ask students to write and say today's date.
- Check answers as a class.

ANSWERS

January, February, March, April, May, June, (July), August, September, October, November, December

Alternative procedure: more confident classes
You could make this into a competitive game by asking students to get into pairs and race against other pairs to write down the months. The first pair to finish and raise their hands are the winners.

2 INTRODUCTIONS

- Have students complete the introductions with words from the table. Remind them that they need to use capital letters at the beginning of a sentence. (See Teaching Tips, *Subject pronouns and possessive adjectives*, page 25.)
- Ask students to compare their answers in pairs.
- Check answers as a class.
- Have students repeat the sentences, paying attention to the contracted forms.

ANSWERS
1 Our 2 his; They 3 My 4 She

3 NATIONALITIES 03

- Ask students to work in pairs to write the nationalities in the table.
- Play the track for students to listen and check their answers.
- Continue the track for students to listen and repeat. Pay special attention to the stress patterns.
- Go around the class, choosing students to say their answers.

ANSWERS / AUDIO SCRIPT 03

Mexico	*Mexican*
Germany	German
Italy	Italian
Japan	Japanese
Colombia	Colombian
Spain	Spanish
the USA	American

Fast finishers
Ask fast finishers to write another nationality for each pronunciation group: *-an*, *-ish*, *-ian* or *-ean*, and *-ese* (e.g., *Jamaican*, *Swedish*, *Australian*, *Korean*, *Chinese*).

Alternative procedure: more confident classes
Ask students to underline the stressed syllable in each country and nationality before you play the track to check their answers. (See underlining in audio script above.)

4 *BE* 04

- Ask students to work in pairs to complete the conversation. Remind them to use contractions where possible.
- Play the track for students to check their answers.
- Have students practice the conversation in pairs, paying attention to the intonation. Then have them switch roles and repeat the procedure.
- Highlight the final falling intonation for a *Wh-* question: *What's your name?* In students' own languages, the intonation range may be narrower. This can make understanding difficult for English learners, and it can make them sound bored or unenthusiastic, so it is important for students to practice this intonation pattern.

ANSWERS / AUDIO SCRIPT 04
2 's/is 3 Are 4 aren't 5 isn't 6 are 7 'm/am
8 are 9 'm/am 10 's/is
See Student's Book, page 7, for audio script.

Alternative procedure: more confident classes
Ask students to work in pairs to change all the facts they can to create a different conversation. Choose random pairs to read their conversations aloud.

5a PERSONAL INFORMATION

- Refer students to the picture story on this page. Ask them to choose one of the students and think of a new name and nationality.
- Ask students to complete the form with their new details.

5b

- Divide the class into pairs and ask them to complete the form with their partner's new information.
- Elicit the questions students will need to ask.

Alternative procedure: less confident classes
Less confident students may prefer to write out the questions first before doing this as a speaking activity.

5c

- Focus students' attention on the prompts and have them introduce their partner to other students. (See Teaching Tips, *Open and closed pairs*, page 24.)

ENGLISH CLASS *Pages 6–7*

THINK AND READ

1

- Ask students to complete words for the things they usually do at school.
- Choose a student to read the answers aloud for the class.

ANSWERS
listen repeat write speak check

2 05

- Focus students' attention on the story. If your students are less confident, you could let them read as you play the audio.
- Ask students to read or listen to the story and check the things they see from Exercise 1.
- Check answers as a class.
- Elicit from the class two or three more things to add to the list (e.g., *spell*, *ask*, *answer*, *raise your hand*, *lend*, *borrow*). Write their ideas on the board.

SUGGESTED ANSWERS / AUDIO SCRIPT 05
read listen write speak
See Student's Book, pages 6–7, for audio script.

RECALL

1 CLASSROOM THINGS 06

- Have students write the letters (a–l) of the things in the picture next to the words.
- Play the track for students to check their answers first.
- Continue the track for students to listen and repeat after checking the answers.

ANSWERS / AUDIO SCRIPT 06
a *board* b table c computer d chair e door f floor
g desk h poster i wall j clock k light l window

Fast finishers
Students who finish early could think of more classroom objects to add to the list (e.g., *pen*, *pencil*, *sharpener*, *pencil case*, *dictionary*, *ruler*, *notebook*, *textbook*, *projector*). At the end of the activity, they could give definitions of the words they have written for other students to guess and add to their lists.

2a COLORS 07

- Refer students to the color boxes and ask them to write the colors.
- Play the track for students to check their answers first.
- Continue the track for students to listen and repeat after checking the answers.

ANSWERS / AUDIO SCRIPT 07
1 *red* 2 orange 3 yellow 4 green 5 blue 6 purple
7 pink 8 brown 9 black 10 white

2b

- Divide the class into pairs to talk about the colors in the classroom.
- Draw students' attention to the model conversation.
- Invite individual students to say some of their sentences.

3a THE ALPHABET 08

- Play the track for students to listen and write the letters in the correct places.
- Continue the track for students to listen and repeat.

ANSWERS / AUDIO SCRIPT 08

/eɪ/	/i/	/e/	/aɪ/	/oʊ/	/u/	/ɑ/
A	*B*	*F*	*I*	*O*	*Q*	*R*
H	C	L	Y		U	
J	*D*	*M*			*W*	
K	E	N				
	G	*S*				
	P	X				
	T					
	V					
	Z					

A B C D E F G H I J K L M N O P Q R S T U V W X Y Z

Alternative procedure: more confident classes
Ask students to write the letters in the correct places *before* playing the track.

Alternative procedure: less confident classes
Ask less confident students to repeat the letters by column. Then point out (in L1 if necessary) that they are grouped by vowel sound and that the symbols at the top are the phonetic symbols for the different sounds.

3b 09 PRONOUNCE

- Play the track for students to listen and repeat the words with the /i/ sound. (See Teaching Tips, *Long and short vowel sounds*, page 32.)

AUDIO SCRIPT 09
See Student's Book, page 6, for audio script.

4a *THIS, THAT, THESE, THOSE*

- Focus students' attention on the table and the arrows to indicate *here* and *there*.
- Ask them to complete the table.
- Choose a student to say the answers.

ANSWERS

	here	there
Singular	this	that
Plural	these	*those*

4b

- Divide the class into pairs to ask each other the names of things in the classroom and how to spell them.
- Draw students' attention to the model conversations and remind them to use *this*, *these*, *that*, and *those*.

Alternative procedure: less confident classes
Ask a few confident students to model the conversations aloud before asking students to continue in pairs.

Extra activity
Ask students if they remember other questions apart from *How do you spell it?* to ask for meaning, pronunciation, spelling, repetition, or clarification; for example, *What does X mean? How do you pronounce/say this word? Could you say that again, please? Could you speak more slowly, please? Can you explain that again, please?*

You could ask students to make posters and display them in the classroom for the first month of class.

5a PLURALS 10

- Play the track for students to listen and write the words.
- Ask students to compare their answers in pairs before you check them as a class.
- Choose a student to read the list of words.

ANSWERS / AUDIO SCRIPT 10
1 this bag 2 this chair 3 this poster 4 this desk
5 this woman 6 this fish 7 this sandwich 8 this tomato

5b

- Ask students to write the plurals of the words. If you want them to include the possessive adjective, remind them that the plural of *this* is *these*. (See Teaching Tips, *English plural nouns*, page 25.)
- Invite different students to write the singular and plural forms of the nouns on the board. Ask the class to check their answers. If there is a mistake, ask a student to come to the board to correct it.

ANSWERS
1 bags 2 chairs 3 posters 4 desks 5 women
6 fish 7 sandwiches 8 tomatoes

6a OBJECT PRONOUNS 11

- Ask students to complete the conversation with the object pronouns in the box.
- Circulate and monitor as they work, helping them with any difficulties. Highlight that for number 4, students need to read on to find the answer (as it mentions *She* in the next line).
- Play the track for students to check their answers.

ANSWERS / AUDIO SCRIPT 11
2 it 3 you 4 her 5 us 6 them
See Student's Book, page 9, for audio script.

6b

- Ask students to say where Marta's glasses are.

ANSWER
They're on her head!

7 SAY GOODBYE

- Ask students to say goodbye to you and the other students when the class finishes.

Homework

Ask students to make an "odd one out" quiz from the vocabulary and grammar in this Starter Unit. Have students write at least three examples to test their partners at the beginning of the next class. Their partners must select the odd one out and justify their choices. Model an example for the class; for example, *fifth, second, first, twelve.* (*Twelve* is the odd one out, as all the others are ordinal numbers.)

1 UNIT WELCOME TO MY WORLD

IN THE PICTURE In a city

Talk about places in a city *Pages 8–9*

STAGE	TIME	FOCUS
GET STARTED		Use some vocabulary from the lesson as an introduction to the theme of places where people live.
WORK WITH WORDS		Recycle vocabulary for places in a city. Listen to a girl talking about places in her city and find them on a map. Listen and complete a conversation with the correct places. Watch a video and decide which of the places you would like to visit.
WRITE AND SPEAK		Use the vocabulary from the lesson to write a list of interesting places in your city and talk about your favorite places.

Get started

Have students close their books. Use this as an opportunity to pre-teach target vocabulary from the lesson. Write these jumbled words on the board: *wnot*, *teters*, *seohu*, *ticy*, *linbuidg*.

Ask students to work in pairs to reorder the words as fast as they can. When the first pair has finished, they should raise their hands.

Check their answers and ask students what theme links all the words together (*places where people live*).

Ask students if they know the names of any places in a town or a city.

Ask students to open their books, look at the unit title, and say what they think the unit is going to be about (*young people describing places where they live around the world*).

ANSWERS
town street house city building

WORK WITH WORDS Places in a city

1a RECALL

- Divide the class into pairs. Ask them to look at the words and cross out the wrong word in each group. Remind them to say why the wrong word is different.
- Set a one-minute time limit and give regular updates; for example, *Thirty seconds to go.*
- Choose a student to say the answers.
- Drill the pronunciation of *building* (/ˈbɪldɪŋ/).

ANSWERS
1 street 2 downtown

1b

Exam-type task

- Ask students to read the descriptions to complete the words for the places.
- Point out that the first letter is given and that there is a short line for each of the other letters in the word.
- Set a time limit of two minutes and give regular updates; for example, *Only 20 seconds left.*
- Invite volunteers to write the answers on the board or check answers as a class.
- Ask students to do the **Work with Words** task on page 69.

ANSWERS
1 theater 2 swimming pool 3 sports center 4 zoo
5 store 6 restaurant 7 movie theater 8 park

Fast finishers
If some students finish earlier than others, ask them to check their answers in pairs.

2

- Refer students to the map and the photos and ask them to say what city it is.

ANSWER
San Francisco, California (in the USA)

3a 12

- Play the track for students to listen to Teresa. Ask them to number the places in the photos marked with a pin in the order they hear them (1–10) and write down another place Teresa talks about.

ANSWERS / AUDIO SCRIPT 12

1 San Francisco International Airport 2 Powell Street Station 3 shopping mall 4 Museum of Modern Art 5 library 6 AT&T Stadium 7 Great America theme park 8 Coit Tower 9 Golden Gate Bridge 10 Ghirardelli Square

Teresa also talks about her apartment and a restaurant.

Hi, welcome to my city! Most visitors arrive at San Francisco International Airport and then take the metro train into the city. Powell Street station is a few blocks from our apartment. My parents have a restaurant on Geary Street, and we live near there.

Our neighborhood is great. There's a shopping mall near the station, and there's an art museum near our apartment too. I love reading, and I go to the library every Saturday with my mom.

In the summer I sometimes watch baseball at AT&T Park with my dad and my brother – my brother is a big baseball fan. Sometimes we go to the Great America theme park too. The theme park is awesome, but my favorite place in San Francisco is Coit Tower. The city looks fantastic from the tower, and you can see San Francisco's famous bridge, the Golden Gate Bridge. At Ghirardelli Square, you can shop and eat chocolate at the famous chocolate factory!

3b 13

- Play the track for students to listen and check their answers.
- Continue the track for students to listen and repeat.

AUDIO SCRIPT 13

1 airport 2 station 3 shopping mall 4 museum
5 library 6 stadium 7 theme park 8 tower
9 bridge 10 square

MOVE BEYOND FOR TEACHERS

San Francisco, California

San Francisco, with a 2012 estimated population of 825,863, is one of the most famous and influential cities in the USA. The hilly city is situated next to one of the biggest natural harbors on the Pacific Ocean. San Francisco was originally established as a Spanish mission in 1776 and later became part of Mexico. It came under the control of the USA in 1846. After gold was discovered nearby in 1848, San Francisco quickly grew to become the cosmopolitan city it is today. San Francisco is now known as an open-minded city that welcomes new ideas. The city has a strong culture of music, literature, movies, and sports.

4a 14 PRONOUNCE

- Play the track for students to listen and repeat the words in the box.

AUDIO SCRIPT 14

See Student's Book, page 8, for audio script.

4b

- Tell students that in English, most two-syllable words are stressed on the first syllable. Draw students' attention to the words in the box in Exercise 4a again and point out that the first syllable of each word is underlined.
- Have students underline the stressed syllable in each word in the box in Exercise 4b.
- Ask individual students to pronounce the words in the box with the correct stress. Then ask the whole class to repeat the words after you.

ANSWERS

<u>awe</u>some <u>base</u>ball <u>ci</u>ty <u>sum</u>mer <u>wel</u>come

5 15

- Ask students to choose the correct words to complete the conversation.
- Allow students to compare their answers in pairs before you play the track for them to listen and check.

ANSWERS / AUDIO SCRIPT 15

2 train station 3 museum 4 mall 5 stadium

See Student's Book, page 10, for audio script.

Extra activity

Have students work in pairs and take turns reading the conversation aloud, paying special attention to the word stress. When they have finished, ask them to switch roles and repeat the procedure.

6 THE MOVING PICTURE

- Tell students they are going to watch a video about different places in San Francisco.
- Play the video and ask students to make a list of all the places they see.
- Divide the class into pairs to compare their answers and discuss whether they would like to visit these places, giving reasons why or why not.
- Ask several students to report what their partner said.
- Play the video again with the volume off. Pause after each activity and ask students to try to remember the exact words of the conversation in each frame.

VIDEO SCRIPT

Hi there! Let me show you my city!
San Francisco is a busy place, and there are a lot of things to do and see. This is the Golden Gate Bridge. It's nearly 1,300 meters long. I think it's the most beautiful bridge in the world.
Ghirardelli Square isn't far from the Golden Gate Bridge. I think the buildings are really cool. It's a great place to hang out with friends or go shopping.
This is the library. It's downtown, next to a big plaza. Sometimes there are free concerts. My friends and I like to listen to music there.
Now we're at Coit Tower. You can see the city from the tall white tower. There's an art museum inside the tower too.
Wow, it's time to leave already. This is the San Francisco airport. It's really modern and there are lots of great shops. Hope to see you here soon! Bye!

WRITE AND SPEAK

7a

- Ask students to work in pairs and make a list of interesting places in their city or area.

7b

- Ask pairs to read their list aloud to another pair to see if they have the same places. Draw students' attention to the model conversations and remind them to talk about their favorite places.

MOVE BEYOND

Ask students to do the **Words & Beyond** exercise on page 69.

Homework

Ask students to rewrite the conversation in Exercise 5 about their city or area, changing as many facts as they can (e.g., names, places, activities). At the beginning of the next class, have students work in pairs and read their conversations aloud for their partners to note down all the changes they hear.

READING Meet San Francisco's sister cities

Identify the type of text

Page 10

STAGE	TIME	FOCUS
GET STARTED		Play a game to recycle key vocabulary to talk about places.
SPEAK AND READ		Identify the type of text (reading subskill). Read an online city guide to Osaka and take notes.
REACT		Discuss why you would or wouldn't like to visit Osaka. Talk about sister cities. Note: Find out about students' sister cities *before the lesson* in case students do not know. Alternatively, if the class has internet access, this can be done in class.

Get started

Divide the class into pairs. Ask students to take turns acting out mimes for the key vocabulary about places (*city*, *theater*, *movie theater*, *tower*, etc.).

SPEAK AND READ

1

- Divide the class into pairs to look at the title of the page and choose the correct explanation for "sister cities."
- Choose a student to report back to the class.

ANSWER
B

MOVE BEYOND FOR TEACHERS

Sister cities

The term *sister city* is used to describe an agreement made between towns and cities in different countries to promote friendship and understanding, as well as trade and tourism. Point out to students that the word *sister* relates to family vocabulary.

2a

- Ask students to think of any tips they know on how to identify a type of text.
- Have students read the HOW TO box and see if they thought of the same tips.
- Ask them to cover the HOW TO box and elicit the three tips on how to identify the type of text. (See Teaching Tips, *Predicting before reading*, page 28.)

2b 16

- Ask students if they know anything about Osaka (Japan's third-largest city by population after Tokyo and Yokohama).
- Have students read the text quickly and try to identify the type of text: A, B, C, or D.
- You could ask students to raise their hands and vote to indicate whether they think the answer is A, B, C, or D to take the pressure off one particular student. Don't play the audio at this point. It is an extra feature, and a suggestion for using it in class is included at the end of the lesson.

ANSWER
C

3

- Ask students to check the tips in the HOW TO box that helped them with Exercise 2b.
- Ask different students around the class to say why the other options were incorrect.

4

Exam-type task

- Explain to students that Teresa is taking notes on San Francisco's sister cities.
- Ask students to read the text again and complete her notes with one word, number, or date in each blank.
- Draw students' attention to the example answer before they start.
- Choose different students to say the answers and where they found the information in the text.

ANSWERS
2 1957 3 2.5 4 puppets 5 under 6 100
7 museum

MOVE BEYOND FOR TEACHERS

Osaka

The National Bunraku Theatre opened in 1984 as a base to preserve and pass on Bunraku, the tradition of puppet drama.

HEP Five is a major shopping mall and entertainment center in the Umeda commercial district of Osaka. The highlight of the shopping mall is the Ferris wheel above the seventh floor, with a height of 106 meters aboveground. The wheel has 52 luxury gondolas that fit up to four people, and each rotation of the wheel lasts 15 minutes.

Osaka Castle is a concrete reconstruction of the original built in 1583. The castle and park are at their colorful best in the cherry-blossom and autumn-foliage seasons.

Alternative procedure: less confident classes

In a less confident class, ask students to match some key words to their definitions before they do Exercise 4. Write these words and definitions in a jumbled order on the board for students to work on in pairs.

main	*most important*
puppet	*a model of a person or an animal that you can move with wires or strings*
under	*in a lower position*
Ferris wheel	*a ride at a fair or park*
roof	*top, outer part of a building*

Fast finishers

Write these words on the board: *main*, *puppet*, *under*, *Ferris wheel*, *roof*. Have fast finishers write definitions with the help of their dictionaries. Ask them to read their definitions aloud when everyone has finished for other students to match to the words on the board.

REACT

5

- Ask students to work in pairs and discuss the questions, giving reasons for their answers.
- Draw students' attention to the PHRASE BYTES box to help them structure their opinions.
- Choose random students to answer the questions.
- Encourage students to expand on why they would or wouldn't like to visit Osaka.

Extra activity

Introduce the idea of borrowed words in the English language. Write these words on the board and ask students if they can identify which countries the words come from:

Food: *pizza, pasta* (Italy), *sushi* (Japan), *tapas* (Spain)

Music: *opera, arpeggio, piano* (Italy)

Add these words from Japan: *bonsai, kamikaze, manga, samurai, sayonara, tsunami, kimono, karaoke, judo, ninja, origami, sumo.*

Divide the class into pairs and ask them to write definitions for at least three words in the lists, using their dictionaries if they need to. Ask if students know any other borrowed words in English.

MOVE BEYOND

Ask students to write the nationalities for the countries in the text.

ANSWERS

Japanese, Australian, Italian, Greek, French, Indian

Recorded reading text 16

The audio could be used for less confident classes to listen while reading the text for the second time. You could also use the audio for checking the answers to Exercise 4, asking students to raise their hands when they hear the relevant information.

Homework

Divide the class into small groups and ask students to choose from the list of San Francisco's sister cities so that each group has a different one. For homework, ask them to do some research individually for an online city guide (e.g., the number of people who live there, what you can do, and any other interesting information) to present to their group at the beginning of the next class. Give students a limit of 150 words.

GRAMMAR *There is/there are*; prepositions of place

Describe what's in a place *Page 11*

STAGE	TIME	FOCUS
GET STARTED		Look at some emoticons and talk about how they are used in informal messages.
READ		Read a chat message for specific information.
STUDY		Use the chat message to help you complete grammar explanations for *there is/there are*. Label pictures with the correct prepositions of place.
PRACTICE		Use *there is/there are* and prepositions of place in written exercises.
SPEAK AND WRITE		Use *there is/there are* and prepositions of place to describe and draw a picture. Write questions and answers about your city using *there is/there are*.

Get started

Draw a simple emoticon on the board, for example, :) , and ask students what we call these symbols in English (*emoticons* – "emotional icons," or "smileys") and what this emoticon means (*I'm smiling*). Ask students to say where we can find them (*emails, text messages, chat rooms, forums*). Ask students why we use emoticons. (*They make messages look friendly and fun and are particularly useful when what you write could be misunderstood.*) Ask students to compare these two sentences:

You always say the same thing. (No emoticon – it looks like a criticism.)
You always say the same thing ;-) (Winking – it looks friendlier.)

Elicit definitions for well-known emoticons and let students come up and draw the corresponding emoticons on the board. For example:

:/	not so good
@}->–	a rose for you
;(	I'm crying.
:-o	Uh-oh!
|-)	Ha ha!
:-||	I'm seriously angry.

READ Grammar in context

1

- Ask students to read the chat messages and say where Owen lives and how many people live there.

ANSWERS

He lives in New York, Texas. Fifteen people live there.

MOVE BEYOND FOR TEACHERS

New York

New York, Texas, was first settled around 1856. The town declined after it was bypassed by the railroad in 1901. In 1992, the town had a Reynolds store and a Baptist church.

New York City is one of the most important cities in the USA and also in the world. New York has been described as the cultural capital of the world, and it exerts a significant impact on commerce, finance, research, technology, and education. New York is also an important center for international diplomacy and home to the United Nations Headquarters.

STUDY

2

- Have students use the chat messages in Exercise 1 to help them complete the examples.
- Check answers as a class.

ANSWERS

are isn't There Is there Are there

Alternative procedure: less confident classes

Ask students to look at Exercise 1 again to help them write example sentences in their notebooks for affirmative and negative sentences, as well as questions and short answers for both *there is* and *there are* in full and contracted forms. For example:

There is / There are	
Affirmative	*There is a zoo. / There's a zoo.* *There are some small houses.* (no contracted form)
Negative	*There is not a zoo. / There isn't a zoo.* *There are not any parks. / There aren't any parks.*
Questions and short answers	*Is there a zoo?* *Yes, there is.* *No, there is not. / No, there isn't.* *Are there any towers?* *Yes, there are.* (no contracted form) *No, there are not. / No, there aren't.*

Extra activity

Ask students to work in pairs and practice reading the chat messages aloud. Then have them switch roles and read the messages again. To make this more fun, and more like a real chat message, students could sit back-to-back. Remind students of the rising intonation in *Yes/No* questions.

3

- Ask students to look at the pictures and complete 1–5 with the correct words in bold from Exercise 1.

ANSWERS

1 in 2 near 3 next to 4 across from 5 between

PRACTICE

4

- Ask students to write sentences about New York City.
- Draw students' attention to the example sentence before they start.
- Let students compare their answers in pairs before you check them as a class. (See Teaching Tips, *Checking answers*, page 24.)
- Remind them to use contracted forms whenever possible.

ANSWERS

2 There's a big park.
3 There aren't any big farms.
4 There are a lot of people.
5 There isn't a beach.
6 There aren't a lot of quiet places.

Extra activity

Recycle vocabulary for classroom objects. Ask students to say sentences about objects in the classroom with *There is ...* , *There isn't ...* , *There are ...* , or *There aren't ...* .

5

- Refer students to the picture and ask them to predict what they think the exercise is going to be about (*a description of a town*).
- Have students complete the sentences about the town using *there is/there are* and prepositions of place.
- Draw students' attention to the example answer before they start.

ANSWERS

2 There's a restaurant near / next to one of the stores.
3 There are some trees behind the museum.
4 There's a bookstore next to / near the museum.
5 There are some tables in front of the café.
6 And there's me in the chair!

Extra activity

Ask students to write two negative sentences about their city, area, or school using *there isn't/there aren't*. Divide the class into pairs and ask them to read their negative sentences aloud for their partner to listen to and correct if necessary.

SPEAK AND WRITE

6

- Divide the class into A/B pairs.
- Explain to students that they are going to describe a picture to their partner for him or her to draw and then compare it with the picture in the book.
- Ask Student As to look at the picture on page 75 and Student Bs to look at the picture on page 76.
- Monitor and note errors and good use of language to go over in a feedback session at the end of the activity.

7a

- Ask students to use the prompts to write the questions for a survey.
- Do the first question together as an example.
- Choose random students to read their questions aloud in a natural way, paying attention to the rising intonation in these *Yes/No* questions.

ANSWERS

1 Is there a theme park in your area?
2 Is there a sports center near your home?
3 Are there any parks?
4 Is there a swimming pool?
5 Are there (any) free concerts in your town?
6 Are there (any) other places for young people?

7b

- Ask students to write their answers.
- Go around the class, asking students to say whether they think their city or town is a good place for young people.

Alternative procedure: more confident classes

In a more confident class, have students answer the questions without preparing their answers first in written form. Have them interview each other and then report back to the class, saying whether their partner's town or area sounds like a good place for young people. Ask students to justify their opinion with examples.

Homework

Ask students to write a chat message between them and a friend about their favorite places in their city, town, or area using *there is/there are*. Refer students to the chat message format in Exercise 1. Remind them to recycle vocabulary about places and to include as many prepositions as they can in their descriptions. They can also use emoticons to add style and emotion! In the next class, divide the class into pairs and ask them to take turns reading their chat message conversations.

LISTENING AND VOCABULARY Meet my family

Listen for the main ideas

Page 12

STAGE	TIME	FOCUS
GET STARTED		Recycle prepositions of place as an introduction to the topic of the lesson.
SPEAK AND LISTEN		Circle family words in a word group. Listen to four students talking about whether they have a big family or a small family (listening subskill).
REACT		Compare and discuss what's good or bad about living in a small family or a big family.
WORK WITH WORDS		Complete sentences with the correct family words and then listen and check.

Get started

Draw a block of apartments on the board and write a name in one of them, for example:

Susan		

Ask students to come up and write different words for members of the family in each of the apartments. For example:

sister		*uncle*
aunt and uncle		*brother*
Susan		*grandparents*
cousin		*mom and dad*

Now draw a 3x3 grid and recycle the prepositions of place from the previous class, writing them in the spaces. For example:

between	*under*	*above*
next to	*near*	*in front of*
across from	*on*	*in*

Each team writes a sentence to describe where the members of Susan's family live, using the correct preposition of place to win the square. For example:

Susan's brother lives between her grandparents and her uncle.

Susan's cousin lives on the first floor.

Susan's sister lives in an apartment on the top floor.

Susan's brother lives above his grandparents.

SPEAK AND LISTEN

1 RECALL

- Ask students to work in pairs and circle the family words. Draw students' attention to Akemi's name before they start.
- Choose a student to read the words aloud.

ANSWERS

father, mom, dad, grandma, grandpa, grandfather, grandmother, brother, sister, child, grandchild – in any order

2a

- Refer students to the HOW TO box and ask a student to read it aloud. (See Teaching Tips, *Listening for the main idea*, page 27.)

2b 17

- Focus on the photos of four students and recycle nationalities by asking the nationality of each one (*Australian*, *Japanese*, *Italian*, *French*).
- Ask students to write a list of the four names.
- Play the track for the class to listen to the students and decide whether they have a big family or a small family. Tell them to write Big or Small next to each name.
- Choose a student to read the answers aloud.
- Ask students which key words (underlined in the audio script) helped them decide their answers.

ANSWERS / AUDIO SCRIPT 17

Riley: small
Akemi: big
Antonio: big (but his nuclear family is small)
Janine: big

Riley: In my family there are just four of us – my mom and my dad, my sister Rose, and me. All of my friends have big families, and I like that. A small family is a little boring.

Akemi: I have four big brothers and they all love watching sports on TV. My parents like watching TV too. My grandparents – my grandma and grandpa – live with us, and they watch TV all the time. Our house is very noisy!

Antonio: I'm an only child, so it's just me and my mom and dad. But I have an uncle, my mom's brother, and two aunts, my dad's sisters. They have kids, and they all live near us, so there are always a lot of aunts, uncles, and cousins in our apartment. I'm never lonely!

Janine: I have a brother and two sisters. My brother and one of my sisters are married. My brother's wife is Lisa, and my sister's husband is Tom. They don't have any kids yet.

MOVE BEYOND FOR TEACHERS

Cultural differences in families

Today, very few homes house more than two generations (i.e., children and parents). Most modern families take one of two forms: nuclear or blended. The nuclear family is a family group consisting of a mother and a father and their children. A variation on this type is the single-parent family. The second most common type of family is the blended family: a family group created by remarriage that includes stepparents, stepsiblings, or both. An extended family includes relatives beyond nuclear and blended family levels (i.e., cousins, aunts and uncles, grandparents, and great grandparents).

3

- Ask students to look back at the HOW TO box and to check the tips that helped them with Exercise 2b.

4 17

- Ask students to read the sentences before listening. Play the track again for students to listen and circle *T* (true) or *F* (false).
- Ask students to compare their answers in pairs before you elicit answers from several different students.

ANSWERS / AUDIO SCRIPT 17

1 F 2 T 3 T 4 F 5 T
See Exercise 2b for audio script.

Alternative procedure: less confident classes

In a less confident class, ask students some follow-up comprehension questions to make sure they have fully understood the listening. You could play the track again if necessary.

How many people are there in Riley's family? (four)

Who are they? (Riley and his mom, dad, and sister, Rose)

What does Riley think about living in a small family? (He says it's boring.)

How many people live in Akemi's house? (nine)

Who are they? (four older brothers, mom and dad, grandparents, and Akemi)

What does Akemi say about living with a big family? (It's very noisy.)

Who lives near Antonio? (his aunts, uncles, and cousins)

How many people live in Antonio's house? (three – Antonio, his mom, and his dad)

How many brothers and sisters does Janine have? (three)

How many brothers does Janine have? (one brother)

How many sisters does Janine have? (two sisters)

REACT

5

- Divide the class into pairs to discuss what's good about a small family and what's good about a big family.
- Draw students' attention to the PHRASE BYTES box to help them structure their answers.

Alternative procedure: more confident classes

Hold a debate.

Divide the class into two groups. Ask each side to prepare arguments for the talking point, choosing either big or small families. Give students five minutes to prepare their arguments.

Write some phrases on the board to help them debate; for example, *We don't agree*; *We think that …* ; *That is true, but … .*

Ask each side to read their arguments aloud one at a time for the other side to reply and give their opinion.

At the end of the debate, ask students to vote on whether they think it is better to live in a small family or a big family.

WORK WITH WORDS Family

6 18

- Have students work in pairs to complete the sentences with the correct words. Point out that each group of three words in the boxes refers to the following three blanks.
- Play the track for students to check their answers.
- Continue the track for students to listen and repeat the words.

ANSWERS / AUDIO SCRIPT 18

1 parents 2 son 3 daughter 4 grandparents
5 granddaughter 6 grandsons 7 uncle 8 aunts
9 cousins 10 married 11 wife 12 husband
See Student's Book, page 14, for first part of audio script.

MOVE BEYOND

Ask students to do the **Words & Beyond** exercises on page 69.

Homework

Ask students to write five sentences about their family: three true and two false. At the beginning of the next class, ask students to read their sentences aloud for a partner to guess which sentences are true and which are false. You could model this activity first by writing sentences about your own family on the board; for example, *I have three brothers. I live with my grandparents.*

GRAMMAR *Have*

Talk about relationships and possessions

Page 13

STAGE	TIME	FOCUS
GET STARTED		Take a quiz using sentences with *have*.
READ AND LISTEN		Read and listen to a conversation to find specific information.
STUDY		Complete grammar explanations for *have*. Use *have* in a chain sentence.
PRACTICE		Use *have/has* in written exercises.
SPEAK		Ask other students questions using *have* and report to a partner.

Get started

(See Teaching Tips, *Test before you teach*, page 29.)

Ask students to work in pairs.

Write the following on the board and ask students to complete the sentences with *has* or *doesn't have* to make them correct.

Our Student's Book:

1 .... *12 units.*

2 .... *a Grammar Database.*

3 .... *a dictionary.*

4 .... *an audio script.*

5 .... *a photo of Australia on page 18.*

6 .... *a list of irregular verbs.*

Set a time limit of three minutes to see how many sentences pairs can complete in this time. The pair with the most points wins the game.

ANSWERS
1 doesn't have 2 has 3 doesn't have 4 doesn't have
5 doesn't have 6 has

READ AND LISTEN Grammar in context

1 19

- Refer students to the pictures in Exercise 1. Ask them what they think the conversation is going to be about.
- Play the track for students to read and listen to the conversation and say who Josh is.
- Choose a student to say the answer and ask him or her to read aloud the lines from the text that give the answer.

ANSWER / AUDIO SCRIPT 19
Josh is Lucy's brother.
See Student's Book, page 15, for audio script.

STUDY

2

- Focus students' attention on the explanations and ask them to complete the examples with the correct words. Encourage them to refer back to Exercise 1 for help.
- Point out to students that we use *have* for possession.
- Check answers as a class.

ANSWERS
have has have doesn't Do; don't have; doesn't

3

- Draw students' attention to the instructions and the model sentences. Check that they understand what to do.
- Choose a student to start a chain sentence. Then ask the student next to him or her to repeat and add to the sentence.
- Continue around the class until each student has had a turn. If you have a large class, you may want to do this in groups.

PRACTICE

4a

- Ask students to complete the description with the correct forms of *have*. Remind them to use contractions where possible.
- Check answers as a class. (See Teaching Tips, *Checking answers*, page 24.)

ANSWERS
2 has 3 don't have 4 have 5 doesn't have 6 have

Fast finishers
Encourage students who finish early to look at the photo and make three sentences with *have*. Tell them to write one false sentence. At the end of the activity, ask students to read their sentences aloud for other students to say which sentence is false.

4b

- Have students write three or four sentences to describe one of their family members.

4c

- Divide the class into pairs and ask students to take turns reading their sentences aloud to their partner.

5a

- Ask students to use the prompts to write questions using *have*.
- Allow students to compare their questions with a partner.
- Check questions as a class. Do not have them ask their questions yet, as they will do this in Exercise 6.

ANSWERS
2 How many cousins do you have?
3 Do you have any pets?
4 Does your family have a house or an apartment?
5 What color hair does your mom have?
6 Do your parents have a car?

5b
- Ask students to write one more question with *have* using their own ideas.

SPEAK

6a
- Have students stand up and walk around the class asking other students the questions in Exercise 5.
- Encourage them to find at least two students with the same answer to each question and write their names.
- Circulate, noting errors and good use of language without interrupting the flow of the activity.

6b
- Divide the class into pairs and ask them to tell their partners about what other students have said.
- Draw students' attention to the model conversations.
- Give feedback to students at the end of the activity, pointing out errors and good use of language. (See Teaching Tips, *Correcting errors effectively*, page 24.)

Alternative procedure
You could put some quiet music on in the background to provide a party-like atmosphere. Encourage students to try to keep the conversation going by making at least one comment. You may want to write some comments on the board in a random order; for example, *That's interesting …* ; *Wow, that's a lot …* ; *What's your dog's name?*; *Which floor is your apartment on?*; *That's a nice color …* ; *What color is their car?*

Homework

Ask students to write an introduction for a famous person's blog. Encourage them to describe the famous person's family and possessions using *have*.

At the beginning of the next class, divide the class into pairs or small groups. Have them take turns reading their introductions aloud for the others to guess who the famous person is.

You could read these model sentences as an example:

I have a car collection. I have a Ferrari. I have a house in Jamaica. I have four gold medals. I have one brother and one sister. (Usain Bolt)

LANGUAGE & BEYOND COMMUNICATE & COOPERATE

Understand different ways to say "hello" *Page 14*

STAGE	TIME	FOCUS
GET STARTED		Think about the differences between formal and informal language when we speak.
SPEAK AND READ		Talk about who you meet on a school day. Look at pictures and say whether the situation is formal or informal.
DO		Compare tips on how to greet people in the USA with how to do it in your own country. Match tips to formal and informal situations.
REFLECT		Discuss what formal and informal greetings are in your own language, how you use them, and why using names is important.
EXTEND		Act out formal and informal situations.

LIFE SKILLS

COMMUNICATE & COOPERATE: UNDERSTAND DIFFERENT WAYS TO SAY "HELLO"
First impressions count! Introducing yourself in the correct way in different social situations is an important life skill. There are many different ways to greet people. In this lesson, students learn some of the most popular and useful expressions for saying hello to friends or other people in relaxed situations and more formal situations and how to sound polite.

Get started

Recycle ways of saying goodbye and other useful language in this quiz to introduce the idea of formal and informal language when we speak.

Write these pairs of sentences on the board. Ask students to work in pairs and choose which sentence is more formal (F) and which is more informal (I) in each of the pairs of sentences.

Excuse me. Do you have the time, please? (F)
Do you have the time? (I)

Thanks a lot. (I)
Thank you very much. (F)

See you later! (I)
Goodbye! (F)

Encourage students to think of when they would use each sentence and who they would be speaking to.

SPEAK AND READ

1

- Ask students to make a list of all the people they meet on a school day and the places they meet them.
- You could write possible places on the board (e.g., *an elevator, a street, a store, the classroom, the playground, an after-school club*).
- Divide the class into pairs to compare their lists.
- Ask a few confident students to report on the people and places they had in common with their partners.

2

- Refer students to the pictures and discuss whether Mary knows the other person in each picture and whether the other person is a friend.

ANSWERS

1 Keesha: Yes, she's a very good friend.
2 Man: No, he's not a friend.
3 Mrs. Matthews: Yes, but she's not a friend.
4 Jerome: Yes, he's a friend.
5 Student: No, she's not a friend because Mary is meeting her for the first time.

Extra activity

Ask students to answer these questions:

When do you think it is important to use formal language? (when we want to be polite or with people we don't know well)

What affects the way we talk to someone? (how well we know them)

What body language usually accompanies formal greetings and informal greetings? (straight back, sit or stand up straight, or a handshake in formal greetings; a hug, a kiss, or more relaxed body language in informal greetings)

DO

3

- Divide the class into small groups and ask them to read the tips and discuss whether they are the same for their country.
- Set a time limit of two minutes.
- Ask a spokesperson from each group to share the group's answers with the class.

MOVE BEYOND FOR TEACHERS

Different customs for saying "hello"

In certain cultures, any type of physical contact in public, such as kissing as a form of greeting someone, is considered taboo. Examples are China and Japan. On the other hand, in most Western European cultures, kissing is accepted and is even a formality, as in the Netherlands, Germany, Spain, France, and Latin America. The number of kisses, however, differs across countries and can depend on gender, age, relationship, and context. In the USA or Australia, hugging is more common than kissing. In Muslim cultures, it is usually appropriate to kiss only members of the same sex – physical contact between males and females is not accepted. British people tend to be reserved, and it is unusual to kiss a person on first acquaintance.

4

- Ask students to match the tips to the pictures. Remind them that the pictures will match to more than one tip.

ANSWERS

b 3 c 5 d 2, 3, 5 e 2 f 1, 4 g 3, 4

REFLECT

5

- Discuss the questions as a class.
- Refer students to the PHRASE BYTES box to help them structure their answers.
- Ask a student to read the REFLECTION POINT aloud. Take a vote to find out whether the class agrees with it.

Alternative procedure: less confident classes

Give less confident students three to four minutes to individually prepare their answers as notes before comparing their answers in pairs. You could generate more ideas by having a "pyramid discussion" by asking pairs to form groups of four and have a group discussion.

EXTEND

6a

- Divide the class into pairs to act out the situations in Exercise 2.
- You may want to ask a few volunteer pairs to model the activity before students begin. (See Teaching Tips, *Open and closed pairs*, page 28.)

6b

- Remind students that you expect to hear them say hello to you and their classmates in English from now on.

Homework

Write other situations on the board for students to act out greetings in pairs (e.g., *at a hotel check-in, in the school hallway, at a doctor's office, at a job interview, at a party*).

For homework, ask students to choose two or three of the situations and write a short conversation in which two people greet each other.

At the beginning of the next class, ask students to read their conversations to the class. Have other students decide what the situation is, who the people are, and how well they know each other.

SPEAKING How do I get there?

Ask for and give directions

Page 15

STAGE	TIME	FOCUS
GET STARTED		Listen to a story about getting lost.
SPEAK		Talk about what you do to find your way in a new place and whether you often get lost.
LISTEN		Listen for general and specific information in four conversations about giving directions. Look at the script and learn polite phrases and questions for asking directions (speaking subskill). Match directions to pictures.
ACT		Role-play asking for directions to places.

Get started

Introduce the topic of the lesson by telling students about a time when you got lost. Students like hearing your own stories, but if you have never been lost, you can adapt the story below. Ask students to write down as many expressions related to giving directions as they can as you tell the story.

Ask for volunteers to write the words on the board. Have students copy down the words to use later on in the lesson.

I'm in Paris, OK, with a friend, and I want to get to an art museum. I have a map, but it's a tourist map and it isn't very good. I turn left; I take a right; I go straight. I'm lost! I stop a man and ask for directions. I ask, "Can you tell me where I am?" He says, "Blah, blah, blah." He doesn't speak English, and I don't speak French. I point to my map and shrug my shoulders [do actions]. *My friend looks at me and thinks, "What are you doing?" but I do it again. The man looks at the map and indicates where we are. The museum is just around the corner.*

SPEAK

1

- Divide the class into pairs to discuss the questions.
- Elicit answers from different students around the class.

LISTEN

2 ▶20

- Refer students to the photos and ask them to predict what they are going to listen to.
- Have students close their books. Play the audio track for them to listen and find out why the last person can't give directions.

ANSWER / AUDIO SCRIPT ▶20

He's lost too.

See Student's Book, page 15, for audio script.

3a

- Ask students to read the tips in the HOW TO box.

3b ▶20

- Play the track again for students to listen and underline polite phrases in Exercise 2.
- Check answers as a class.

ANSWERS / AUDIO SCRIPT ▶20

1 Excuse me Thank you 2 please Thanks
3 please Thanks 4 Excuse me Sorry
See Student's Book, page 15, for audio script.

3c ▶21

- Play the audio track for students to listen and repeat the questions. (See Teaching Tips, *Intonation in questions*, page 32.)

AUDIO SCRIPT ▶21

1 Can you tell me the way to the shopping mall?
2 How do I get to the library, please?
3 Can you tell me the way to the station, please?
4 How do I get to the stadium?

4a

- Ask students to match the directions to the pictures.

ANSWERS

1 c 2 b 3 e 4 a 5 d

4b ▶22

- Play the track for students to listen and repeat the sentences.

AUDIO SCRIPT ▶22

See Student's Book, page 15, for audio script.

ACT

5a ▶23

- Divide the class into A/B pairs.
- Tell Student As to ask for directions to the places in the box. Remind students to repeat and check the directions.
- Tell Student Bs to look at the map on page 75 and give his or her partner directions.
- Draw students' attention to the PHRASEBOOK to help them structure their conversation. These phrases are recorded, so they could be used for students to practice pronunciation and intonation.
- Monitor and note errors and good use of language to go over in a feedback session at the end of Exercise 5b.

5b

- Tell Student Bs to ask for directions to the places in the box. Remind students to repeat and check the directions.
- Tell Student As to look at the map on page 75 and give his or her partner directions.
- Monitor and note errors and good use of language to go over in a feedback session at the end of the activity.
- Give students feedback at the end of the activity on mistakes and good use of language.

Alternative procedure: less confident classes
Ask two of the more confident students to demonstrate the activity to the class before the other students begin their conversations.

Extra activity
Divide the class into pairs. Draw a simple map of a town and ask students to come up and write names of places (e.g., *shopping mall*, *movie theater*, *post office*).

Ask students to work in pairs to give each other directions from one place on the map to another without naming the destination. When they arrive, they say the name of their destination to see if they have followed the directions correctly.

Homework

Ask students to write directions from the classroom to a place on the school's campus or nearby in the neighborhood, no more than a five-minute walk away. At the beginning of the next class, their partners must listen and figure out where the final destination is. In a less confident class, demonstrate the activity first. Ask students to listen to you and figure out the final destination.

WRITING Hello from Cartagena

Use correct punctuation *Page 16*

STAGE	TIME	FOCUS
GET STARTED		Play a letter game and begin to find out about the country of Colombia.
SPEAK AND READ		Say what you know about Cartagena. Clarify how to use correct punctuation (writing subskill).
PRACTICE		Add punctuation to an email.
DISCUSS		Talk about your city or a city you have visited.
WRITE		Write and edit an e-postcard about a town or city.
SHARE		Exchange e-postcards with other students and vote on the most interesting place to visit.

Get started

Play a game of *Snowman* (see Games, page 29) using the word *Colombia*.

Ask students a few general questions about Colombia; for example, *What's the capital of Colombia?* (Bogotá); *What's the name of the currency?* (Colombian peso); *What language do they speak?* (Spanish); *How many people live there?* (about 48 million people).

Elicit other information that students know about Colombia (e.g., the names of famous Colombians).

SPEAK AND READ

1

- Refer students to the title and the photo and elicit what they know about Cartagena.
- Focus students' attention on the architecture. Ask them to describe it and say whether it reminds them of the architecture in another city.

MOVE BEYOND FOR TEACHERS

Cartagena

Cartagena is located on the northern Caribbean coast of Colombia. The city is known for its beautiful Spanish architecture and is the most visited city in Colombia. Because of the beauty of Cartagena, many meetings and conventions are held there.

Cartagena is the fifth-largest city in Colombia, with a population of over 1 million people. The city was named a UNESCO World Heritage Site in 1984 because of its lovely architecture and history. Today, Cartagena hosts the Cartagena Film Festival, the oldest in Latin America.

2

- Have students read the e-postcard and check the things Angelica writes about.
- Ask students to add two more things.

ANSWERS
a tower parks shopping malls old buildings churches
Other things mentioned: squares, a castle, modern buildings, a soccer stadium

3a

- Ask students to read the tips in the HOW TO box. Check that they understand how each type of punctuation is used.

3b

- Ask students to find one example of each punctuation mark in Angelica's e-postcard. (See Teaching Tips, *Punctuation*, page 30.)
- Choose different students to read their examples aloud.

Fast finishers
Ask students to write an example sentence for each tip in the HOW TO box.

PRACTICE

4

- Ask students to add punctuation to Jessie's email.
- Allow students to compare their answers in pairs before you check them by inviting students to come to the board and write a sentence.

ANSWERS
Hi, Angelica.
Thanks for your e-postcard.
Cartagena looks amazing in the photo.
I can't speak Spanish. Do a lot of people in Colombia speak English?
Write soon!
Jessie

DISCUSS

5

- Explain to students that they are going to write an e-postcard from an interesting town or city.
- Divide the class into pairs or small groups to talk about their city or a city they have visited. Ask them to talk about fun and interesting places there. This will help them think of ideas for the e-postcard they are going to write. Suggest that they make some notes about their ideas in preparation for Exercise 6.

WRITE

6

- Explain to students that they are now going to write their e-postcards and check them.
- Direct students' attention to the writing plan to help them plan their e-postcards. Give them three minutes for planning.
- Ask students to write their e-postcards and check them. Set a time limit of 10 minutes for this.
- Remind students to check the points in the plan to make sure they have followed the instructions correctly.

Alternative procedure

Ask students to write the first draft of their e-postcards and then exchange their texts with a partner. Write the following criteria on the board and ask students to refer to them and check each other's work:

Does the e-postcard start and finish well?

Has your partner followed the writing plan?

Is it interesting?

Are the spelling and punctuation correct?

Is there a lot of different vocabulary?

Is the grammar correct?

Encourage the pairs to read each other's postcards and give comments and suggestions for improvement before students write their final e-postcards.

SHARE

7

- Ask students to read their e-postcards to other students in the class.
- Have students vote on which postcard is from the most interesting place.

Homework

Ask students to write an e-postcard to tell a pen pal about their town or city. Have students bring their e-postcards to the next class to share. Divide the class into pairs and ask students to tell their partner about the interesting places and things their pen pal can do when visiting.

VOCABULARY Places in a city

1

- Ask students to look at the picture and say what they can see (*a town square with different types of buildings*).
- Have students complete the places they can see in the picture and places that are not in the picture.
- Check answers as a class. (See Teaching Tips, *Checking answers*, page 28.)

ANSWERS
1 square 2 library 3 museum 4 bridge 5 tower
6 airport 7 station 8 stadium 9 shopping mall
10 theme park

Family

2

- Ask students to complete the text with the words in the two boxes.
- Let students compare their answers in pairs before you check them as a class.

ANSWERS
1 parents 2 Aunt 3 husband 4 Uncle
5 daughter 6 son 7 cousins 8 married 9 wife
10 granddaughter 11 grandson 12 grandparents

GRAMMAR *There is/there are*; prepositions of place

3

- Ask students to choose the correct words and phrases.
- Allow them to compare their answers in pairs.
- Check answers as a class.

ANSWERS
1 There isn't 2 there's 3 There are 4 there are
5 behind 6 there's 7 next to

Have

4

- Ask students if they know the meaning of the word *gadget* (*a small piece of equipment that uses technology*) and elicit examples (e.g., *computer*, *laptop*, *cell phone*).
- Ask students to complete the exercise with the correct forms of *have*.
- Choose a student to read the text aloud.
- Have students work in pairs to talk about the gadgets they have.

ANSWERS
1 have 2 don't have 3 don't have
4 have 5 has 6 doesn't have 7 do (you) have

Extra Resources

Go to the Teacher's Resource Center at mee2.macmillaneducation.com for:

- videos, video worksheets, and video scripts;
- extra vocabulary at two levels of difficulty;
- extra grammar at two levels of difficulty;
- culture lessons, with full teacher's notes;
- life skills lessons, with full teacher's notes;
- Speaking Database materials;
- the *Move Beyond* Level 1 wordlist
- downloadable PDF and Word tests for Unit 1;
- tips for using the Grammar Database;
- extra reading materials;
- and more!

Go to Workbook pages 84–95 for further practice material.

2 UNIT NIGHT AND DAY

IN THE PICTURE Around the world

Talk about your daily routine

Pages 18–19

STAGE	TIME	FOCUS
GET STARTED		Brainstorm vocabulary about night and day as an introduction to the topic of the lesson.
WORK WITH WORDS		Look at a satellite picture of the sun's light on the world and match daily activities to pictures. Distinguish between *before* and *after*. Watch a video about different times and activities around the world.
SPEAK		Use the vocabulary from the lesson to compare your daily routines with a partner's routines and find three differences.

Get started

Have students close their books. Draw two columns on the board and label them *Night* and *Day*.

Divide the class into pairs and ask them to copy the column headings on a piece of paper. Give them two minutes to think of as many words as they can that they associate with *Night* or *Day* and write them in the correct columns. Give an example of each if necessary (e.g., *sun*, *moon*).

Ask students to stop when the time limit is up and count how many words they have in each column.

Invite students to come to the board and write their words in the columns. Correct any misspelled words.

Ask students if they prefer the nighttime or the daytime and ask them to give reasons why.

Alternative procedure: less confident classes

In a less confident class, write these words on the board:

afternoon, *blue sky*, *dark*, *evening*, *noon*, *midnight*, *moon*, *morning*, *stars*, *sunrise*, *sunset*

Ask students to write them in the correct column, *Night* or *Day*, and then add one more word of their own to each column.

ANSWERS

Night: dark, evening, midnight, moon, stars, sunset
Day: afternoon, blue sky, noon, morning, sunrise

WORK WITH WORDS Daily activities

1a RECALL

- Divide the class into pairs to say the times on the clocks using the words in the box.
- Choose different students to say the answers.
- Drill the times chorally to remind students of stress in these phrases.

ANSWERS

1 It's nine o'clock.
2 It's half past seven. / It's seven thirty.
3 It's a quarter past/after eleven. / It's eleven fifteen.
4 It's a quarter to three. / It's two forty-five.
5 It's twenty past/after eight. / It's eight twenty.
6 It's ten to ten. / It's nine fifty.

Alternative procedure: less confident classes

Less confident students may need more practice with saying the time before moving on to the next activity. Ask students to think of the question we normally use when we want to ask for the time (*What time is it, please?*) and how we usually answer (*It's …*). Write the question and answer on the board.

Ask students to write down five different times. Then have students work in pairs, taking turns asking the time and answering with a time from their list.

1b

- Tell students that they are going to tell their partner from Exercise 1a at what times they do the five activities in the box.
- Draw students' attention to the model sentence.
- Set a two-minute time limit for this activity.
- Choose different students to tell the class when they do each activity.
- Ask students to do the **Work with Words** task on page 70.

2a

- Ask students to continue working in pairs. Refer them to the photo and have them tell each other what they can see.
- Draw students' attention to the PHRASE BYTES box to help them structure their answer.
- Ask students why some countries are light and some countries are dark in the photo. If they need help, ask them to think about the connection between the photo and the title of the unit.

- Choose a student to write the explanation on the board. Then "improve" it as a class, adding more words and working toward a full explanation together.

> **SUGGESTED ANSWER**
> It shows the sun's light on the world at that time and how some parts are in daylight (facing the sun) and others in the dark (facing away from the sun).

2b
- Ask students to match the photos to the messages in the speech bubbles.
- Choose individual students to say which activity in bold they can see in each photo.

> **ANSWERS**
> a message 3: do my homework
> b message 1: wake up
> c message 4: go home
> d message 2: get to school

Fast finishers
Have students try to guess which country each photo is from and recycle nationalities (photo a – *Japan/Japanese*; photo b – *USA/American*; photo c – *Ireland/Irish*; photo d – *Chile/Chilean*).

2c
- Ask students to match the other activities in bold in the messages to the pictures.
- Draw students' attention to the example answer before they start.
- Point out to students that we also say *brush my teeth* and that you can *brush* or *comb* your hair, depending on whether you use a brush or a comb.

> **ANSWERS**
> 2 take a shower 3 brush my teeth 4 pack my bag
> 5 get dressed 6 brush my hair

Extra activity
Ask students to put the activities in the order they do them. Then ask them to compare their answer in pairs to see if their order is the same as their partner's.

3 ▶24
- Play the track for students to listen and repeat all the daily activities in bold in the messages.

> **AUDIO SCRIPT** ▶24
> wake up take a shower get dressed brush my hair
> pack my bag get to school do my homework brush my teeth
> go home get home

4a
- Ask students to complete the sentences with *before* or *after*.

4b
- Divide the class into pairs and ask them to compare their answers and to discuss any differences.
- Check answers as a class.

> **ANSWERS**
> 1 after 2 before 3 after 4 before 5 after 6 after

5 THE MOVING PICTURE ▶
- Explain to students that they are going to watch a video about different times around the world.
- Play the video and ask students to take notes on where the speakers are from.
- Divide the class into pairs for students to compare their answers.
- Choose different students to read their notes aloud.
- You may want to play the video again with the volume off. Pause each time the clocks stop and ask students to try to remember the relevant time and the exact words each speaker says.

> **ANSWERS / VIDEO SCRIPT**
> 1 Paris 2 Quito 3 Tokyo 4 London 5 New York
> 6 Tokyo 7 Quito 8 Los Angeles
>
> 1
> **Viviane:** My name's Viviane. I get to school at eight o'clock, and school starts at half past eight.
>
> 2
> **Juan Carlos:** I'm Juan Carlos. I have lunch at school at a quarter past 12.
>
> 3
> **Misaki:** My name's Misaki. I get home at a quarter to six and do my homework.
>
> 4
> **Harry:** I'm Harry. My second class finishes at eleven o'clock.
>
> 5
> **Olivia:** My name's Olivia. I wake up at a quarter to seven. I get dressed and brush my hair.
>
> 6
> **Misaki:** It's a quarter after nine. Time to take a shower, brush my teeth, and pack my bag.
>
> 7
> **Juan Carlos:** I have dinner with my family at eight o'clock.
>
> 8
> **Drew:** I'm Drew. I can't sleep. What time is it? Oh no! It's a quarter after two in the morning!

SPEAK

6
- Ask students to work in pairs and compare their daily activities to find three differences between their routines. Teach or elicit that *routine* means your usual way of doing things, especially when you do them in a fixed order at the same time.
- Draw students' attention to the PHRASE BYTES box to help them structure their answers.
- Have students share their conversations with the class and report the differences they found in their daily routines.

MOVE BEYOND

Ask students to do the **Words & Beyond** exercise on page 70.

> **Homework**
> Ask students to write a page for their blog describing their daily routines. Ask them to write one false sentence. At the beginning of the next class, ask students to work in pairs and read their texts aloud for their partner to guess the false sentences.

READING Midnight sun

Find specific information

Page 20

STAGE	TIME	FOCUS
GET STARTED		Play a game to recycle talking about countries and focus on the country Norway.
SPEAK AND READ		Find specific information in a school blog message about Tromsø, a town in Norway (reading subskill). Complete sentences about facts and activities in Tromsø and find three differences from your daily activities.
REACT		Discuss whether Tromsø is a good place to live and what activities you want to see or do there.

Get started

Play a game of *Twenty Questions* (see Games, page 29) to recycle vocabulary for talking about countries and introduce Norway.

MOVE BEYOND FOR TEACHERS

Norway

Norway is part of the continent of Europe, but it isn't in the European Union. It is the farthest north of any European country. Its capital city is Oslo, the currency is the Norwegian krone, and it is a monarchy. The population of Norway is 5 million, and the language spoken is Norwegian (and Sami in some parts of the country).

SPEAK AND READ

1a

- Divide the class into pairs. Ask them to look at the photos and to say where they think the town of Tromsø is.
- Refer students to the PHRASE BYTES box to help them structure their answers.
- Choose several students to say their answers, but do not confirm answers at this point.

1b

- Ask students to look at the school blog post and say who the students in Tromsø are writing to (*their new friends in Austin, Texas*).
- Have students read the first lines of the school blog post to check their answer to Exercise 1a.

ANSWER

Tromsø is in the north of Norway.

MOVE BEYOND FOR TEACHERS

Tromsø

The Norwegian city Tromsø /ˈtrʊmsø/ is the largest city and the largest urban area in northern Norway. The city center of Tromsø contains the highest number of old wooden houses in northern Norway, the oldest house dating from 1789. The zone where the Northern Lights appear is a circle around the North Magnetic Pole. Tromsø is situated in the middle of this zone, and as a result, you have a good chance of seeing the Northern Lights from there.

2a

- Ask students to think of any tips they know on how to find specific information in a text. (See Teaching Tips, *Reading for specific information*, page 28.)
- Refer students to the HOW TO box and ask if they thought of the same tips.
- Ask them to cover the box and try to remember the four tips without looking.
- Elicit from students how these tips can help them.

2b 25

- Ask students: *Do you think winter days in Norway are short or long?* Have students read the article quickly and complete the sentences about Tromsø. Don't play the audio at this point. It is an extra feature, and a suggestion for using it in class is included at the end of the lesson.
- Have students compare their answers in pairs before you check them as a class.

ANSWERS

1 above 2 60 3 Midsummer's Eve 4 dark 5 winter
6 4:30 (in the afternoon)

Alternative procedure: less confident classes

In a less confident class, ask students to match the important words in the text to the same words in each sentence (e.g., *the Arctic Circle*, *24 hours a day*, *June 23rd*) and check these before students do the exercise.

3

- Ask students to check the tips in the HOW TO box that helped them with Exercise 2b.

4a

- Ask students to read the text again and write down three differences between daily activities in Tromsø and their daily activities.
- Draw students' attention to the example answer before they start.
- Choose different students to read their sentences aloud.

4b

- Have students compare their sentences in pairs to find out whether they are the same or different.
- Choose several students to read their sentences aloud.

Fast finishers

Write these numbers on the board: *60*, *24*, *23*, *2:15*.

Ask students to find what they refer to in the text and write the answers in their notebooks. At the end of the activity, fast finishers can "test" the rest of the class.

ANSWERS

There are 60 days of summer when the sun shines 24 hours a day.
On June 23rd they celebrate Midsummer's Eve.
The school day ends at 2:15.

REACT

5

- Divide the class into pairs and ask them to share their answers to the questions, giving reasons for their answers.
- Draw students' attention to the **PHRASE BYTES** box to help them structure their opinions.
- Choose several pairs to report their answers to the class.
- Discuss as a class whether Tromsø is a good place to live and what students want to see and do there.

MOVE BEYOND

Ask students to find prepositions of place in the blog post and to make a list as in the example.

ANSWERS

in + Austin / Tromsø / the north of Norway / the snow
above the Arctic Circle
to + the beach / a café
at home

Recorded reading text ▶25

Use the audio for checking the answers to Exercise 2b. Play the audio track, pausing it to confirm the answers.

Homework

Ask students to write a school blog post to friends in an English-speaking country and say why their town or city is a good place to live. Remind students to use *there is/ there are* and *have* to talk about important festivals and activities at different times of the year. In the next class, choose a few students to read their blog posts aloud and ask whether the rest of the class had similar information in their blogs.

GRAMMAR Simple present affirmative; prepositions of time

Talk about when you do things

Page 21

STAGE	TIME	FOCUS
GET STARTED		Recycle seasons, months of the year, and daily routines.
READ		Read a description comparing life in Buenos Aires and Tokyo.
STUDY		Use the description to complete grammar explanations for the simple present affirmative and prepositions of time.
PRACTICE		Complete texts using the simple present affirmative and prepositions of time. Practice the pronunciation of the /ɪz/ sound in verb endings.
WRITE AND SPEAK		Write notes for a video message and present the message to other students.

Get started

Draw the sun on the left side and the moon on the right side of the board.

Ask students to say the names of the seasons and months when there is less or more sunshine. You may want to point out that the length of the days in different seasons varies little or not at all in countries close to the equator. Use this opportunity to drill the seasons and months because these are needed in the lesson.

Divide the class into pairs and ask them to brainstorm as many daily activities as they can, from when they get up to when they go to bed. Set a time limit of three minutes for this.

Stop students and ask them to count the number of activities they have thought of to see who has the most. Invite students to come to the board and write their activities in the correct places.

Have students work in small groups and act out different activities for other students to guess.

READ Grammar in context

1

- Refer students to the photos and ask them what they know about Buenos Aires and Tokyo and what they think the text is going to be about.
- Ask students to read the descriptions and say in what two ways Buenos Aires and Tokyo are different.

ANSWERS

There is a time difference of 12 hours, so when it is nighttime in one country, it is daytime in the other.
The seasons are different. Summer starts in December in Buenos Aires and in June in Tokyo.

MOVE BEYOND FOR TEACHERS

Buenos Aires and Tokyo

Buenos Aires is located in eastern Argentina on the Río de la Plata river. It is the capital and largest city in Argentina, with 15.2 million people in the greater metropolitan area. Seventy-five percent of the population of Buenos Aires is of Spanish or Italian descent.

Tokyo is the capital of Japan. It is the largest city in the world. More than 35 million people live in the Tokyo metropolitan area. Tokyo is located in the southeastern part of Honshu, Japan's main island. The original name of Tokyo was Edo. When the emperor of Japan moved from Kyoto to Edo in 1868, the name was changed to Tokyo.

STUDY

2

- Have students complete the examples with the correct words from Exercise 1.
- Check their answers as a class.

ANSWERS
lives goes; finishes studies

Alternative procedure: less confident classes

Ask students to draw two columns and label them *I/you/we/they + verb* and *he/she/it + verb*.

Have students underline all the simple present verbs in the text – except for *is* and *are* – and write the verb in both forms in the correct column.

Check answers as a class. Then ask students to complete the examples in Exercise 2.

I/you/we/they + verb	*he/she/it* + verb
live	lives
go	goes
finish	finishes
study	studies
talk	talks
call	calls
start	starts

3

- Ask students to use Exercise 1 to help them complete the explanations with *at*, *in*, and *on*.
- If it's appropriate as a topic in your country, you can also add that we say *at Easter*, *at Christmas*, etc.

ANSWERS
on in at

Extra activity

Ask students to write these time expressions in a vertical list on the right side of the page in their notebooks: *Tuesday, ten o'clock, the spring, weekends, 1997, the afternoon, July, June 23rd*. Next, have students write the prepositions *at*, *in*, and *on* on the left side of the page and match the time expressions to the prepositions with lines or arrows. Encourage students to write one more example for each preposition.

ANSWERS
at + ten o'clock
in + the spring, 1997, the afternoon, July
on + Tuesday, weekends, June 23rd

PRACTICE

4

- Have students look at the photo and complete the description with the simple present form of the verbs.
- Draw students' attention to the example answer before they start.
- Let students compare their answers in pairs before you check them as a class.

ANSWERS
2 fly 3 crosses 4 comes 5 goes 6 have
7 rains 8 stays

Extra activity

Ask some simple comprehension questions about the text: *Where does Luis Alberto live?* (Puerto Ayora in the Galápagos Islands); *Where are the Galápagos Islands?* (on the equator); *What time does the sun come up and go down?* (at six o'clock); *When are the two main seasons?* (from December to May and June to November).

5

- Have students complete the description with *at*, *in*, and *on*.
- Draw students' attention to the example answer before they start.
- Ask different students around the class to read the answers aloud.

ANSWERS
2 in 3 on 4 at 5 at 6 in 7 At 8 In 9 On

6a 26 PRONOUNCE

- Play the track for students to listen and circle the verbs with an /ɪz/ sound at the end.
- Check answers as a class.

ANSWERS / AUDIO SCRIPT 26
Verbs with an /ɪz/ sound at the end: *brushes, relaxes, uses, watches*
See Student's Book, page 21, for audio script.

6b 27

- Have students read the explanation.
- Play the track for students to listen and repeat the verbs.

AUDIO SCRIPT 27
See Student's Book, page 21, for audio script.

WRITE AND SPEAK

7a

- Divide the class into pairs and ask them to write notes for making a video message about their country, town or city, and daily life. Encourage them to look at Exercises 1, 4, and 5 to help them.
- Circulate and help students with any difficulties at this stage.

7b

- Tell students to decide who will say each part of their video message and give them time to practice.
- Ask students to present their video messages to other students (either in small groups or to the whole class).
- Have students take notes on each other's presentations and ask questions at the end.

Alternative procedure: more confident classes

In order to encourage students to listen carefully to each other's presentations, ask them to write one false sentence in their video message. Students listen for the false sentence and say what it was at the end of each presentation.

Homework

Have students write three or four lines about a country, town, or city of their choice, excluding their own. Ask them to use the text in Exercise 4 as a model. At the beginning of the next class, put students in pairs to present their texts without saying the name of the country or place for their partner to guess.

LISTENING AND VOCABULARY Let me show you around

Use sounds to help you understand *Page 22*

STAGE	TIME	FOCUS
GET STARTED		Recycle vocabulary and grammar worked on so far.
SPEAK AND LISTEN		Listen to a boy talking about his house and decide what's in each room. Use sounds to help you understand (listening subskill).
REACT		Compare your home to the boy's house and find things that are similar or different.
WORK WITH WORDS		Match photos to words for furniture and other things in the home. Listen to a girl describing her apartment to check your answers. Describe a room in your house for your partner to guess.

Get started

Play a game of *Three in a Row* (see Games, page 33) to recycle vocabulary and grammar that students have seen so far, for example:

prepositions of place	prepositions of time	describing routines
nationalities	family	time
have	give directions	*there is/there are*

Questions

Say three sentences using *under/next to/behind.*	Say three sentences using *at/in/on.*	Describe three daily routines.
Say three nationalities and say the language they speak.	Say six words related to family vocabulary words.	(Draw three clocks on the board.) Say these times.
Say three sentences using *I/you/he + have.*	Give directions to the cafeteria.	Say three sentences to describe the classroom using *there is/there are.*

SPEAK AND LISTEN

1 RECALL

- Divide the class into pairs to recycle vocabulary they know for rooms in a house.
- Set a time limit of three minutes for this. You could ask students to race against other pairs to see who can think of the most words.
- Draw a very basic house on the board for students to come up and label as this will help students visualize the task.

2a

- Ask students for ideas on how using sounds in listening activities can help them understand.
- Refer students to the HOW TO box and ask a student to read the ideas aloud for the class.
- Check to find out whether students have thought of similar or different ideas.
- Point out to students that using background noises and tone of voice when listening is an effective strategy to help identify and understand what is being said. The noises in the background in these short conversations provide students with a lot of contextual clues as to what the people are doing, in the same way as pictures and diagrams provide students with clues to make sense of reading texts.

2b 28

Exam-type task

- Focus on the photo of Matthew and recycle descriptions of people. Ask students how old Matthew is and what his bedroom might look like. Explain to students that they are going to listen to Matthew talk about his house.
- Make sure students understand the vocabulary in the exercise.
- Point out that this is a typical exam-type task and that they will not need all of the letters a–h.
- Play the track for students to listen and match the things in each room to the rooms.
- Ask students to take turns reading the answers aloud.

ANSWERS / AUDIO SCRIPT ▶28

1 f 2 b 3 d 4 h 5 c

Matthew: Hi, I'm Matthew and this is my home. The tour starts in my bedroom. It's small, but there's a lot of space for all my things in the closet and on the shelves. This is my collection of harmonicas. This door's the bathroom. We have a nice shower in here.
This is my sister's room. I hardly ever go in here. She never cleans her room, so it's usually a mess ... yep, it's a mess. Let's look in the closet. She has all her old teddy bears. ... This is my parents' room. Parents always get the big room. ... OK, let's go down to the living room. ... There's the TV, and there's the armchair. Mom always sits there. Hi, Mom!
Mom: Shhh!
Matthew: We often watch movies at night. I always sit on the sofa, but Meow is there now. Say your name, Meow! And here's the kitchen, with the dishwasher, stove, refrigerator, and ... dinner. Mom sometimes cooks, but Dad usually makes dinner. Hi, Dad!
Dad: Hi, Matt.

MOVE BEYOND FOR TEACHERS

Lunch, dinner, or supper?

Lunch, the midday meal, in some regions of the USA and the UK is called *dinner*. *Supper* is the name for an informal evening meal for some people, although it is often used interchangeably with *dinner*. *Dinner* traditionally had been used to refer to the main and most formal meal of the day, which, from the Middle Ages until the 18th century, was most often the midday meal. When the evening meal became the main meal, it was referred to as *dinner* and the lighter midday meal was called *luncheon* (*lunch*).

3

- Ask students to look back at the HOW TO box and to check the tips that helped them with Exercise 2b.

Extra activity
Encourage students to say all the sound effects they can remember from the audio. Play the track again if necessary.

4 ▶28

- Play the track again for students to match the sentence halves.
- Have students compare their answers in pairs before checking answers as a class.

ANSWERS / AUDIO SCRIPT ▶28

2 d 3 f 4 b 5 a 6 e
See Exercise 2b for audio script.

Extra activity
In a less confident class, ask students some follow-up comprehension questions to make sure they have fully understood the listening. You could play the track again if necessary. Ask: *Where does Matthew's tour start?* (in his bedroom); *What musical instrument does he play?* (the harmonica); *What's in his sister's closet?* (teddy bears); *What furniture is in the living room?* (a TV, an armchair, and a sofa); *And the kitchen?* (a dishwasher, a stove, and a refrigerator).

REACT

5

- Divide the class into pairs and ask them to compare their homes with Matthew's house.
- Have students find at least one thing that is similar and one thing that is different.
- Elicit responses from several different students.

WORK WITH WORDS Furniture and other things in the home

6a

- Ask students to work in pairs to match the photos to the words in the box. Do not check answers yet, as they will check them in Exercise 6b.

Fast finishers
Have fast finishers think of more furniture and things in the home, using their dictionaries if necessary. At the end of the activity, ask students to draw the furniture on the board for others to guess what it is in English.

6b ▶29

- Play the track for students to listen to Amanda describe her apartment and check their answers to Exercise 6a.
- Point out to students that Amanda says the words in the same order as the photos.
- Ask students if they can remember the three background sounds (*the cabinet door*, *the refrigerator door*, *the sound of curtains being opened or closed*).

ANSWERS / AUDIO SCRIPT ▶29

1 stove 2 dishwasher 3 cabinet 4 refrigerator 5 sofa
6 armchair 7 carpet 8 lamp 9 curtains 10 closet
11 bookshelf 12 shelf (shelves)

Hi, I'm Amanda, and this is our apartment. ... This is the kitchen. There's the stove and the dishwasher. There are a lot of cabinets to put things in. And there's my favorite thing, the refrigerator. ... This is the living room. There's a big sofa and an armchair in here and a nice carpet on the floor. ... My bedroom's here. That's my desk with a lamp on it, the window and curtains, ... my closet, where I keep my clothes, my bookshelf, and the shelves where I put other things.

7 ▶30

- Play the track for students to listen and repeat the words.
- You could recycle word stress and ask students to underline the stressed syllable in each word. (See underlining in audio script.) Remind students that in two-syllable words, the stress usually falls on the first syllable.

AUDIO SCRIPT ▶30

1 stove 2 dishwasher 3 cabinet 4 refrigerator 5 sofa
6 armchair 7 carpet 8 lamp 9 curtains 10 closet
11 bookshelf 12 shelves

8

- Have students think of a room in their house, but not necessarily their bedroom.
- Draw students' attention to the examples of rooms in a house and the key language for structuring descriptions.
- Divide the class into pairs and ask students to describe what is in the room they are thinking of for their partners to guess the room.
- Circulate and help students with any difficulties. Note errors and good use of language to go over in a feedback session at the end of the activity.

Alternative procedure: less confident classes
Less confident students may want to prepare notes about what they are going to say before doing the speaking exercise. You could model this activity first in front of the class before students continue in pairs. Encourage students to use a variety of rooms.

MOVE BEYOND

Ask students to do the **Words & Beyond** exercises on page 70.

Homework

Ask students to write a script as if they are doing a video tour of their house, starting from the bedroom and going through at least three other rooms. Encourage them to use *there is/there are*, *have*, and the vocabulary for furniture and other things in the home. At the beginning of the next class, have students read their scripts aloud to their partners for them to write down all the furniture words they hear.

GRAMMAR Simple present with adverbs of frequency

Talk about how often you do things

Page 23

STAGE	TIME	FOCUS
GET STARTED		Recycle simple present verbs for daily routines. Talk about what a perfect teenager does or doesn't do.
READ		Read a description for specific information.
STUDY		Complete grammar explanations for the simple present with adverbs of frequency.
PRACTICE		Use the simple present and adverbs of frequency in written exercises.
SPEAK		Ask other students questions about how often they do different activities and tell the class about interesting information you have found out.

Get started

Pre-teach some of the new vocabulary in the lesson by asking students these questions: *What's the opposite of "get up early"?* (get up late); *How can you describe a room that isn't neat?* (messy); *What's the opposite of "remember"?* (forget); *Can you always find your keys and phone?* (students' own answers); *Do your parents get angry with you?* (students' own answers).

Ask students about a "perfect teenager." *Does a perfect teenager get up early or late? What is the perfect teenager's room like? How does a perfect teenager help around the house?*

READ Grammar in context

1

- Refer students to the photo in Exercise 1. Ask students: *Do the girls look similar?* (yes, they are identical twins); *What do you think the description is about?* (similarities and differences they have).
- Set a time limit of one minute to encourage students to read quickly.
- Choose a student to say the answer. Ask the student to read aloud the words from the text that give the answer.

ANSWER
Yes, they are. (*But we're good friends ...*)

Fast finishers
Write these definitions on the board for students to find the words in the text: *on one occasion* (once); *happens up to a point in time and then stops* (until); *used for saying people are with each other* (together).

STUDY

2

- Ask students to complete the chart with the words in bold in Exercise 1.
- Invite a student to read the explanation about word order aloud. Ask students to complete the examples.
- Check answers as a class.

ANSWERS
From top to bottom: never, hardly ever, *sometimes*, often, *usually*, normally, always
Word order: always; is/'s

PRACTICE

3

- Ask students to complete the sentences with the adverbs of frequency in Exercise 2. Point out that they should use the percentages (0–100%) to help them.
- Choose different students to say the answers.

ANSWERS
2 usually/normally 3 always 4 sometimes 5 often
6 hardly ever

Alternative procedure: less confident classes
As a whole class, match the percentages to the adverbs of frequency before students do the exercise.

4

- Ask students to put the words in order to make sentences.
- Have students compare their answers in pairs before you check them as a class.

ANSWERS
2 She never remembers her homework.
3 She hardly ever eats vegetables.
4 She often loses her phone.
5 She sometimes sleeps on the sofa.
6 She is always happy.

5a

- Have students add an adverb of frequency to each sentence to make it true for them.
- Circulate and monitor as they work, helping students with any difficulties they may have with word order.

ANSWERS
1 My bedroom is [adverb of frequency] messy.
2 I [adverb of frequency] take a shower in the morning.
3 I'm [adverb of frequency] late for school.
4 I [adverb of frequency] do my homework in the living room.
5 I [adverb of frequency] do my English homework.
6 I [adverb of frequency] watch TV in the evening.

5b

- Draw students' attention to the model question beginnings.
- Divide the class into pairs and ask students to compare their answers.
- In a class discussion, invite different students to report on what their partner has said.

Alternative procedure: less confident classes
Ask different students to write the sentences in Exercise 5a on the board for the class to refer to the first time they do Exercise 5b. Then partially erase the sentences and ask students to repeat the exercise with a different partner.

SPEAK

6a

- Ask students to write three questions with *How often ... ?* to ask other students.

6b

- Encourage students to ask at least three other students their questions and write the students' answers.
- Circulate, noting errors and good use of language without interrupting the flow of the activity.

6c

- Invite students to tell the class one interesting thing.
- Give feedback at the end of the activity, pointing out errors and good use of language.

Homework
Ask students to look at the sentences in Exercise 4 and change them so that all of them are true for them except one. Have students read their sentences aloud to a partner at the beginning of the next class for the partner to guess the false sentence.

LANGUAGE & BEYOND GET ORGANIZED

Organize your things Page 24

STAGE	TIME	FOCUS
GET STARTED		Recycle word order in the simple present with adverbs of frequency and talk about being organized.
READ		Match teenagers to photos of their bedrooms and say who you are most like.
DO		Order steps for organizing your bedroom and plan how to organize your room.
REFLECT		Discuss why it is good to be organized and different ways to organize your things.
EXTEND		Decide how to organize or reorganize your classroom or another room in the school or your house.

LIFE SKILLS

GET ORGANIZED: ORGANIZE YOUR THINGS
Some students never have enough time, always lose things, or turn in homework late. This lesson focuses on finding solutions to help students plan and prioritize to create a neater personal space. Developing systems for getting and staying organized is a life skill that allows you to have more time to focus on your life and leads to success at school and in adult life.

Get started

Divide the class into pairs. Ask students to tell their partner three things they do to make sure they're organized, either at home or at school. Remind them to include adverbs of frequency in their sentences.

Encourage students to share their ideas with the class.

READ

1

- Divide the class into pairs and ask them to match the teenagers to their bedrooms. Have students say who they are most like.
- Point out to students that we use *to be like someone/ something* when we compare one thing to another. Students may confuse this with *to like someone*, which we use to express a preference. Clarify the difference between *I like* and *I'm like* by giving some examples of each.
- Check answers as a class. Choose several students to say who they are like and why; for example, *I'm like Anna because my room's always messy*.
- You could point out to students that we use words such as *really* and *very* before adjectives to modify them. *Really* and *very* make the adjectives they go before stronger.

ANSWERS
Photo 1: Kara Photo 2: Ida Photo 3: Anna

DO

2

- Divide the class into pairs and ask them to put the steps for organizing their bedrooms in the correct order. Draw students' attention to the first step as an example before they start.
- Allow two minutes for this.
- Choose a student to read the order aloud for the class to agree on.

ANSWERS
2 Start 3 Choose 4 Plan 5 Finish

3a

- Explain to students that they are going to organize or reorganize their rooms.
- Ask students to follow the steps in Exercise 2 and draw a simple plan of their organized room.
- Set a time limit of three minutes for this.

3b

- Divide the class into pairs and ask them to show each other their plans. Tell them to explain where things are in their plans and why.
- Draw students' attention to the model conversations to help them structure their answers.
- Invite students to share with the class any major changes they are planning for their bedrooms.

Fast finishers
Students who finish early can find three things in the text we use to organize ourselves (e.g., *boxes*, *labels*, *bags*). Ask them to think of more things to add to the list (e.g., *charts*, *cabinets*, *folders*, *lists*, *schedules*, *shelves*, *suitcases*, *closets*).

REFLECT

4

- Discuss the questions as a whole class.
- Ask two students to read aloud one REFLECTION POINT sentence each.
- Ask whether everyone agreed with the steps for organizing a bedroom or if they have a different way of organizing themselves.

Alternative procedure: less confident classes
Give less confident students three or four minutes to prepare their answers individually in outline form before comparing their answers in pairs. You could generate more ideas by asking pairs to become groups of four, and then have a group discussion.

EXTEND

5

- Ask students to work in small groups to decide how to organize or reorganize the classroom or another room at school or one of their houses.
- Allow students five minutes for this task.
- Encourage students to present their ideas to the class to close the activity.

Homework

Ask students to write five steps for preparing themselves for an exam, following the same format as the steps in Exercise 2: *1 Get ready*; *2 Start*; *3 Choose*; *4 Plan*; *5 Finish*. At the beginning of the next class, ask students to read aloud their ideas for making the ideal plan for preparing for an exam. You could make a notice or poster to display students' ideas when they are about to take an exam.

SPEAKING When's the next one?

Ask for and tell the time when you travel Page 25

STAGE	TIME	FOCUS
GET STARTED		Recycle telling the time and the 12- and 24-hour clock times.
SPEAK		Talk about when you travel on buses and trains and how to say the times on bus and train schedules.
LISTEN		Listen for general and specific information in two conversations at a bus stop and a train station. Look at the script and learn questions for asking the time and ways of making time to think (speaking subskill). Practice saying the time using the 12- and 24-hour clock times.
ACT		Role-play asking and telling the time in two travel conversations.

Get started

Recycle telling the time by writing these phrases on the board: *a quarter past/after, half past, a quarter to*.

Ask students to draw a clock for each of the time expressions.

Divide the class into pairs and have students take turns looking at each other's clocks and asking for and saying the time.

Now ask students to say the times on their clocks to each other using the 24-hour clock times.

SPEAK

1

- Divide the class into pairs and ask them to answer the questions.
- Elicit answers from the class.

ANSWERS
2 16:30 = sixteen thirty; 19:05 = nineteen oh five

Alternative procedure: less confident classes
You can expand on question 2 if you feel students are not familiar with telling the time using the 24-hour clock times. Ask students how we say these times in 12-hour clock time and what times are given in transportation schedules (*the times the train or bus arrives or leaves*).

LISTEN

2 31

- Ask students to close their books.
- Play the audio track for students to listen to the conversations and find out what the people do next.
- Elicit answers from the class.

ANSWERS / AUDIO SCRIPT 31
Mary and Paul have a snack.
Angel and David walk to the sports center.

Mary: Excuse me. What time is the next train to New York?
Agent: Well, there's one at 17:45.
Mary: Seventeen forty-five? Oh yes, five forty-five! What time is it now?
Agent: It's 20 after five.
Mary: Thanks. ... Do we have time for a snack?
Paul: Uh ... yes. We have 25 minutes.
Mary: Good. I'm really hungry.

Angel: Excuse me. When's the next bus to the sports center?
Woman: Let's see ... I think it's at 1:05, but check the schedule.
Angel: Thanks. ... What time is it now?
David: It's twelve thirty.
Angel: How long do we have until it leaves?
David: Uh, let me think ... Thirty-five minutes.
Angel: Let's walk. It's only 15 minutes on foot.

3 31

- Play the track again for students to listen and complete the conversations.
- Point out to students that *How long ... ?* is used to ask questions about amounts or periods of time.

ANSWERS / AUDIO SCRIPT 31
1 What time is 2 What time 3 Do we have 4 When's
5 How long
See Exercise 2 for audio script.

4 32

- Play the track for students to listen and repeat the questions.
- Draw students' attention to the falling intonation in *Wh*-questions.

AUDIO SCRIPT 32
1 What time is the next train to New York?
2 What time is it now?
3 Do we have time for a snack?
4 When's the next bus to the sports center?
5 How long do we have until it leaves?

5a

- Ask students to think of ways to make time to think when they are having a conversation in English and why it is important.
- Have a student read the tips in the HOW TO box aloud.
- Compare the tips in the box with the ideas students thought of.

5b

- Ask students to underline examples of making time to think in the conversations.

ANSWERS
See underlining in audio script in Exercise 2.

6a 33

- Play the track for students to listen and draw the times on the clocks.

ANSWERS / AUDIO SCRIPT 33

1 eight thirty 
3 five oh five 
2 nineteen forty-five 
4 a quarter to four 

6b 34

- Divide the class into pairs. Ask students to say the times in Exercise 6a in two or three different ways.
- You could do the first one together with the class as an example.
- Go around the class, inviting different students to say the times.
- Play the track for students to listen and repeat all the times.

ANSWERS / AUDIO SCRIPT 34
1 eight thirty / half past eight / twenty thirty
2 nineteen forty-five / a quarter to eight / seven forty-five
3 five oh five / five past five/ seventeen oh five
4 a quarter to four / three forty-five / fifteen forty-five

ACT

7 35

- Divide the class into groups of four, Students A, B, C, and D.
- Explain to students that they are going to practice two travel conversations and then present them to other groups.
- Ask Students A and C to look at page 75 and follow the instructions.
- Ask Students B and D to look at page 76 and follow the instructions.
- Draw students' attention to the **PHRASEBOOK** to help them structure their conversations. These phrases are recorded if you would like to play them.
- Have students present their conversations to other groups. Give students feedback at the end of the activity on errors and good use of language.

Extra activity

Play a game called *The Alphabet Race* to recycle the alphabet and methods of transportation.

Go around the class, asking pairs to say a way to travel for each letter of the alphabet except *O, Q,* and *X*. You could ask students to come up and write them on the board.

SUGGESTED ANSWERS

airplane, balloon/bicycle/bike/boat/bus, camel/canoe/car/cruise ship, donkey, elephant, ferry/foot, go-kart, helicopter/horse/hot air balloon, inflatable boat, jet, kayak, limousine, metro/motorcycle, naval ship, pedicab/pickup truck/plane, raft/rocket/rollerblades, sailboat/scooter/ship/skates/skis/submarine/subway, taxi/tractor/train/tram/truck, underground/unicycle, van, wagon, yacht, zeppelin

Homework

Ask students to write all the times in Exercises 1 and 2 in two or three different ways.

WRITING My favorite room

Use *also* and *too* *Page 26*

STAGE	TIME	FOCUS
GET STARTED		Recycle rooms and places in a house and simple present verbs.
SPEAK AND READ		Talk about pen pals and whether students would like to have one. Read a message from a girl to her pen pal. Learn how to use *also* and *too* (writing subskill).
PRACTICE		Use *also* and *too* in a written exercise.
DISCUSS		Talk about your favorite room in your house and what you do there.
WRITE		Write a description of your favorite room for a pen pal.
SHARE		Read your description and listen to other students' descriptions. Find out which room most students choose as their favorite.

Get started

Write these fill-in-the-blank sentences in a list on the board:

1 The car is in the ________ . *2 You have dinner in the* ________ . *3 You grow flowers in the* ________ . *4 You brush your teeth in the* ________ . *5 You watch TV in the* ________ . *6 You cook in the* ________ . *7 You sleep in your* ________ . Divide the class into pairs and ask students to think of the correct parts of a house to complete the sentences.

Elicit answers from different students around the class and write them on the board. Discuss reasons why students might give different answers.

Erase everything but the names of the rooms. Ask students to reconstruct the sentences and check their answers.

SUGGESTED ANSWERS

1 garage 2 dining room 3 yard 4 bathroom
5 living room 6 kitchen 7 bedroom

Alternative procedure: less confident classes

Write the names of the rooms on the board in a jumbled order to help less confident students.

SPEAK AND READ

1

- Divide the class into pairs and ask students to take turns asking and answering the questions.
- Discuss answers as a class.

MOVE BEYOND FOR TEACHERS

Benefits of having a pen pal

Although the way we communicate has changed radically, many teachers still arrange international pen pal exchanges for their students. Benefits include real practice in reading and writing skills, widening teenagers' horizons to include other ways of life and different cultures, and promoting the key skills needed to develop a friendship.

2

- Ask students to read Judy's message to her pen pal and decide what her favorite room is.
- Choose a student to say the answer and read the words in the text aloud that helped him or her decide on the answer.

ANSWER
Judy's favorite room is the kitchen. (*big table, oven*)

3a

- Ask students to read the tips in the HOW TO box.

3b

- Have students underline examples of *also* and *too* in the message in Exercise 2.
- Choose different students around the class to read their examples aloud.

ANSWERS
... and it also has a lot of light.
... it's normally quiet too.
It's also really warm ...

PRACTICE

4

- Ask students to complete the description with *also* and *too*.
- Encourage students to compare their answers in pairs before you elicit them from different students around the class.

ANSWERS
1 too 2 also 3 too 4 also

Fast finishers
Encourage students to find four adjectives describing rooms in the texts in Exercise 2 and Exercise 4 (*favorite*, *big*, *quiet*, *warm*). Ask them to think of more adjectives they can use to describe rooms in a house (e.g., *small*, *comfortable*, *pretty*).

DISCUSS

5

- Explain to students that they are going to write a description of their favorite room for a pen pal.
- Divide the class into pairs to tell each other about their favorite rooms in their houses.
- Remind students to say why the room is their favorite, what is in the room, and what they do in the room at different times of the day.

WRITE

6

- Tell students that they are now going to write a description of their favorite room. Draw their attention to the points in the writing plan to help them prepare. Encourage them to make some notes before they start writing.
- Ask students to write their descriptions and check them. Set a time limit of 10 minutes for this.
- Remind students to check the points in the plan to make sure they have followed the instructions correctly.

Alternative procedure
Ask students not to write the name of the room so other students can guess it in Exercise 7.

SHARE

7

- Ask as many students as possible to read their descriptions aloud to the class. If you have a large class, you may want to do this in groups. Encourage students to ask questions to find out more information about their classmates' favorite rooms.
- Take a class vote to find out which room is the most popular among all of the students.

Homework

Ask students to make a poster presentation of their ideal bedroom. Have them write a short text to describe the main features of the room and add pictures and photos to make it more visual. Suggest looking in magazines and catalogs for ideas. Have students work in groups to present their ideal bedrooms to each other at the beginning of the next class. At the end of the activity, ask the groups to vote on their favorite bedroom.

VOCABULARY Daily activities

1

- Ask students if they know anything about what time Americans do these things every day: *get up, start/ finish school, have lunch, go to bed*.
- Have students complete Mike's blog for his friends with the verbs in the box.
- Encourage students to say what they like and don't like about Mike's new routine.
- Check answers as a class.

ANSWERS

1 wake 2 take 3 get 4 brush 5 brush 6 get
7 go 8 get 9 do 10 pack

Furniture and other things in the home

2

- Ask students to complete the words in Mike's blog. Point out that the first two letters of each word are given.
- Ask students to compare their answers in pairs before you check them as a class.
- Encourage students to say whether they think Mike prefers where he lives now or where he lived before. (*It's smaller, the furniture is old, and there's no washing machine. He probably preferred living in the house.*)

ANSWERS

1 closet 2 bookshelf 3 shelves 4 cabinet
5 carpet 6 lamp 7 curtains 8 sofa 9 armchair
10 stove 11 refrigerator 12 dishwasher

GRAMMAR Simple present affirmative; prepositions of time

3

- Ask students to complete the blog with the correct form of the verbs or with *at*, *in*, and *on*.
- Allow them to compare their answers in pairs.
- Check answers by choosing different students around the class to say the answers.

ANSWERS

1 starts 2 ends 3 in 4 At 5 eat 6 On
7 plays 8 play

Simple present with adverbs of frequency

4

- As an introduction, ask students what they usually do on weekends.
- Have students complete the sentences with the adverbs of frequency in the box.
- Choose individual students to read the sentences aloud.
- Ask students whether their weekend is similar or different.

ANSWERS

1 I always get up late.
2 We usually go shopping.
3 I often watch a movie with friends.
4 We sometimes have lunch with my parents' friends.
5 I hardly ever forget to do my homework.
6 I never get bored.

Extra Resources

Go to the Teacher's Resource Center at mee2.macmillaneducation.com for:

- the Speaking section of Progress Check Units 1&2;
- a downloadable project linked to Units 1–2;
- videos, video worksheets, and video scripts;
- extra vocabulary at two levels of difficulty;
- extra grammar at two levels of difficulty;
- culture lessons, with full teacher's notes;
- life skills lessons, with full teacher's notes;
- Speaking Database materials;
- the *Move Beyond* Level 1 wordlist;
- downloadable PDF and Word tests for Unit 2;
- tips for using the Grammar Database;
- extra reading materials;
- and more!

Go to Workbook pages 96–107 for further practice material.

PROGRESS CHECK 1&2

Preparing for the Progress Check

The Progress Check can be done either as a review of the two preceding units or as a formal test. For the first Progress Check, it is a good idea to have students prepare as thoroughly as they can so that they get into the habit of regularly reviewing what they have learned. Reassure the class that the Progress Check contains only material that they have covered in the previous two units.

Vocabulary review

- Before you start, review days and times. Ask students what day and time it is and write these at the top of the board.
- Then write the following in a list on the board and ask students to write the words for each of the places.

  1 You watch plays here. 2 You swim here. 3 You play sports here. 4 You see animals here. 5 You buy things here. 6 You eat meals here. 7 You watch movies here. 8 You walk and play games here.
- If some students need help, you could give them the first letter of each word.
- Divide the class into pairs and give them two minutes to list as many places to visit in a town as they can. After two minutes, choose several students to give some answers. Then ask students to turn to pages 8–9 to check their answers and find out whether they missed any.
- Draw a family tree on the board with a boy, Daniel, at the bottom. Add people's names to show he has a sister, brother, mother, father, aunt, uncle, grandparents, and cousins, but don't include these terms on the board.
- Give students three minutes to work in pairs and complete the family tree with words that show who the people are in relation to Daniel.
- After checking the answers, ask further questions (e.g., *Daniel is Maria's … ?*) to elicit some of the family words.
- To review daily routines, ask students to write as many things as they can think of that they do *before* noon in one column in their notebooks. Then ask them to write as many things as they can that they do *after* noon in their notebooks. Then allow them to open their books to pages 18–19 and fill in any activities that they missed from their daily routines. Ask them to write them in chronological order and to write a time next to each activity.
- Give students one minute to compare their answers with a partner. Then ask the class a few questions; for example, *Who brushes their teeth before 7:30 a.m.? Who gets home after 4 p.m.?*
- Ask students to turn to page 22 and give them two minutes to look at the house and furniture vocabulary. Then divide them into pairs and ask them to close their books and sketch a simple house in a notebook, labeling rooms and adding and labeling furniture in the appropriate rooms.

Grammar review

- To remind the class of the grammar they have studied so far in the units, have a "race" in which students go through their books and tell you the main grammar points from each unit (Unit 1: *There is / there are*; prepositions of place; *Have*; Unit 2: Simple present affirmative; prepositions of time; Simple present with adverbs of frequency).
- Ask students for an example sentence or as many examples as possible of each. Correct mistakes as you go and, if there are any frequent areas of error, do a more extended review of the language. Ask students to read over the grammar explanations on pages 11, 13, 21, and 23 and the Grammar Database on pages 64–65.

Optional warm-up activities

These activities are suitable when you are not using the Progress Check as part of a formal test.

READ Exercise 1

- Tell students that this type of exercise is multiple choice and ask them to look at the example given.
- Ask students to read over the sentences so they can see what the text is about and familiarize themselves with the topic. Then ask them to look closely at the types of words given in the examples (subjects, prepositions of place, verbs, etc.). Ask them to think of what types of words can come before or after these, or any rules they know regarding where the example words go in a sentence. Don't ask students to give you answers or confirm any answers at this point.
- Point out that looking at the types of words and the position of the blank in multiple-choice sentences can be very useful in eliminating wrong answers and choosing the correct one.

LISTEN Exercise 2

- Refer students to the listening activities and the HOW TO boxes they covered on pages 12 and 22. Ask them which tips they thought were most useful.
- Remind students that listening isn't a passive activity and that they shouldn't just sit back while the audio is playing. They should use the time they have in a test to predict what they will hear. If they do this, what they hear will make more sense to them.
- One way to help them predict is to use the pictures if there are any in the exercise.
- Divide the class into pairs and give them two minutes to write as many things as they can see in all the pictures in Exercise 2. Have a quick feedback session.
- Draw students' attention to the clocks in question 2 and ask them to say the times in their heads.
- Divide the class into pairs and ask them to discuss the differences among the stations in question 5.
- Point out to students that they have gathered a lot of useful information before hearing the audio and that they will now be much better focused on what they are listening for.

WRITE Exercise 4

- Coming up with ideas for a writing task may be difficult for some students. Encourage them to look closely at Kim's email to see exactly what information they need to include. They can number the points to include if necessary and then check these off when they check their writing.
- Apart from the things Kim asks for, ask them to think about what other things they could include.
- Finally, ask them to think about how they are going to start and end their email to Kim.

Doing the Progress Check

READ Exercise 1

- If you have decided not to do the full warm-up, give students a minute to read over the exercise, looking at the sentences and examples. Ask them to notice the types of words and what comes before and after each blank.
- Focus students' attention on the **Test-Taking Tips** and remind them that this type of task is very common in standardized English exams.
- Have students read the sentences about Melissa's hometown and choose the best word (A, B, or C) for each blank.
- Remind students to use the strategies given to eliminate any wrong answers and to read their answers to themselves to make sure they sound correct.

PROGRESS CHECK 1&2

ANSWERS
1 B 2 A 3 C 4 B 5 C

LISTEN Exercise 2

36

- If you have decided not to do the full warm-up, refer students back to the techniques they studied on pages 12 and 22.
- Then focus students' attention on the **Test-Taking Tips** and ask them to read through the tips and think about how they may be useful.
- Encourage students to spend one or two minutes looking at the pictures to predict what type of information and words they may hear.
- Point out that they will hear each conversation twice and there will be an example first. Remind them that one strategy is to eliminate one option when they listen for the first time.

ANSWERS / AUDIO SCRIPT 36

1 B 2 C 3 A 4 B 5 B

Narrator: **1** Which is Susan's room?
Girl 1: Is this your room, Susan?
Susan: Yep.
Girl 1: It's nice. I hardly ever clean mine, so it's always a mess.
Susan: My room is normally a little messy, but it's never very messy.
Narrator: Now listen again.

Narrator: **2** What time does the train leave?
Boy 1: Excuse me. What time is the next train to Boston?
Woman: Uh ... let's see ... there's one at 2:05.
Boy 1: What time is it now?
Boy 2: It's five to two.
Boy 1: Um ... so it leaves in 10 minutes ...
Boy 2: I want to have a snack.
Boy 1: Sorry, when's the next one?
Woman: It's at 2:50.
Boy 2: Hmm. Ten to three. Let's take that one.
Boy 1: OK.
Narrator: Now listen again.

Narrator: **3** Where's the noise from?
Girl: What's that noise?
Mom: What noise?
Girl: Listen. Is it the stove?
Mom: No. The stove never makes noise. Maybe it's the dishwasher, or the refrigerator. They're sometimes noisy.
Girl: Oh, Mom, look! There's water coming out of the dishwasher!
Mom: Oh no! You're right!
Narrator: Now listen again.

Narrator: **4** Which is the right note?
Mark: Hi, Jack!
Jack: Hey, Mark!
Mark: Listen. Are you free tonight?
Jack: No, my soccer game is tonight. It's every Monday. Why?
Mark: I have a great new video game!
Jack: Really? OK, what about Wednesday?
Mark: Um, no, tomorrow's better for me. Is that OK for you?
Jack: Uh ... OK, yeah. What time?
Mark: At seven. At my house.
Jack: Great, see you then!
Narrator: Now listen again.

Narrator: **5** Which is the right station?
Woman: Excuse me. How do I get to the bus station, please?
Girl: Which one? There's the main station and a small one just around the corner.
Woman: The main station.
Girl: OK, you go straight ahead until you see a park on the left. The park's in front of the station. You can't miss it.
Woman: Thanks.
Narrator: Now listen again.

WRITE Exercise 3

- Focus students' attention on the **Test-Taking Tips** and ask them to follow the tips as they do the exercise.
- Ask students to read the descriptions and complete the family words.

ANSWERS
1 parent 2 aunt 3 husband 4 daughter 5 grandfather

WRITE Exercise 4

- Ask students to read Kim's email and elicit who they have to write to and what they need to include.
- Remind them to include a beginning and ending in their email, but explain that they shouldn't spend too long thinking about this.
- Finally, remind students of the word limit and encourage them to check this by counting the words. Also remind them to check their spelling, grammar, and punctuation.

MODEL ANSWER
Hi, Kim.
I always get to school at 8:30. I normally have lunch at school. I go home at 4 o'clock and do my homework. I usually go to bed at 10 o'clock.
Bye!
Luke

After the Progress Check

Optional game

Creating a chain story as a class works well to practice the simple present tense and the vocabulary for daily routines. Start the story by saying: *Sara has a busy day. She wakes up at six o'clock. At 6:10 a.m. she … .* Write this at the top of the board and ask a student to continue the story. Each student continues the story by adding an original sentence, which you write on the board. Encourage students to use *before* and *after* when they can. When the story gets too long, start again with a new situation.

Feedback and extension

After the Progress Check has been graded, provide feedback to the class as a whole and individually as much as possible. Ask students which parts they found the most difficult and how they think they could improve their grades next time.

READ Exercise 1

- Review the example sentence as a class. Ask students why it couldn't be A (*it's physically impossible*).
- Then go through each item 1–5 and try to eliminate one answer each time based on either grammar or possibility (e.g., *in item 1* it *is impossible, as* are *can't correctly come after* it*; in item 3 the only word that can grammatically fit before the verb* go *is* often, etc.).
- Remind students that the more they can read in English in their spare time (e.g., online or in magazines), the more confident they will be in the reading sections of exams.

LISTEN Exercise 2

- Hand out copies of the audio script to students and ask them to read through and discuss with a partner where they made mistakes.
- As with the reading part of the exam, look at ways they would have been able to eliminate incorrect answers.
- If there were any answers that many students mistakenly chose, spend a little more time going over reasons why they should have eliminated them.
- Remind students that, as with the reading, the more time they can spend listening to English in their spare time, the more accustomed they will be to accent, pronunciation, and intonation. Ask students where they think they can find English to listen to (*songs, radio, television,* etc.).

WRITE Exercise 3

- Elicit family words from the class and make a list on the board.
- Choose one of the words on the board and ask students to give a description of the word (e.g., *niece: your brother's or sister's daughter*).
- Ask students to choose three or four of the family words on the board and to write a description for each word.
- Divide the class into pairs and ask them to read their descriptions for their partners to listen and say the correct family words.

WRITE Exercise 4

- Write the model answer on the board, along with:
  1 another email that doesn't respond to all the criteria needed
  2 an email that answers the questions but is significantly over the word count
  3 an email with lots of spelling and grammatical errors
- Divide the class into pairs and give them five minutes to look through the four emails. Ask them to identify which is the best answer and why. Ask them to give reasons why they think the other three could lose points and what the student should do to improve them.

3 CLASSMATES

IN THE PICTURE School subjects

Talk about school subjects

Pages 30–31

STAGE	TIME	FOCUS
GET STARTED		Sort classroom language into categories and use some of the vocabulary from the lesson.
WORK WITH WORDS		Recycle vocabulary related to the classroom and school subjects. Complete a school schedule. Watch a video of teenagers talking about their favorite school subjects. Complete sentences to describe your schedule.
SPEAK		Use the vocabulary from the lesson to write a definition of three school subjects for a partner to name.

Get started

Recycle classroom language. Write these three categories on the board: *Actions*, *Questions*, *Expressions*.

Ask students to categorize these phrases: *Open your books*; *Time's up!*; *Underline the words in bold*; *How do you pronounce "chemistry"?*; *Good work!*; *How do you spell that?*

Divide the class into pairs and ask them to race against each other to think of more phrases for each category in three minutes. Ask students to stop when the time is up and count how many phrases they have for each category.

Invite students to come to the board and write their phrases in the correct categories. Correct any misspelled words.

Put the title of the unit on the board: *Classmates*. Elicit from students the meaning of the word (*people in your class at school*) and ask them what they think the unit is going to be about (*everything related to school*).

ANSWERS

Actions: Open your books; Underline the words in bold
Questions: How do you pronounce "chemistry"?; How do you spell that?
Expressions: Time's up!; Good work!

WORK WITH WORDS School subjects

1 RECALL

- Focus students' attention on the photo of a classroom in the USA and elicit similarities and differences between it and the classroom they are in now.
- Divide the class into pairs and ask students to write words for the different categories. Draw students' attention to the examples and the photo to help give them ideas.
- Set a time limit of three minutes.
- Choose different students to give their answers.
- Ask students to do the **Work with Words** task on page 71.

2

- Have students match the icons on the photo to the US school subjects.
- Elicit any more school subjects students may know (e.g., *biology*, *chemistry*, *physics*, *social studies*, *French*).
- Point out that we use capital letters when we talk about languages as school subjects, but other subjects don't need a capital letter.
- Find out from students which subject doesn't have an icon (*music*), but don't check answers at this point.

3a ▶37

- Play the track for students to check their answers to Exercise 2 first.
- Continue the track for students to listen and repeat as the answers are given again.

ANSWERS / AUDIO SCRIPT ▶37

a art b health c English d history e languages
f PE (physical education) g drama h geography
i computer science j math k science l music

3b

- Ask students to create an icon for the missing subject in Exercise 2 (*music*).
- Have students come to the board and draw their icons.
- Vote on the best icon. Point to each icon and ask students to raise their hands. Ask a volunteer to count the number of votes for each icon and name the winner.

Extra activity
Divide the class into pairs and have students act out the school subjects for their partner to guess.

4 38

- Focus students' attention on the schedule and ask them to complete the sentences.
- Use this opportunity to recycle days of the week using the short forms in the schedule as prompts.
- Play the track for students to check their answers.

ANSWERS / AUDIO SCRIPT 38
1 homeroom 2 history 3 lunch 4 math 5 drama
6 Science; health
See Student's Book, page 32, for audio script.

Alternative procedure: less confident classes
Recycle saying the time by asking comprehension questions about the schedule to help orient students before they do Exercise 4: *What time do they start school every morning?* (8:30 a.m.); *What time do they have lunch?* (11:50 a.m.–12:30 p.m.); *When do they finish school?* (3:30 p.m.).

5 39

- Play the track for students to listen and complete the schedule with the school subjects.
- Let students compare their answers in pairs before you check them as a class.
- Ask students if they like this school schedule and whether it is similar to or different from their own.

ANSWERS / AUDIO SCRIPT 39
1 English 2 music 3 languages 4 art 5 geography
6 PE
1 Our first class on Monday is English.
2 We have music on Tuesday afternoon.
3 We have languages three times a week from ten o'clock to 10:50. I study French.
4 Our last class on Wednesday is art.
5 Geography is on Tuesday, Thursday, and Friday before lunch.
6 The week ends with two hours of PE.

Extra activity
Ask students to study this audio text in order to reconstruct all the information they remember. Play the track again for students to write down what they hear. Keep playing the track until a student thinks he or she has a perfect version of the text and calls out *Stop!* Divide the class into groups of three or four to compare their sentences. Invite students to come to the board and write their sentences to check. Ask students to underline all the prepositions of time to recycle this grammar point.

6 THE MOVING PICTURE

- Explain to students that they are going to watch three teenagers talking about school subjects.
- Play the video and ask students to write down which subjects the students like and why.
- Let students compare their answers in pairs before you check them as a class.
- You might want to play the video again with the volume off. Pause after each activity and ask students to try to remember the exact words of the conversation in each frame.

ANSWERS / VIDEO SCRIPT
Charlotte: drama because it's fun to act, sing, and dance; it's creative, and she likes being with her friends in drama class
Holly: math because she enjoys algebra, and she likes to have one right answer
Aaron: PE because he likes trying new sports and games, and geography because he likes learning about sports in other countries

Robert: Hey, everyone! It's time for *What's Cool in School*. We're talking about our favorite school subjects today. I'm Robert, and I'm here with three of my classmates. They're going to tell you about their favorite – and not so favorite – subjects. First, it's Charlotte.
Charlotte: My favorite school subject's drama because it's fun to act, sing, and dance. It's very creative. I can be other people or animals or even a machine. I love being with my friends in drama class. We laugh all the time. And Ms. Lowell is the best drama teacher in the world. Hey, Ms. Lowell! Drama class is awesome.
Robert: Next we go to Holly.
Holly: Well, one of my favorite subjects is math because I enjoy algebra. Maybe some people think it's strange, but I like to have one right answer. I don't really like history. There are so many dates and too much information, and then they expect us to remember it all.
Robert: Let's move on to Aaron.
Aaron: My favorite subject is PE. I like to have fun and do different sports. We do a lot of different activities in PE class. I like to try new games. Oh, and I play on the soccer team after school. I like to swim and play basketball and tennis. I also like geography because I like learning about sports that people play in different countries. But I don't like drama or singing. I try not to take those classes.
Robert: Thanks for your thoughts. And that's *What's Cool in School* for today.

7

- Ask students to complete the sentences about their school schedules.
- Have students compare their sentences in pairs and report any differences they found in their school routines and likes and dislikes.

Fast finishers
Ask fast finishers to create an "odd one out" activity (i.e., one item of a group is different and doesn't fit in with the rest of the group) from the vocabulary in this lesson to test the rest of the class. You could write an example on the board; for example, *languages, art, history, science* (*science is the odd one out, as the others are arts and humanities subjects*).

SPEAK

8

- Divide the class into pairs and ask them to complete the tasks.
- Circulate and monitor as students work, helping them with any language difficulties.

Alternative procedure: less confident classes
First choose pairs to model this activity for the class before asking students to continue by themselves.

MOVE BEYOND

Ask students to do the **Words & Beyond** exercise on page 71.

Homework

In class, you could brainstorm some ideas to encourage students to be creative; for example, new school subjects (*cooking, yoga, making video games, school newspaper, independent study*), different schedules (*start at ten o'clock, 40-minute classes, three-month vacations, classes Monday through Thursday!*), regular rest periods, physical activities every 40 minutes, etc.
For homework, ask students to write notes on how they could improve their school schedules. At the beginning of the next class, divide the class into small groups and ask students to present their ideal schedules to one another. Ask each group to report the best ideas to the class.

READING An interview

Understand the main ideas

Page 32

STAGE	TIME	FOCUS
GET STARTED		Play a game to recycle school subjects.
SPEAK AND READ		Read quickly to understand the main ideas in a text about a school (reading subskill). Complete a reporter's notes and answer questions about the school.
REACT		Say whether you like the Evelyn Grace Academy building and how the school is different from your school.

Get started

Play a game of *Snowman* (see Games, page 33) to recycle school subjects.

SPEAK AND READ

1

- Divide the class into pairs to ask and answer the questions.
- Choose different students to give their answers. Start a class discussion about what students like about their school.

2a

- Encourage students to think of any tips they know about how to understand the main ideas in a text. (See Teaching Tips, *Predicting before reading*, page 28.)
- Refer students to the HOW TO box to see whether they thought of the same tips.
- Ask them to cover the box and try to remember the three tips without looking.

2b ▶40

- Have students read the interview and check the information Jon talks about. You could set a time limit of two minutes to encourage students to read quickly. Don't play the audio at this point. It is an extra feature, and a suggestion for using it in class is included at the end of the lesson.
- Let students compare their answers in pairs before you check them as a class. When you discuss the subjects that Jon likes, remind students that Jon is British and point out that in the UK, people say "maths" instead of "math."

ANSWERS
the building the number of students the schedule
the subjects

MOVE BEYOND FOR TEACHERS

The education systems in the UK and the USA

In the UK, the education system is divided into five stages: early years, primary, secondary, further education, and higher education. Students have to attend school until they are 16 years old.

In the USA, the education system is also divided into five main levels: preschool, elementary school, middle/junior high school, high school, and postsecondary education. By law, most US states require that children attend school until they are 16 years old. Most students finish school, and they graduate from high school when they are 18 years old.

3

- Ask students to check the tips in the HOW TO box that helped them with Exercise 2b.

4

Exam-type task

- Have students read the interview again and complete the reporter's notes.
- Point out to students that this type of information transfer activity is a typical task in many standardized English exams.
- Choose different students to read their answers aloud.

ANSWERS
Student name: Jon
Year: 8
Nº students: around 800
School times: 8:30-3:15
Favorite subject: maths
Rules: wear a uniform, can't take phones inside the school

Extra activity
Ask students to compare the rules in their school and any other schools they know with the rules of the Evelyn Grace Academy. In a less confident class, have students write the rules down before they do this as a speaking activity.

5
- Ask students to write their answers to the questions.
- Let students compare their answers in pairs before you check them as a class.

ANSWERS
1 They walk along a running track.
2 Jon starts school at 8:30 a.m.
3 He takes classes in dance and music.

MOVE BEYOND FOR TEACHERS

Evelyn Grace Academy

The Evelyn Grace Academy is a nonselective, coeducational secondary school in South London. The building, designed by architect Zaha Hadid, was awarded the 2011 Stirling Prize for architecture. You can find a "video prospectus" on the school's website to show students what life is like at the school. Search for *Evelyn Grace Academy Brixton.*

Fast finishers
Ask students to write an extra comprehension question about the interview to ask the class at the end of the activity; for example, *Where is the school?* (South London); *What subjects do they have in Year 8?* (science, history, math, and English).

REACT

6
- Divide the class into pairs to discuss the questions.
- Draw students' attention to the PHRASE BYTES box to help them structure their opinions.
- Invite students to share their answers with the class and encourage them to expand on how the Evelyn Grace Academy is similar to or different from their school.

MOVE BEYOND

Ask students to continue working in pairs and to take turns asking and answering the questions in the interview about their school.

Recorded reading text 40
Use the audio in Exercises 4 and 5 as an alternative to having students read the text again. Ask them to close their books and listen for the specific information. Then have them open their books again and read to check.

Homework

Ask students to write notes to design and describe their perfect school to prepare to give a presentation on it in the next class (about three minutes for each presentation). During the presentation stage, encourage other students to ask questions, such as: *Where do the students study?* At the end of the presentations, have a group discussion about whose school would work best in the real world.

GRAMMAR Simple present negative; questions and short answers

Use negative verbs and ask and answer questions *Page 33*

STAGE	TIME	FOCUS
GET STARTED		Use the simple present to ask and answer questions about everyday activities.
READ AND LISTEN		Read and listen to an interview to find out how Bella's school is different.
STUDY		Use the interview to complete examples of the simple present negative, questions, and short answers.
PRACTICE		Produce target language in written exercises and complete *Wh-* questions.
SPEAK		Talk about your everyday routine and tell the class some interesting facts about your partner.

Get started

Write one true and four false sentences about yourself on the board; for example, *I speak French. I have a bicycle. I play computer games. I watch TV every night. I cook every day.*

Have students ask you questions to find out which sentence is true. Monitor to check students' knowledge of simple present questions and short answers. Encourage them to say *Do … ?* and answer *Yes, I do* or *No, I don't* where possible.

Ask students to vote on which sentence is true. Then give them the correct answer.

Ask students to make the four false sentences negative. Monitor to check students' knowledge of simple present negative sentences.

READ AND LISTEN Grammar in context

1 41
- Refer students to the photo and ask them what they think the text is going to be about.
- Play the track for students to read and listen to the interview and decide in what way Bella's school is different.
- Choose a student to say the answer.
- Ask students if they think Watershed School sounds interesting.

ANSWER / AUDIO SCRIPT 41
They don't spend all day in classrooms. They go out of the classroom to learn in the real world.
See Student's Book, page 33, for audio script.

MOVE BEYOND FOR TEACHERS

Watershed School, Colorado, USA

Watershed School is a pioneering private middle school and high school located in Boulder, Colorado. It has an innovative and experiential program in which students experience adventure and learn by doing. The curriculum revolves around learning expeditions, considered to be the most productive method of education; for example, children learn geography and biology in a canoe in a nearby river or in the woods. In addition to traditional sports such as football, students practice yoga, mountain biking, and playing Frisbee.

STUDY

2

- Ask students to complete the examples using Exercise 1 to help them.
- Check answers together as a class.

ANSWERS
don't spend   doesn't believe   Do; Does; have   do   doesn't

PRACTICE

3a

- Ask students to write the complete questions.
- Let students compare their answers in pairs before you check them as a class.

ANSWERS
2 Does she like it?
3 Does she think her school is typical?
4 Why does she think it's different?
5 How do they learn in the real world?

3b

- Ask students to write the answers to the questions, making sure they use short answers where possible. Refer them to Exercise 1 to help them with their answers. Draw students' attention to the example sentence.
- Let students compare their answers in pairs before you check them as a class.

ANSWERS
2 Yes, she does.
3 No, she doesn't.
4 Because they don't spend all day in classrooms.
5 They go to local farms and organizations and visit other cities and countries.

Fast finishers
Have fast finishers change affirmative answers from Exercise 3b to negative and vice versa.

4

- Have students complete the text with the simple present form of the verbs.
- Check answers as a class.

ANSWERS
1 don't go   2 doesn't go   3 don't work   4 don't spend
5 don't like   6 doesn't interest

5

- Ask students to complete the questions with the question words in the box.
- Remind them that they can use each word only once.
- Choose different students around the class to read the answers aloud.

ANSWERS
1 How   2 Where   3 When   4 What   5 Who   6 Why
7 Which

SPEAK

6a

- Divide the class into pairs to ask and answer the questions in Exercise 5.
- Draw students' attention to the model conversation.
- You could point out that you are going to ask them to write their partner's answers for homework, as this will make them listen more intently.
- Monitor and note errors and good use of language to go over in a feedback session at the end of the activity.

Alternative procedure: less confident classes
In a less confident class, let students prepare their answers in written form before doing this as a speaking activity. Circulate and monitor as they work, helping students with any language difficulties. You could ask a more confident pair to model this activity for the class before students continue by themselves in pairs.

Alternative procedure: more confident classes
In order to encourage students to listen carefully to each other's answers, ask students to give one false answer for their partner to guess.

6b

- Invite students to tell the class two interesting facts about their partner.

Extra activity
You could develop this into a class survey by collating the results on the board.

Write some prompts; for example, *All of us ... , Most students ... , Some students ... , None of us ... .*

Divide the class into small groups and ask students to write some conclusions using the prompts; for example, *Most students walk to school.*

Homework

Ask students to write their partner's answers to the questions in Exercise 5. At the beginning of the next class, ask students to read their sentences aloud to their partner to check that they have written the correct information.

LISTENING AND VOCABULARY Dress code

Listen for specific information

Page 34

STAGE	TIME	FOCUS
GET STARTED		Brainstorm different categories of clothes and talk about dress codes.
SPEAK AND LISTEN		Listen to students talking about their school clothes and follow tips for listening for specific information (listening subskill).
REACT		Discuss with a partner which school clothes you like from the photos and what you wear to school.
WORK WITH WORDS		Learn vocabulary for clothes and accessories. Practice the /oʊ/ sound. With a partner, design a school uniform for your school.

Get started

Have students close their books. Write these categories on the board:

Men's clothes
Unisex
Women's clothes

Divide the class into small groups and ask students to think of clothes vocabulary for each category. Set a time limit of three minutes and give regular updates; for example, *One minute to go.*

Stop students and give them one minute to check the organization of their lists. Ask students to count how many words they have in total and congratulate the winning team.

Write *Dress code* on the board and ask students what this means and which situations may have a dress code (*a set of rules about how you can dress, e.g., at school, a job, a fancy restaurant, a party, a wedding*).

Alternative procedure: less confident classes
Write clothes vocabulary on the board for students to categorize (e.g., *coat, dress, jacket, jeans, shirt, shorts, skirt, T-shirt, pants, tie*). Ask them to add at least two more words to each list.

SPEAK AND LISTEN

1 RECALL

- Divide the class into pairs and ask them to answer the questions.
- Choose different students to give their answers.

ANSWERS
1 jacket, jeans, pants, shirt, skirt, T-shirt
2 Students' own answers

2 42

- Play the track for students to listen to three teenagers talking about school clothes and match the names to the photos.
- Let students compare their answers in pairs before you check them as a class.

ANSWERS / AUDIO SCRIPT 42

1 c 2 b 3 a

Gilberto: My name is Gilberto, and I'm from Puerto Rico. Our school uniform is pretty casual. We wear blue shirts, gray pants, socks, and sneakers. In winter we wear exercise pants and exercise jackets. Our uniform is really comfortable!

Eva: I'm Eva. I'm from Italy. Our school uniform is very traditional. We wear a jacket, a white shirt, and black shoes. The boys wear a tie. It's red. Girls don't wear pants. We wear skirts. We also have clothes for PE – a white T-shirt, shorts – they're blue ... and white socks. We wear a coat, a scarf, and gloves when it's cold.

Zoe: Um ... my name's Zoe. I'm from San Diego. We don't have a school uniform at our school. We wear our normal clothes. This is my sister's shirt, but the jeans, the belt, and the black sneakers are mine. We can wear jewelry too, like earrings. I have a backpack for my stuff. When it's cold, we usually wear a hoodie or a sweater.

3a

- Ask students if they know any tips on how to listen for specific information. (See Teaching Tips, *Listening for specific information*, page 27.)
- Refer students to the HOW TO box and ask them to read the tips.
- Check to see if students have thought of similar or different ideas.

3b 42

- Play the track again for students to match the information to the correct photo.
- Encourage students to compare their answers in pairs before you elicit them from different students around the class.

ANSWERS / AUDIO SCRIPT 42

1 b 2 c 3 b 4 a 5 b
See Exercise 2 for audio script.

MOVE BEYOND FOR TEACHERS

School uniforms

School uniforms in England have been around since the Middle Ages. From the time of Henry VIII, uniforms were called "bluecoats" because blue was the cheapest dye available and showed humility among all children. The first school to introduce a uniform was Christ's Hospital, and its is the oldest uniform of any school. Today, the British government encourages schools to have a uniform, as it can promote positive behavior and protect children from social pressures to dress in a particular way.

In the USA, school uniforms are worn primarily in private schools. However, it is becoming more common for some public schools to have uniforms as well.

4

- Ask students to look back at the HOW TO box and to check the tips that helped them with Exercise 3b.

REACT

5

- Divide the class into pairs to discuss the questions.
- In a class discussion, invite students to share their answers with the class.

Alternative procedure: more confident classes

Hold a class debate. Write the following question on the board: *Do you think school uniforms are a good thing? Why or why not?* Ask students to stand in a line, from 0 = completely disagree to 10 = totally agree, and divide the class into two groups accordingly – one half in favor of school uniforms and the other half against. Remind students that the important thing is to defend their point of view in this activity. Give groups three minutes to prepare their arguments. After the debate, ask students to vote to see if anyone changed sides.

WORK WITH WORDS Clothes and accessories

6a

- Have students match the pictures to the words in the box. Do not check answers at this point.

Fast finishers

Have fast finishers think of more clothes vocabulary. They can use their dictionaries if necessary. At the end of the activity, ask students to draw the clothes items on the board for others to guess what they are in English.

6b ▶43

- Play the track for students to listen and check their answers first.
- Continue the track for students to listen and repeat the words after checking the answers.

ANSWERS / AUDIO SCRIPT ▶43

a scarf b earrings c sweater d coat e tie f belt
g gloves h shorts i exercise jacket j exercise pants
k backpack l hoodie

MOVE BEYOND FOR TEACHERS

American English versus British English

You could point out to students that Americans say *sweater* and *sneakers* and the British tend to say *jumper* and *trainers*. Also, in American English, *trousers* are called *pants*. This can cause confusion because the word *pants* refers to underwear in British English.

7 ▶44 PRONOUNCE

- Play the track for students to listen and underline the /oʊ/ sound in the words. (See Teaching Tips, *Long o sound*, page 28.)
- Play the track again for students to listen and repeat.
- Point out to students that the lips are relaxed and in a rounded position. Say: *o, o, oh*. The tongue is in a relaxed, neutral position in the middle of the mouth.

ANSWER / AUDIO SCRIPT ▶44

cl<u>o</u>thes c<u>oa</u>t ph<u>o</u>t<u>o</u> h<u>o</u>me Z<u>o</u>e

Extra activity

Ask students to think of two or three more words with the /oʊ/ sound (e.g., *note, hope, boat*).

8 ▶45

- Ask students to complete the quotes with words from Exercise 6a.
- Let students compare their answers in pairs before you play the track for them to check.

ANSWERS / AUDIO SCRIPT ▶45

1 earrings 2 backpack 3 exercise pants; exercise jackets
4 coat; scarf; gloves 5 hoodie 6 tie
See Student's Book, page 36, for audio script.

Extra activity

Ask students to match the sentences to the three teenagers in Exercise 2.

ANSWERS

1 Zoe 2 Zoe 3 Gilberto 4 Eva 5 Zoe 6 Eva

9

- Divide the class into pairs and ask them to design a school uniform for their school.
- Ask students to present their ideas to the class.
- You may want to take a class vote on the best idea for a school uniform.

Alternative procedure: less confident classes

Discuss together as a class different types of clothes and patterns students could choose from, and write ideas on the board. Use this opportunity to recycle colors.

Write some prompts on the board. For example:

Features: *It has long/short sleeves / buttons / zippers.*

Patterns: *checkered, plaid, flowered, polka dot, striped, solid*

Material: *It's made from cotton/polyester/wool/silk.*

MOVE BEYOND

Ask students to do the **Words & Beyond** exercise on page 71.

Homework

Ask students to write six headings – *Head, Neck, Body, Hands, Legs*, and *Feet* – and then list all the words for clothes from the lesson under the appropriate part of the body where they're worn. Ask them to look up new words in their dictionaries and add at least one more example to each category. In the next class, write the headings on the board and ask students to call out the clothes they wrote for each section. Ask students to add to their lists any words they didn't include.

GRAMMAR Possessive *'s*, *whose*, and possessive pronouns

Talk about possessions and relationships Page 35

STAGE	TIME	FOCUS
GET STARTED		Recycle simple present *Wh-* questions and clothes vocabulary.
READ AND LISTEN		Read and listen to a conversation in a locker room.
STUDY		Complete grammar explanations for possessive *'s* and *whose*. Complete a table with possessive pronouns.
PRACTICE		Use possessive forms in written exercises.
SPEAK		Talk about possessions and identify who they belong to.

Get started

Recycle simple present *Wh-* questions and clothes vocabulary. Write questions on the board in a jumbled order. For example:

dresser / do / think / Who / is / good / you / a / ? (Who do you think is a good dresser?)

sneakers or shoes / do / Which / you / prefer, / ? (Which do you prefer, sneakers or shoes?)

Divide the class into pairs and ask them to order the questions correctly.

Ask students to take turns asking and answering the questions. Elicit answers from several students. Review the meaning of the *Wh-* question words with the class (*Why* to ask about a reason; *When* to ask about time; *Which* to ask about a choice; *How* to ask about manner; *What* to ask about a thing; *Where* to ask about a place; *Who* to ask about a person).

READ AND LISTEN Grammar in context

1 46

- Refer students to the picture in Exercise 1 and ask: *Where are the students?* (In a locker room); *What do you think the teacher is saying?* ("Is this your coat?" / "Whose coat is this?"); *Is the locker room neat?* (no, it's a mess); *Where are the clothes?* (they're on the floor); *Does the teacher look happy?* (no, he doesn't).
- Play the track for students to read and listen to the conversation and decide who the coat belongs to.
- Choose a student to say the answer and to read aloud the words from the text that give the answer.

ANSWER / AUDIO SCRIPT 46

The coat belongs to Mr. Ford. (No, sir. It's yours.)
See Student's Book, page 35, for audio script.

STUDY

2

- Ask students to complete the examples with words from Exercise 1.
- Let students compare their answers in pairs before you check them as a class.
- Point out to students that *Whose* is another important question word and that we use it for asking about an owner. We say *Whose bag is this?* Ask students to add this new *Wh-* question word to their list and write its meaning.

ANSWERS

Harry's students' Whose

3

- Ask students to read the explanation and complete the table with possessive pronouns. Remind them to use Exercise 1 to help them. (See Teaching Tips, *Subject pronouns and possessive adjectives*, page 25.)
- Let students compare their answers in pairs before you check them as a class.

ANSWERS

mine yours ours

PRACTICE

4

- Ask students to complete the sentences with the words in parentheses. Remind them to add an apostrophe (') in the correct place and an s if necessary.
- Invite different students to come to the board and write the answers.

ANSWERS

1 Dan's 2 my parents' 3 Chloe's
4 our neighbors' (*our neighbor's* would be correct if there were only one neighbor, but the Student's Book gives *neighbors* as plural)
5 Kath's 6 the students'

Fast finishers

Ask fast finishers to find six words related to clothes and accessories in this lesson (*exercise jacket*, *sneakers*, *coat*, *gloves*, *earrings*, *bag*).

5 47

- Ask students to complete the conversation with the words in the box.
- Play the track for students to listen and check their answers.

ANSWERS / AUDIO SCRIPT 47

1 Whose 2 yours 3 mine 4 Martin's 5 his 6 Whose
7 theirs 8 hers 9 brother's 10 school's
See Student's Book, page 37, for audio script.

SPEAK

6

- Divide the class into pairs to do the tasks.
- Draw students' attention to the model conversation.
- Circulate, noting errors and good use of language without interrupting the flow of the activity.

- Give feedback to students at the end of the activity, pointing out errors and good use of language.

Alternative procedure: less confident classes
You could do this as a class before asking students to continue in pairs. Ask different students to choose some items from their pockets or bags (keys, phones, wallets, cosmetics, pens, etc.). Hold the items up as you choose them to make sure everyone knows their names. Put the items in a bag and pull them out one by one, asking: *Whose phone is this ... ?* The class must point to the owner and say: *It's his phone.* Pretend you haven't heard the answer so that students must say it in another way (e.g., *It's John's phone / It's his*) and ask the student: *Is it yours?* The student must respond with *Yes, it's mine* or *No, it isn't mine*.

Homework

Dictate these sentences to students: *Are these his gloves? That's my coat. Is this your backpack? These are her earrings. Those are our coats. Do they have their sneakers?*

Circulate while you are dictating, checking that students have written the sentences down correctly. In a less confident class, ask a student to come up and write the sentences on the board to check that everyone has transcribed the sentences correctly before they do their homework.

Ask students to change the possessive adjectives and nouns to possessive pronouns for homework. At the beginning of the next class, let students compare their answers in pairs before you check them as a class.

ANSWERS
Are these his? That's mine. Is this yours?
These are hers. Those are ours. Do they have theirs?

LANGUAGE & BEYOND KNOW YOURSELF

Understand your learning style Page 36

STAGE	TIME	FOCUS
GET STARTED		Make a paper airplane, following instructions, and think about different learning styles.
READ AND LISTEN		Read a website article and find out what type of learner you are.
DO		Talk about what type of learning activities you like best and decide whether the activities are good for visual, auditory, or kinesthetic learners.
REFLECT		Discuss the learning styles of your classmates and how knowing your learning style can help you.
EXTEND		Find out what other students are good at and see if it matches that person's learning style.

LIFE SKILLS

KNOW YOURSELF: UNDERSTAND YOUR LEARNING STYLE
In this lesson, students examine the three most common types of learning styles: auditory, visual, and kinesthetic. To learn, we depend on our senses to process the information around us. Most people tend to use one of their senses more than the others. Knowing that other people can have different learning preferences helps us communicate our message effectively in a way that more people can understand. Recognizing their own strengths and understanding how to relate to others can help students make the most of their learning potential and later on make more effective career choices.

Get started

Ask students to take out a sheet of paper. Tell them they are going to make a paper airplane (or a similar paper creation or piece of origami of your choice).

First, write the instructions on the board and draw diagrams:

1 Fold your paper in half lengthwise and open it up again. 2 Fold the top corners down toward the center fold. 3 Fold the top triangle down. 4 Fold the top corners to the center fold line about 3 cm above the point of the triangle. 5 Fold the point of the triangle up. 6 Fold the plane in half along the center fold line. 7 Fold the wings down to the bottom edge of the airplane. 8 Fly your plane!

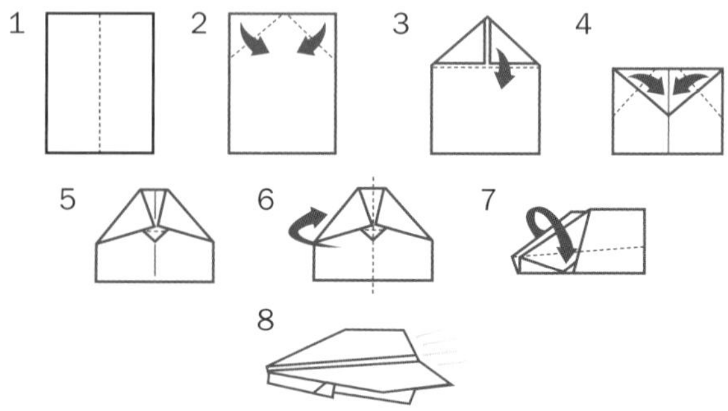

Then read the instructions aloud for students to follow. Finally, demonstrate the process.

Write the words *auditory*, *visual*, and *kinesthetic* and ask students to match these learning styles to each of the three techniques.

Discuss the meaning of each word initially if necessary.

Discuss as a class which technique students found easier and why.

MOVE BEYOND FOR TEACHERS

Multiple intelligences

H. Gardner's concept of multiple intelligences is commonly viewed as a model of learning styles. According to this point of view, the following types of learning styles can be identified:

Visual learners learn best if they can see the teacher's body language and facial expressions; they tend to prefer sitting at the front of the classroom to avoid visual obstructions. They tend to think in pictures and learn best from visual displays. They like to take detailed notes. About 65 percent of people are visual learners.

Auditory learners learn best through explanations and discussions; they like to talk things through and listen to what others have to say. Written information is not as helpful to them. They like to read texts aloud and enjoy recording their voices.

Kinesthetic learners learn best through a hands-on approach; they like to actively explore the physical world around them and may find it hard to sit still for long periods.

READ AND LISTEN

1a

- Ask students to read the quiz and follow the instructions. Point out that they can circle more than one choice for each quiz item.

1b 48

- Play the track for students to read and listen and decide what type of learner they are. Point out that they may be a mixture of types.

AUDIO SCRIPT 48

See Student's Book, page 36, for audio script.

2

- Divide the class into pairs to discuss whether they agree with the quiz results.
- Draw students' attention to the PHRASE BYTES box to help them structure their answers.
- In a class discussion, encourage students to talk about their learning styles and say why they agree or disagree with the quiz results.

DO

3

- Ask students to look at the typical classroom activities and check the activities they like doing.
- Elicit answers from several different students.

4

- Divide the class into pairs and ask them to say whether the activities in Exercise 3 are good for auditory, visual, or kinesthetic learners and to explain why.
- Draw students' attention to the PHRASE BYTES box to help them structure their answers.
- Choose several students to say their answers and give their reasons.

ANSWERS

reading: b listening: a speaking: a pronunciation: a
project work: a, b, c role-play: a, c

Extra activity

Read characteristics of the three main learning styles aloud in a random order and ask students to call out *auditory*, *visual*, or *kinesthetic*.

Auditory learners

They sit where they can hear. They talk to themselves. They like reading aloud. They learn by hearing and listening.

Visual learners

They take detailed notes. They sit at the front. They close their eyes to remember something. They like to see what they are learning. They like illustrations and colorful presentations.

Kinesthetic learners

They need to be active. They speak with their hands and with gestures. They like to take a hands-on, tactile approach. They love activities such as cooking, construction, and art. They love being outdoors.

REFLECT

5

- Encourage students to talk about the questions as a class before they read the REFLECTION POINT.

Alternative procedure: less confident classes

Give less confident students three or four minutes to prepare their answers individually in outline form before comparing their answers in pairs. You could generate more ideas by asking pairs to become groups of four, and then finally hold a class discussion.

EXTEND

6

- Divide the class into groups and allow students five minutes to ask and answer questions about what they are good at to find out whether the results match that person's learning style or styles. Direct students' attention to the model conversation.
- Have groups choose a representative to present their conclusions to the class to close the activity.

Fast finishers

Write these jobs on the board and ask fast finishers to match them to the three main learning styles: *actor*, *artist*, *athlete*, *English teacher*, *interpreter*, *journalist*, *PE teacher*, *politician*, *writer*.

When all students have finished, ask fast finishers to explain their answers and encourage the class to add one more job to each learning style.

ANSWERS

Auditory: English teacher, interpreter, politician
Visual: artist, journalist, writer
Kinesthetic: actor, athlete, PE teacher

Homework

Dictate these sentence beginnings and ask students to think about them carefully and complete them according to their learning style:

1 I learn best when I … 2 I like to do these things to review for tests: … 3 I prefer to study in … 4 Taking notes is … 5 My English notebook is …

At the beginning of the next class, divide the class into pairs and ask students to guess what their partner has written in each sentence. You could use the information you gather from these questions to plan future lessons adapted to the most prevalent learning style.

SPEAKING What are they like?

Describe people

Page 37

STAGE	TIME	FOCUS
GET STARTED		Recycle simple present questions and vocabulary for talking about personality, appearance, and nationality.
SPEAK		Think of words and phrases to describe people and compare with other students.
LISTEN		Listen to a conversation in which people are being described. Describe two people (speaking subskill).
ACT		Describe people in the class for others to identify.

Get started

Recycle simple present questions and vocabulary for talking about personality, appearance, and nationality. Draw a seven-pointed star on the board and write answers to questions about a famous woman around it (e.g., *green, blonde or brown, 1.51 m, the piano, unusual clothes, singing and songwriting, the USA*).

Explain to students that the star gives information about a famous woman. Ask students: *What are the questions?* Give an answer example if necessary; for example, *Her eyes are green. What question do you need to ask to find out this information?* Elicit from students *What color are her eyes?* Cross out the word *green* from the star.

Elicit more questions to eliminate the rest of the clues.

Suggested questions: *What color are her eyes? What color is her hair? How tall is she? What instrument does she play? What does she wear? What does she like? Where is she from?*

When they have asked you all the questions, ask them to guess who the famous person is (*Lady Gaga*).

Ask students to draw a seven-pointed star and write answers to questions about a famous person around it. Divide the class into pairs and have them take turns asking each other questions to guess who their partner's famous person is.

When they have all finished, ask them to tell the rest of the class who the famous people were and what they found out about them.

SPEAK

1a

- Divide the class into pairs and have them think of two words or phrases to complete the sentences. Draw students' attention to the example.

1b

- Ask students to compare their answers in small groups.
- Elicit answers from several different students and invite them to write them on the board. Check spelling and drill the pronunciation of the words.

SUGGESTED ANSWERS

2 jeans, glasses 3 football, reading 4 blue, brown
5 long, curly 6 French, funny

Alternative procedure: less confident classes

Write the suggested answers on the board in a jumbled order for students to complete the sentences. Ask students to add one or two more words or phrases for each sentence.

LISTEN

2 ▶49

- Focus students' attention on the photos.
- Play the audio track for students to listen and write the four names under the correct photos.
- Play the track again, pausing to check the answers.

ANSWERS / AUDIO SCRIPT ▶49

Claire 2 Leo 1 Manuel 6 Laura 3

Rita: Here's the list of students for the school play.
Miguel: Oh, thanks. Who's Claire?
Rita: You know her.
Miguel: No, I don't. What does she look like?
Angela: Uh, she has long wavy brown hair and brown eyes. She always wears T-shirts.
Miguel: Huh. Well, what's she like?
Angela: She's really nice. She plays the guitar and sings.
Rita: And Leo is the Colombian guy. You know, he's tall. He has big brown eyes. He loves sports.
Miguel: Oh yeah. And Manuel and Laura?
Angela: They're friends. Manuel isn't very tall, just average height. He has dark hair and wears glasses. Laura has long blond hair. She's pretty funny.
Miguel: OK. Well, let's see if they can act.

Alternative procedure

Describe the photos together as a class before students listen to the conversation.

3 ▶49

- Play the audio track again for students to listen and write the missing words to complete the conversation.

ANSWERS / AUDIO SCRIPT ▶49

See underlining in audio script in Exercise 2.

Extra activity

Divide the class into pairs and ask them to take turns reading the conversation aloud.

4 ▶50

- Ask students to match the sentence halves.
- Play the track for students to listen and check their answers.
- You could play the track again for students to repeat the sentences and highlight the difference in pronunciation of *he's* /hiz/ and *his* /hɪz/.

ANSWERS / AUDIO SCRIPT ▶50

1 c 2 e 3 d 4 a 5 b
See Student's Book, page 39, for audio script.

Fast finishers
Ask fast finishers to write the opposites of all the adjectives in the lesson (e.g., *long/short*, *wavy/straight*, *tall/short*). Have different students read one of the opposites aloud to test the class at the end of the activity.

5
- Ask students to write five sentences to describe the two other people in the photos.
- Elicit sentences from students around the class.

Alternative procedure: more confident classes
Have students exchange texts and give each other feedback on errors and good use of language.

Extra activity
In many standardized English exams, students are asked to describe a photo or a picture. You can help prepare students by playing a game called *Forty Seconds!*

Describe first photo – 10 seconds

Describe second photo – 10 seconds

Invent it! – describe their characters – 10 seconds

Invent it! – describe their likes and dislikes – 10 seconds

ACT

6 51
- Divide the class into groups of three or four and ask them to complete the tasks.
- Draw students' attention to the PHRASEBOOK to help them with their descriptions of two people in the class.
- Monitor and note errors and good use of language to go over in a feedback session at the end of the activity.
- Have students take turns presenting their descriptions to the class for other students to identify the people.
- Give students feedback at the end of the activity on errors and good use of language.

Extra activity
Ask students to find a photo of someone in the Student's Book and to describe the person. Ask the class to look through the book to see if they can find the photo.

Homework

Ask students to find a photo of a famous person (e.g., a pop star, sports personality, or TV star) and write a description of the person's appearance. At the beginning of the next class, divide the class into pairs and ask students to take turns describing the famous people for their partner to guess. Encourage students to bring in their photos of the people to show each other and discuss after the description activity.

WRITING Things we do and like

Use *and*, *or*, and *but*

Page 38

STAGE	TIME	FOCUS
GET STARTED		Recycle grammar and vocabulary you have learned in the unit so far.
SPEAK AND READ		Ask and answer questions in a class questionnaire. Learn about connectors *and*, *or*, and *but* (writing subskill).
PRACTICE		Produce target language in a written exercise.
DISCUSS		Talk about things and activities you like and dislike in school and outside of school.
WRITE		Write a questionnaire about activities that students like and dislike.
SHARE		Exchange questionnaires with other students and answer their questions. Read students' answers to your questionnaire.

Get started

Play a game of *Three in a Row* to recycle vocabulary and grammar that students have seen so far. For example:

clothes	simple present questions and short answers	possessive *'s*
possessive pronouns	school subjects	accessories
simple present negative	*Whose … ?*	learning styles

Draw the grid above on the board. Divide the class into two teams. Have teams take turns choosing a cell in the grid. Give the team the instruction for that cell (see Instructions grid). If the team answers correctly, they "take" the cell. The aim is to get three cells in a row.

Instructions

Say 10 items of clothing.	Make three simple present questions and answer them.	Change this sentence to one with the possessive *'s*: *The sneakers belong to Sally.*
Say all the possessive pronouns.	Say six school subjects.	Say six accessories.
Make these sentences negative: *I like shopping. He wears glasses.*	Make a question with *Whose … ?* and answer it.	Name the three learning styles.

SPEAK AND READ

1

- Divide the class into pairs and have students complete the tasks. First, have students ask and answer the questions in the class questionnaire and write their partner's answers.
- Then ask students to compare their answers with other students in the class to see if their answers are similar.
- You might want to ask students to raise their hands for each option in questions 1–3 to find out which options the majority chose. For question 4, you could elicit answers from different students around the class and ask the class to raise their hands if they had the same or a similar answer.

2a

- Ask students to read the tips in the HOW TO box.
- Point out to students that the words *and*, *or*, and *but* are three very common conjunctions in English.

2b

- Have students underline examples of *and*, *or*, and *but* in the questionnaire in Exercise 1.
- Choose students at random from around the class to read their examples aloud.

ANSWERS

... we do and like; ... English, math, or geography?; ... never, sometimes, or often?; Pop, rock, and classical ... ; ... but it's raining.

PRACTICE

3

- Have students choose the correct word (*and*, *or*, or *but*) to complete the sentences. Remind them to refer to the HOW TO box to help them decide on their answers.
- Allow students to compare their answers in pairs before checking answers as a class.

ANSWERS

1 and 2 but 3 or 4 but 5 and 6 or

Fast finishers

Ask fast finishers to write a fill-in-the-blank sentence with *and*, *or*, or *but*, making sure they refer to the HOW TO box for use and meaning. They can use the sentences to test each other when they have finished the activity.

DISCUSS

4

- Explain to students that they are going to write a questionnaire about things they like and dislike in school and outside of school.
- Divide the class into small groups to ask each other what they like and dislike in school and what they like and dislike outside of school. Encourage them to make a list of the answers they hear.

WRITE

5

- Go over the points in the writing plan with the class. Refer them back to the examples of questions they saw in the questionnaire in Exercise 1.
- Ask students to write four questions for their questionnaires, including one situation similar to question 4 in the questionnaire in Exercise 1. Tell them that at least two of their questions should be about activities outside of school. Remind them to refer to the lists they made in their groups. Tell them to give three possible answer options in each question.
- Tell students that they should write their questions using simple present verbs and that they should use *and*, *or*, and *but* in their questions and answer options. Remind them to refer to the HOW TO box if necessary.
- Set a time limit of 10 minutes for this. Monitor and offer help as necessary.
- Encourage students to check the points in the writing plan to make sure they have followed the instructions correctly.

SHARE

6

- Ask students to exchange their questionnaires with other students in the class. Tell them to write their answers and then exchange the questionnaires back so they can read the answers to their questions.
- Ask students to share some of their questions and the most interesting answers with the class.

Homework

Ask students to write the answers to their questionnaire in a short report to present at the beginning of the next class. Have students write some conclusions at the end of their report using *All of my classmates ... ; Most of my classmates ... ; Some of my classmates ... ; None of my classmates ...* .

VOCABULARY School subjects

1

- Elicit from students what a link in a website is (*a word or image in a computer document that you can click on in order to move to a related document, word, or image*).
- Ask students to complete the names of the school subjects. Point out that the first letter and often the last letter of each word is given.
- Go around the class, choosing different students to read the answers aloud.

ANSWERS
1 art 2 health 3 drama 4 English 5 geography
6 history 7 computer science 8 languages 9 math
10 music 11 physical education 12 science

Clothes and accessories

2

- Ask students to look at the pictures and write the names of the clothes and accessories.
- Allow students to compare their answers in pairs before checking them as a class.
- Encourage students to say what they think about the Lunar Middle School uniform.

ANSWERS
1 belt 2 tie 3 earrings 4 sweater 5 coat
6 gloves 7 scarf 8 shorts 9 hoodie
10 exercise jacket 11 exercise pants 12 backpack

GRAMMAR Simple present negative; questions and short answers

3

- Ask students to complete the questions and answers. Remind them that some are short answers.
- Have them compare their answers by reading the conversation aloud in pairs.
- Check answers together as a class.

ANSWERS
1 What do you do?
2 Do you like
3 I do
4 Why do you think
5 doesn't end
6 Do students wear
7 they don't
8 Do the students enjoy

Possessive 's and possessive pronouns

4

- Ask students to complete the sentences with possessive 's and possessive pronouns.
- Choose different students to read the answers aloud.

ANSWERS
1 ours 2 mine 3 's 4 's; his 5 '; theirs
6 's; hers 7 yours

Extra Resources

Go to the Teacher's Resource Center at mee2.macmillaneducation.com for:

- videos, video worksheets, and video scripts;
- extra vocabulary at two levels of difficulty;
- extra grammar at two levels of difficulty;
- culture lessons, with full teacher's notes;
- life skills lessons, with full teacher's notes;
- Speaking Database materials;
- the *Move Beyond* Level 1 wordlist;
- downloadable PDF and Word tests for Unit 3;
- tips for using the Grammar Database;
- extra reading materials;
- and more!

Go to Workbook pages 108–119 for further practice material.

UNIT 4 WHAT'S GOING ON?

IN THE PICTURE Staying in and going out

Talk about activities

Pages 40–41

STAGE	TIME	FOCUS
GET STARTED		Sort activities into categories using the verbs *do*, *go*, and *play*.
WORK WITH WORDS		Review and learn verb phrases to talk about free-time activities. Watch a video of a teenager talking about what she does when she goes out.
SPEAK		Talk about what you do on weekends.

Get started

Write three columns on the board with the headings *Do*, *Go*, and *Play*.

Recycle words that collocate with them; for example, *(do) exercises*, *(go) on the internet*, *(play) games*. Write the activities in the appropriate columns.

Divide the class into small teams and have students think of as many words as they can in one minute to put in the columns.

Invite students from each team to come to the board and add words to the columns.

Ask students which activities they do at school and which ones they do in their free time.

WORK WITH WORDS Activity verbs

1a RECALL

- Divide the class into pairs and have students match the words in the two boxes.
- Explain that some of the verbs can be used more than once. Refer students to the photos to help them.
- Set a time limit of one minute for this.

1b ▶52

- Play the track for students to check their answers.
- Choose students to share their answers with the class. Have the class repeat the phrases to practice pronunciation.
- Ask students to do the **Work with Words** task on page 72.

ANSWERS / AUDIO SCRIPT ▶52

go on the internet	go shopping	go swimming	
go to the movies	listen to music	meet friends	play soccer
play the piano	play video games	read a book	ride a bike
watch television			

Extra activity

Put the verbs from Exercise 1a on the board and circle each verb. Elicit some examples of words that collocate with the verbs and connect them with a line to the appropriate verb (e.g., *go shopping*).

Have students think of more words that collocate with the verbs (e.g., *go home*, *play tennis*, *ride a horse*, *read blogs*) and then invite them to come to the board and connect their words to the correct circles. For example:

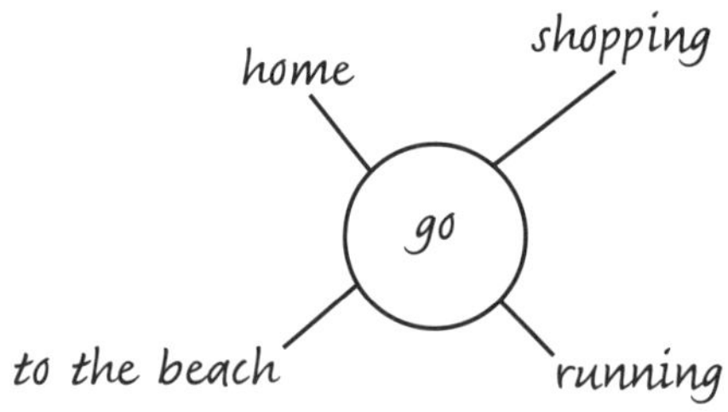

Have students copy the diagrams in their notebooks. Explain that they should add new words to their diagrams as they come across them and that they should review them frequently.

2

- Ask students to describe the activities in the photos and say what they all have in common. (*They're all activities people do in their free time.*) Ask if they have ever read books or watched movies or sporting events outside.
- Divide the class into A/B pairs and have students do the tasks. Set a time limit of three minutes.
- Stop the activity and ask students to share their answers with the class.

3 ▶53

- Have students complete the sentences and match them to the photos.
- Play the track for students to check their answers. After each sentence, ask students which photo goes with it.
- Check pronunciation of difficult words (e.g., *laugh* and *leave*) and drill if necessary.

ANSWERS / AUDIO SCRIPT 53

1 sit; listen to – photo a 2 start – photo d
3 send; put on – photo f 4 stay in; laugh – photo e
5 go; open – photo c 6 leave – photo b
See Student's Book, page 42, for audio script.

4a

- Have students match the words to their opposites in Exercise 3 and then compare their answers in pairs.
- Do not confirm answers yet.

4b 54

- Play the track for students to listen and check their answers.
- Continue the track for students to listen and repeat the words.

ANSWERS / AUDIO SCRIPT 54

1 get, *send* 2 come, go 3 cry, laugh 4 end, start
5 go out, stay in 6 arrive, leave 7 close, open 8 stand, sit
9 take off, put on 10 talk to, listen to

Extra activity

Divide the class into pairs and have students close their books. Ask students to take turns saying a word from the list in Exercise 4a. Their partner should say the opposite word.

5 THE MOVING PICTURE

- Explain to students that they are going to watch a video about Holly and what she does in her free time.
- Ask students to watch the video and write down when Holly usually goes out and what she does.

ANSWERS / VIDEO SCRIPT

She usually goes out on Saturday afternoons and Sunday mornings. On Saturday afternoons she meets her friends and they go to the mall or to see a movie, or they just relax and do nothing.
On Sunday mornings she goes for a walk in the park and plays with their dog. She often goes swimming or rides her bike with her best friend, Joanna.

Hi, everyone. I'm Holly, and I love my time off from school. Here's what I do on a typical weekend! On Saturdays I always get up late. I usually have a big breakfast. Then I call my friends. We get together and do normal things like listen to music. I read magazines with my best friend, Joanna. In the afternoon I usually go out. I meet my friends at the mall. Sometimes we go to see a movie ... or just relax and do nothing. In the evening I stay in. I normally watch a movie on TV with my mom, my dad, and my brothers. They don't like it when I talk during the movie. Then I go to bed at 9:30 or 10. On Sunday mornings... I go for a walk in the park and play with Sammy, our dog. I often go swimming or ride my bike with Joanna. I go home at lunchtime. In the afternoon I do homework. On Sunday evenings I usually chat with my cousin in Canada on the internet. I hardly ever watch TV on Sundays. I go to bed at around 9 because I have to get up early for school the next day. Good night!

6

- Focus students' attention on the schedule and check that they understand *a.m.* (*morning*) and *p.m.* (*afternoon/ evening*).
- Encourage students to use a variety of verbs from Exercise 4a to write notes about their weekend activities.

SPEAK

7

- Have students read the instructions and focus on the example.
- Model the task by having a strong student ask you some of the questions. For more confident groups, encourage students to ask extra questions; for example, *What video games do you play? Who do you go out with?*
- Divide the class into pairs and set a time limit of three minutes to do the task. To encourage students to listen closely to their partner, have them write down their partner's answers.
- Monitor and note errors and good use of language to go over in a feedback session at the end of the activity.
- Stop the activity and invite students to tell the class what they found out about their partner.

MOVE BEYOND

Ask students to do the **Words & Beyond** exercise on page 72.

Homework

Have students write a paragraph for a personal profile on a social networking site about what a classmate does on the weekends. Advise students to be sensitive about the information they gather in case there are any privacy issues involved, and only include information that could be considered public. In the next class, collect and display the profiles around the classroom. Set a time limit of five minutes for students to read the profiles. Then have students work in small groups to try to remember one thing about each student in the class.

READING Singing in the rain

Understand the order of messages *Page 42*

STAGE	TIME	FOCUS
GET STARTED		Talk about how we communicate with family and friends and about social networking sites.
SPEAK AND READ		Talk about the things you read. Read instant messages that describe an event in progress and discuss how to understand the order of messages (reading subskill).
REACT		Talk about the videos you like to watch and whether you would like to participate in an online video.

Get started

Write *communication* on the board and elicit different ways we communicate with our family and friends (e.g., *letters, emails, telephone, internet, instant messages*). Write students' additional ideas on the board. Ask students if they use social networking sites or apps to communicate with people. Elicit four or five examples of sites or apps they use (e.g., *Facebook, Twitter, Google+, Instagram, WhatsApp)*. Draw a 5x5 grid on the board and write the sites and apps they mention in the top row. For example:

	Facebook	Twitter	WhatsApp	Instagram
Carla				

Have students copy the grid in their notebooks and write their names in the first column. Tell students which apps or sites you use and check the appropriate columns. Ask students to check the boxes for the apps or sites they use. Divide the class into small groups and explain that they are going to ask each other questions to find out what apps and sites the group members use and who they talk to. Choose a student to model the activity with you. Give students three minutes to ask each other questions and complete the grid. Stop students after three minutes and invite them to share their findings.

SPEAK AND READ

1

- Refer students to the instructions for Exercise 1 and explain that messages can include text messages, Twitter posts, and social networking status updates.
- Divide the class into pairs and have students answer the questions.
- Encourage students to use adverbs of frequency in their responses; for example, *I sometimes read blogs but not often*. Ask extra questions; for example, *What comics do you read?*
- Choose several students to report to the class what their partner has said.

2 55

- Ask students to read the text quickly and discuss the question in pairs. Don't play the audio at this point. It is an extra feature, and a suggestion for using it in class is included at the end of the lesson.
- Invite students to share their answers with the class.

MOVE BEYOND FOR TEACHERS

Flash mobs and viral videos

The text in Exercise 2 features two people using an instant messaging service to communicate. The event being described is a flash mob. This is when a lot of people suddenly gather in a public place, do something for a short time, and quickly go away again. These events are often video recorded and uploaded to video-sharing websites such as YouTube. A search on YouTube will return a range of staged events, many of them involving singing or dancing. "Singing in the Rain" was a popular choice for flash mobs, as well as the "Harlem Shake," but new ones crop up all the time.

3a

- Ask students how we normally read a text in English (*from top to bottom and from left to right*).
- Choose students to read the tips in the HOW TO box aloud.
- Ask students if they read messages like the one in Exercise 2 and, if so, where they usually read them.

3b

- Explain that students should put the events in the messages in the order they happen.
- Ask which event is first and have students write a *1* next to it in their books.
- Have students order the rest of the events.
- Let students compare their answers in pairs before you check them as a class.

ANSWERS

1 People arrive and leave by bus.
2 Music starts playing.
3 The man opens an umbrella.
4 The woman walks toward the man.
5 The man and woman dance to the music.
6 The dancers take off their hats.

Fast finishers

Ask fast finishers to find things in the photo that are mentioned in the text; for example, *umbrellas, performers, station floor, (people) smiling, (people) dancing*.

4

- Ask students to check the tips in the HOW TO box that helped them with Exercise 3b.

5

- Have students choose the correct description in pairs. Check the answer as a class.

ANSWER

B

REACT

6

- Divide the class into pairs and have students discuss the questions with their partners.
- Refer students to the PHRASE BYTES box to help them structure their discussion.
- Choose several students to give feedback about their partners' responses.

MOVE BEYOND

Ask students to do the **Move Beyond** task.

Ask them if they watch video clips on sites such as YouTube. Elicit examples of videos clips they like.

Give students five minutes to write a description of their favorite video. While they are doing this, circulate and make notes of errors and good use of language. (See Teaching Tips, *Giving feedback on written work*, page 26.)

Choose several students to read their texts aloud to the class. Ask the other students to say which videos they would like to see.

Extra activity

Explain to students that the event described in the text is called a flash mob. If you have access to the internet, find an example before class to show to students; a YouTube search for *flash mobs* will return plenty of results.

You could play the flash mob clip with students sitting in pairs with half the students sitting with their backs to the screen opposite a partner facing the screen. Ask the students facing the screen to describe the activity on screen to their partners as it progresses. Students often enjoy this live reporting activity.

At the end of the clip, ask students to write a short description in their pairs. Model an example. For less confident groups, write some sentence beginnings on the board, e.g., *There are …* ; *They are in/at …* ; *They are singing/dancing/jumping*, etc.

Choose pairs to read their descriptions to the class. For homework, you could ask students to find another flash mob clip that they like and write a short description.

Recorded reading text ▶55
Use the audio to help drill the present progressive. Play selected sentences from the audio (e.g., the questions in the present progressive); pause after each sentence and have students repeat the sentence, paying attention to word stress.

Homework

Write the title *How we communicate* on the board. Ask students to copy the title in their notebooks and tell them to survey five people about how they communicate. Suggest that students ask two family members, their best friend, a teacher, and a neighbor. Students should then write a short text (30–50 words) about their findings under the title *How we communicate*. You could suggest that students illustrate their texts with drawings or photos from magazines. Have students present their findings at the beginning of the next class. (Allow about three minutes per student.)

GRAMMAR Present progressive

Talk about what's happening now and future arrangements *Page 43*

STAGE	TIME	FOCUS
GET STARTED		Listen to and discuss a story about telling the truth and telling lies.
READ AND LISTEN		Read and listen to a phone conversation between two friends talking about what they are doing now and later.
STUDY		Read grammar explanations for the present progressive and complete examples.
PRACTICE		Practice using the present progressive and focus on the pronunciation of the /ŋ/ sound at the end of verbs in the progressive form.
SPEAK		Talk about what's happening in photos.

Get started

Pre-teach the words *lie* and *believe*. Put the following definitions on the board and ask students to match the words: *think something is true* (*believe*); *say something that isn't true* (*lie*).

Search on the internet for a simple illustration from the story "The Boy Who Cried Wolf" to project on the board, or alternatively, draw simple pictures of a boy, some sheep, a mountain, a wolf, a village, and some villagers on the board. Elicit the vocabulary from the class. Model pronunciation and do a choral drill of the words. Tell students that you are going to tell a story and that they should use the pictures to predict what the story is. Divide the class into pairs to make their predictions. Then invite students to share their ideas with the class. Tell the following story and ask students to listen and check their ideas. Repeat the story if necessary.

The Boy Who Cried Wolf

There is a boy who takes care of sheep on a mountain. One day he is bored, so he goes to the village and says, "Help! There's a wolf." The villagers go to the mountain, but there isn't a wolf. They say, "You're lying," and they go back to the village.

The next day the boy is bored again, so he goes to the village and says, "Help! There's a wolf." The villagers go to the mountain, but there isn't a wolf. They say, "You're lying again. Why do you always lie?'" and they go back to the village.

On the third day, the boy sees a wolf on the mountain, so he goes to the village and says, "Help! There's a wolf." This time the villagers don't believe him and they say, "We don't believe you. You're telling lies again." So the boy goes back to the mountain, and he sees that the wolf has eaten his sheep.

Write the following questions on the board and ask students to discuss them with a partner: *Why is the boy on the mountain?* (he's taking care of some sheep); *Why does the boy tell lies?* (because he's bored); *Why don't the villagers believe the boy on the third day?* (because he always lies); *What is the point of the story?* (if you lie a lot, people won't believe you when you tell the truth).

Choose students to share their answers with the class.

READ AND LISTEN Grammar in context

1 ▶56

- Explain to students that they will read and listen to a phone conversation.
- Play the track for students to read and listen to find out where Juan is.

ANSWER / AUDIO SCRIPT ▶56
He's probably at home; he's *not* in Times Square, New York.
See Student's Book, page 45, for audio script.

STUDY

2

- Read the instructions aloud and choose different students to read the grammar rules for "Present progressive with present-time expressions" to the class.
- Ask students to complete the examples. Remind them to look back at Exercise 1 for help.
- Let students compare their answers in pairs before you check them as a class.
- Invite students to share their answers with the class. Point out that we usually use contractions when we are speaking.

- Refer students to the section on "Present progressive for the future" and ask them to find words in the conversation in Exercise 1 to complete the example. Highlight that Juan and Ben are talking about the future and ask concept-checking questions; for example, *Is Ben with Ann now? Do Ann and Ben have plans to meet? When is he meeting her?* (See Teaching Tips, *Present progressive for future arrangements*, page 25.)
- Refer students to the time expressions and explain that they're a good way to know that we are talking about the future. Ask students if they can think of any more time expressions for the future (e.g., *on Friday*, *tomorrow evening*, *next Tuesday*).

ANSWERS
'm 're; taking aren't/'re not; talking
Are am 'm not; isn't
'm meeting

Extra activity
Write the following progressive forms from the text on the board: *doing*, *standing*, *shopping*, *having*.

Divide the class into pairs and ask students to write the base forms.

Elicit the spelling rules and then refer students to the spelling rules in the Grammar Database on page 67.

PRACTICE

3
- Read the instructions and refer students to the example. Then ask them to complete the story using the present progressive form of the verbs.
- Let students compare their answers in pairs. Then choose students to share their answers with the class.

ANSWERS
2 'm playing 3 's/is looking 4 're playing 5 isn't winning
6 'm running

4
- Ask students to look at the picture and explain that Juan is telling another story.
- Have students write four sentences using the present progressive.
- Ask students to compare their answers in pairs and then ask several students to share their answers with the class.

Alternative procedure: more confident classes
For more confident classes, have students write as many sentences as they can in one minute.

Alternative procedure: less confident classes
For less confident classes, put some sentence prompts on the board (e.g., *sit in the park*, *sit on the bench*, *watch TV*, *people / go for a walk*, *people / look at me*) and ask students to form sentences using the prompts to help them.

5 57 PRONOUNCE
- Play the track for students to listen.
- Model the /ŋ/ sound and have students repeat it.
- Continue the track for students to listen and repeat.

AUDIO SCRIPT 57
See Student's Book, page 45, for audio script.

6a
- Ask students to read the instructions. Then elicit the first question: *What are you doing right now?*
- Have students form the questions and then write their own answers. Let them compare their questions and answers in pairs before you check them as a class.

ANSWERS
1 What are you doing right now?
2 Who are you sitting next to?
3 Is your teacher talking?
4 Is it raining outside?
5 Are you meeting friends later?
6 What are you doing next weekend?

6b
- Read the first question aloud and model the task with a student.
- Divide the class into pairs for them to ask and answer the questions.
- Monitor and note errors and good use of language to go over in a feedback session at the end of the activity.

SPEAK

7
- Have students read the instructions and the examples and look back at pages 40 and 41. Encourage them to recycle the vocabulary from page 40.
- Give students 15 seconds to look at the photos and two minutes to do the activity. Encourage students to say as many sentences as possible.
- Stop students and invite them to share their sentences with the class.

Homework

Ask students to imagine they are on vacation and writing a short email to their best friend. They should include the following information: where they are, what they're doing, what they're wearing, what they can see happening, and what they're doing this evening.

Ask them to write their email in 30–50 words. At the beginning of the next class, divide the class into small groups and ask them to read their emails to each other. Ask students to decide in their groups who is having the best vacation.

LISTENING AND VOCABULARY Soundscape

Identify the type of audio *Page 44*

STAGE	TIME	FOCUS
GET STARTED		Talk about places you've been and the types of things you've heard in the last week. Recycle adverbs of frequency.
SPEAK AND LISTEN		Talk about different types of audio and where you usually hear them. Listen and identify different types of audio (listening subskill).
REACT		Write an announcement and a conversation.
WORK WITH WORDS		Learn words to describe places in public buildings. Design and present a plan of a building to other students.

MOVE BEYOND FOR TEACHERS

Soundscapes

A soundscape is like a landscape made from sounds and signifies the combination of sounds that we hear around us. It helps give meaning to the world around us, along with the things we see, touch, smell, and taste. For example, we know we're in a kitchen if we can see cabinets, a sink, kitchen utensils, etc. In the same way, the sounds of a faucet running, someone chopping vegetables, and the background sound of a refrigerator also tell us that we're in a kitchen. This contextual knowledge is also a useful way for us to make sense of the language we are hearing and a useful strategy for students when doing listening activities.

Get started

Give students one minute to think of all the places that they've been in the last week. Give them some examples of places you've been (e.g., *the supermarket*, *at home*, *the subway*). Then ask them to think of all the things they've heard in those places (e.g., *a conversation*, *music*, *an announcement*, *an elevator*, *the television*). Give them one minute to make a list. Divide the class into pairs. Ask them to say some of the things on their list while their partner guesses where they heard each sound. Write two headings on the board: *Places* and *Things we hear (audio)*. Invite students to come to the board and add some of their words under the headings. Divide the class into small groups and ask them to discuss how often they hear the things on the list. Encourage them to use adverbs of frequency and to explain their answers; for example, *I never hear announcements because I don't travel by train.* Set a time limit of three minutes. At the end of the task, ask students which things they hear most often.

SPEAK AND LISTEN

1

- Divide the class into pairs and have students answer the question.
- Choose different students to share their ideas.

2a

- Choose a student to read the tips in the HOW TO box aloud. Check that students understand each tip.

2b 58

- Play the track for students to listen and match the excerpts to the types of audio in Exercise 1.
- Let students compare their answers in pairs before checking them as a class.

ANSWERS / AUDIO SCRIPT 58

1 audio tour 2 conversation 3 announcement 4 lesson

1
Welcome to the Science Museum. You are now standing in the museum's main hall. To your right is the gift shop, and next to the gift shop is the coffee shop. Our tour starts on the second floor. Please use the elevator or the stairs in front of you.

2
Mia: Hey, Joe. What's happening?
Joe: I'm looking for the restrooms. Do you know where they are?
Mia: They're on the first floor.
Joe: Thanks. Um ... How do I get there?
Mia: Go down the elevator and turn right. The restrooms are across from the gift shop.

3
This is an announcement for Neil Thompson. Neil Thompson – please come to the information desk, where your mother is waiting for you. The information desk is on the first floor. It's next to the main museum entrance across from the ticket office. Thank you.

4
OK. Are you all listening? Please be quiet and listen. This room is called Making the Modern World. It has some of the museum's famous objects, including Stephenson's Rocket. Now, Stephenson's Rocket isn't a rocket – it's a train.

Extra activity

Refer students to the tips in the HOW TO box and then ask them to listen again and answer the following questions: *1 Who's speaking? 2 Who's the information for? 3 What sounds do you hear?*

Stop after each track and have students compare their answers in pairs. Choose students to share their answers with the class before listening to the next excerpt.

ANSWERS

Audio tour
1 a museum guide 2 visitors to the museum
3 no specific sounds, but it sounds like it's listened to through headphones
Conversation
1 two friends 2 one friend is giving information to the other
3 café sounds
Announcement
1 a receptionist in the museum 2 Neil Thompson (a visitor)
3 sounds of the museum; it sounds like a PA system
Lesson
1 a teacher or museum guide 2 a group of students
3 students talking

3

- Ask students to check the tips in the HOW TO box that they used to help them with Exercise 2b and discuss as a class.

REACT

4

- Read the instructions aloud and elicit more examples of places (e.g., *an airport*, *a concert*, *an art gallery*).
- Have students do the task in pairs. Circulate and offer help as needed.

Extra activity

When students have written their announcements and conversations, have them practice reading their texts aloud. Put two pairs together, and while one pair is reading, the other pair should listen and guess where the place is and who the speakers are.

WORK WITH WORDS Places in public buildings

5

- Have students match the icons to the words and then compare their answers in pairs.
- Check answers as a class. Check pronunciation of the words and model and drill as needed. Highlight that in compound nouns such as *coffee shop*, *ticket office*, and *information desk*, the first word is stressed.

ANSWERS

a stairs b elevator c ticket office d restrooms
e coffee shop f entrance g information desk h first floor
i gift shop j second floor

6 ▶58

Exam-type task

- Ask students to listen and choose the correct answers.
- Play the track again and stop after each excerpt.
- Let students compare their answers in pairs before you check them as a class.

ANSWERS / AUDIO SCRIPT ▶58

1 B 2 A 3 C 4 C

See Exercise 2b for audio script.

7

- Read the instructions aloud and divide the class into pairs. Explain to students that they have five minutes to draw and label their plan. Suggest some buildings that students might choose, making sure they don't all choose their school.
- Stop students after five minutes. Explain that they will describe their plan to another pair for them to guess the place.
- Refer students to the places in Exercise 5 and the prepositions of place in Exercise 6: *in front of*, *next to*, *on (the first floor)*, *at the top of (the stairs)*. Ask students to use these expressions in their descriptions.

MOVE BEYOND

Ask students to do the **Words & Beyond** exercise on page 72.

Homework

Ask students to design three or four icons for places you can find in an airport, hospital, or station. At the beginning of the next class, have students guess the places each other's icons represent and decide which icon is the best. Students can then come and draw their best icon on the board.

GRAMMAR Present progressive and simple present

Talk about how often you do things *Page 45*

STAGE	TIME	FOCUS
GET STARTED		Recycle vocabulary for musical instruments and types of music. Talk about where and how you listen to music.
READ AND LISTEN		Read and listen to an excerpt from a radio show talking about a pop group.
STUDY		Find examples of the target language in a text and complete grammar explanations about the present progressive and the simple present.
PRACTICE		Use the present progressive and the simple present in written exercises.
SPEAK		Find out about the music a classmate listens to and whether he or she plays an instrument.

Get started

Divide the class into pairs and have students brainstorm different musical instruments. Set a time limit of one minute for them to think of as many instruments as possible.

Choose students to share their answers and make a list on the board.

Choose a student to stand up and mime a musical instrument from the list for the others to guess.

Have students raise their hands to guess. If a student gives the correct answer, it's his or her turn to mime playing an instrument for the group.

Repeat the process with different genres of music (hip hop, jazz, etc.).

Finally, divide the class into groups of three or four and have them ask each other where they listen to music (*at concerts*, *on an MP3 player*, *with friends*, *on their own*, etc.).

Invite representatives to tell the class about their group.

READ AND LISTEN Grammar in context

1 59

- Ask students to read and listen to the radio show and answer the question.
- Choose a student to give the answer.

ANSWER / AUDIO SCRIPT 59

They're playing at the FIBArk Festival.
See Student's Book, page 47, for audio script.

Alternative procedure: more confident classes

With more confident students, have students listen with their books closed to answer the question. Then have them compare their answer in pairs before reading the text to check.

Extra activity

Divide the class into pairs and ask students to write three questions about the radio show; for example, *Where is Red Bandana from?* Monitor and help students as needed. Then have students work with another pair to ask and answer the questions. At the end of the activity, choose students to ask the class their questions.

STUDY

2a

- Ask students to underline the present progressive verbs in Exercise 1 and circle the simple present verbs.

ANSWERS

Present progressive: You're listening, I'm playing, is touring, they're giving
Simple present: love, live, plays, sings, plays, plays, plays, sings

2b

- Ask students to complete the explanations with time expressions from the text.
- Let students compare their answers in pairs before choosing students to share their answers with the class.

ANSWERS

Present progressive: Right now, today
Simple present: usually, sometimes

PRACTICE

3

- Read the instructions and have students read through the sentences. Explain that the sentences form a complete text about Amy and her cousin Saul.
- Ask students to circle the correct words in each sentence and then compare their answers in pairs.
- Choose students to read the answers aloud.

ANSWERS

1 is going out 2 usually stays in 3 's visiting 4 lives
5 doesn't go out 6 is taking

4

- Have students write the correct forms of the verbs in parentheses.
- Choose different students to read the answers aloud.

ANSWERS

1 I like 2 I usually listen to 3 I'm listening to 4 I'm learning
5 I have 6 I'm going

Fast finishers

Ask fast finishers to choose four of the sentences from Exercise 4 and write them in the negative form.

ANSWERS

1 I don't like different types of music.
2 I don't usually listen to pop or hip hop.
3 This month I'm not listening to a lot of classical guitar music.
4 I'm not learning to play the guitar right now.
5 I don't have classes on Fridays.
6 I'm not going to a class in a few minutes.

5a

- Ask students to complete the questions with the correct forms of the verbs in parentheses.
- Circulate and help students with any difficulties.
- Choose students to read the questions aloud.

ANSWERS

1 Do you like music? 2 do you normally listen to
3 are you listening to 4 Are you learning

5b

- Answer one of the questions yourself and write the answer on the board as an example.
- Have students write their own answers to the questions in Exercise 5a.
- Monitor students and help them as needed.

SPEAK

6

- Read the instructions and divide the class into pairs.
- Ask students to cover their answers for Exercise 5b and to ask and answer the questions in Exercise 5a.
- Ask students what they found out about their partners.

Alternative procedure

As an alternative to the survey, a *Find Someone Who …* activity would give students the chance to move around and talk to different students.

As students are writing their answers to Exercise 5b, circulate and take notes on students' answers. They don't need to be notes on all the questions, just one or two points for each student; for example, *Jordi sometimes listens to classical music. Marta is listening to a lot of Lady Gaga right now.*

On the board, write *Find a student who …* , followed by a list of the things you noted; for example, *… sometimes listens to classical music, … is listening to a lot of Lady Gaga right now.*

Explain to students that they should circulate and ask the questions in Exercise 5a to find the students who match the points on the board. They have five minutes to find a different person for each of the points. At the end of the activity, check answers as a class. Use this information to do a quick survey on musical tastes in the class and write the results on the board.

Homework

Ask students to write a short description of a band or a singer they like and are listening to right now. Ask them to include the following information: where the band or singer is from; what type of music they play; what instruments they play; if they are giving any concerts right now.

At the beginning of the next class, have students ask and answer questions in small groups about each other's chosen bands or singers.

LANGUAGE &BEYOND *GET THINKING*

Find ideas and information *Page 46*

STAGE	TIME	FOCUS
GET STARTED		Decide on the best gift idea for people you know and talk about good and bad gift ideas.
READ AND SPEAK		Read and answer questions about an online forum message asking for advice on how to organize a celebration. Suggest ideas for organizing a celebration.
DO		Read responses to the forum message and choose an idea. Discuss what information is relevant and where it can be found.
REFLECT		Reflect on situations in which you need to find information, ways in which you find it, and where you find it.
EXTEND		Discuss ideas for a day trip and where you can find the relevant information.

LIFE SKILLS

GET THINKING: FIND IDEAS AND INFORMATION
This life skills lesson deals with finding ideas and information. As teenagers gain more independence, they'll have to make more decisions for themselves. The ability to generate ideas and find relevant information will help them make better decisions. It's also worth pointing out that decisions are often made with other people, so in this lesson students not only think about and evaluate different ways of gathering information but also put into practice what they have studied in a collaborative decision-making task.

Get started

Draw a grid on the board with these names down the side: *mom*, *brother*, *grandma*, *best friend*, *teacher*. Write these gift ideas across the top: *some earrings*, *a CD*, *a novel*, *a personalized mug*, *a trendy T-shirt*, *an orchid*, *a mirror*. Ask students to copy the grid into their notebooks. Explain that these are different gift ideas and pre-teach any new words (e.g., *personalized mug*, *trendy*, *orchid*).

Ask students to look at the list of people and decide whether the gift ideas are good or bad and why. Ask them to put a check or an X in each of the boxes. Set a time limit of two minutes.

Divide the class into pairs and ask students to compare their answers, to comment on their classmates' suggestions, and to offer more ideas.

READ AND SPEAK

1

- Refer students to the texts and picture and ask what they can see.
- Have students read Vic245's forum message and answer questions 1 and 2.
- Divide the class into pairs and have students compare their answers for questions 1 and 2 with their partner and then answer question 3 together.
- Choose several students to share their answers with the class.

ANSWERS
1 It's her 13th birthday next week.
2 She needs to decide what to do and organize everything.
3 Students' own answers.

DO

2

- Ask students to read the instructions and elicit some of the vocabulary from the message (e.g., *pizza place*, *have a sleepover*).
- Ask students to read the answers to Vic245's message and then to work in pairs to compare their ideas from Exercise 1 with those in the text.
- Elicit from the class the ideas that are mentioned in the text. Then ask them to work with a partner to decide which idea is the best. Point out that they can include their own ideas.
- Monitor and note errors and good use of language to go over in a feedback session at the end of the activity.
- Invite students to share their ideas with the class.

Extra activity
Ask students to focus on some of the verb phrases from the text. Write these verbs in a column on the left side of the board: *spend*, *see*, *have*, *make*, *stay*, *find*, *order*, *watch*, *have*. Write these words and phrases in a column on the right: *a pizza place*, *something to eat*, *a movie*, *DVDs*, *a sleepover*, *food*, *the day there*, *in a music video*.

Have students close their books and match the two halves of the verb phrases. When students have finished, ask them to compare their answers with the text.

3

- Have a student read the questions aloud.
- Draw students' attention to the expressions in the PHRASE BYTES box to help them structure their answers.
- Divide the class into groups of three or four and ask them to discuss the questions.
- Monitor and note errors and good use of language to go over in a feedback session at the end of the activity. (See Teaching Tips, *Correcting errors effectively*, page 24.)
- Choose a student from each group to share the group's answers with the class.

- Write any errors and good use of language on the board. Highlight good use of language and have students correct the errors.

REFLECT

4

- Divide the class into small groups to discuss the questions. After a few minutes, call on different students to give their answers.
- Have students read the REFLECTION POINT and say whether they agree or disagree.

EXTEND

5

- Read the instructions and then divide the class into small groups.
- Set a time limit of five minutes for students to make a list of activities, decide on two activities they are going to present to the class, and think about the information they need and where they can get it. Monitor and help students as needed.
- Stop students at the end of the time limit and ask them to prepare their presentations. Ask them to decide which student will present the ideas.
- Invite students from each group to present their ideas and ask the other students to take notes while they listen. Ask students to vote on their favorite idea at the end.

Alternative procedure: less confident classes

If students are unable to come up with ideas for activities, have a class brainstorming session. Write the ideas on the board. Return to the procedure above, letting students refer to the points on the board.

Homework

Ask students to plan a day trip to surprise a friend. Encourage them to think about what that person likes to do and then to do some research about interesting places and events.

At the beginning of the next class, have students share their ideas with a partner.

SPEAKING At the tourist information office

Ask for information

Page 47

STAGE	TIME	FOCUS
GET STARTED		Recycle words to describe places in a town or city.
SPEAK		Talk about what tourists can visit and do in your town. Talk about where they can get information about sights and events.
LISTEN		Listen to a conversation in which people ask for information in a tourist information center (speaking subskill).
ACT		Prepare and act out a scene in a tourist information office, asking for information and using polite expressions.

Get started

Recycle words to describe places in a town or city. This vocabulary will be activated in the speaking section.

Draw a word snake on the board with these words: *museum*, *park*, *stadium*, *airport*, *theater*, *movie theater*, *subway, shopping mall*, *station*, *art gallery*, *market.* A word snake is a string of words that are written together with no spaces between words. The words are usually written in an up-and-down, curvy pattern that looks like the shape of a snake.

Divide the class into pairs and explain that students have to find the words and write them in their notebooks. Choose students to share their answers with the class.

Write the following categories on the board: *Transportation*, *Entertainment/Culture*, *Shopping*. Check that students understand what each of the categories is and ask them to put the words from the word snake in the correct categories. Invite students to come to the board and write the words in the correct categories. When all the words are on the board, ask students if they can think of any more words to go in each category.

ANSWERS

Transportation: airport, subway, station
Entertainment/Culture: museum, park, stadium, theater, movie theater, art gallery
Shopping: shopping mall, market

SPEAK

1

- Divide the class into pairs and have students ask and answer the questions.
- Choose students to share their answers with the class.

LISTEN

2 ▶60

- Choose a student to read the instructions aloud.
- Play the audio track for students to listen and decide where Cathy and Ray are.
- Ask students to read the conversation to check their answers.
- Choose a student to say the answer and give reasons.

ANSWERS / AUDIO SCRIPT ▶60

They aren't in the USA. They ask the assistant if she speaks English and they talk about pesos, not dollars.

Cathy: Excuse me. Do you speak English?
Assistant: Yes, I do.
Cathy: Good. Can I ask a question?
Assistant: Yes, of course.
Cathy: Where's the Museum of Popular Art?
Assistant: It's in the historic part of the city near Alameda Park.
Cathy: Thank you.
Assistant: You're welcome.

Cathy:	Sorry, I have another question. How do we get there?
Assistant:	You can walk. It takes about 10 minutes. Or you can take the subway.
Ray:	Can I ask something else?
Assistant:	Of course.
Ray:	When does it open? And what time does it close?
Assistant:	Let me check ... On Thursdays it opens at 10 a.m. and closes at 6 p.m.
Ray:	And how much does it cost?
Assistant:	It costs 40 pesos. Or it's free on Sundays. How long are you staying?
Ray:	We're only staying two days.
Assistant:	Well, enjoy your stay!
Cathy:	Thank you for your help.
Assistant:	You're welcome.

MOVE BEYOND FOR TEACHERS

What's the USA?

USA stands for United States of America. The USA consists of 50 states, 48 of which are contiguous on the North American continent. Alaska and Hawaii, although not connected to the rest of the states, are also part of the USA. The currency of the USA is the US dollar. The USA does not have an official language, but most government business is conducted in English, and the primary language spoken in the USA is English.

3a

- Ask students to complete the questions with the question words in the box.
- Monitor and offer help as needed, but do not confirm answers at this point.

3b 61

- Play the track for students to listen and check their answers. Then check answers with the class.
- Continue the track for students to listen again and repeat the questions. Remind students that intonation is important when we're asking for information. (See Teaching Tips, *Intonation in questions*, page 28.)

ANSWERS / AUDIO SCRIPT 61

2 Where 3 How much 4 When 5 What 6 How

See Student's Book, page 49, for audio script.

4 60

- Have students work in pairs to write the questions in the correct places in the conversation in Exercise 2.
- Play the track again for students to listen and check their answers.

ANSWERS / AUDIO SCRIPT 60

See underlining in audio script in Exercise 2.

5a

- Have students read the tips in the HOW TO box. You could choose one student to read them aloud to the class.

5b

- Have students complete the tasks and then compare their answers in pairs.
- Choose students to share their answers with the class.

ANSWERS

1 Excuse me. Do you speak English?
Can I ask a question?
Yes, of course.
Thank you.
You're welcome.
Sorry, I have another question.
Can I ask something else?
Of course.
Thank you for your help.
You're welcome.

2 You're welcome.

ACT

6 62

- Play the track for students to listen and practice the questions and answers in the PHRASEBOOK.
- Read the instructions for the tasks and divide the class into groups of three to write a short scene set in a tourist information office.
- Ask each group to think of a famous city. They should include sights and monuments from the city but not the name of the city. Explain that there should be an assistant and two friends talking in the scene and encourage students to use the questions and answers in the PHRASEBOOK.
- Set a time limit of five minutes. Circulate and help students as needed.
- When students have finished, ask them to spend two or three minutes practicing their scene.
- Ask students to act out the scene. Encourage them to do this without their notes.
- Have the other students listen and try to identify the city.

Alternative procedure: less confident classes

For less confident students, role-playing a scene can be stressful, especially if they are afraid they won't remember their lines or are self-conscious about performing in front of their classmates. One option is to allow students to just read their scripts. Another option is to have them prepare prompts from their scripts. The prompts would be key words from the questions and answers. For example:

Speak English?

Yes

Question?

Yes

Museum of Popular Art?

The extent of these prompts can be varied from one group to another and so can be adapted to suit the confidence level of each of the groups. However, students should be encouraged to use as few words as possible in the prompts and to look at them only if absolutely necessary.

Homework

Ask students to think of two celebrities and imagine that they are asking for information in a tourist information center in a famous city. Have students write a conversation of 15–20 lines using the questions and expressions from the PHRASEBOOK. At the beginning of the next class, ask students to read each conversation in groups of three, choose the best one, and act it out for the class. If there isn't time for all groups to perform, allow them initially to volunteer so that the more willing and confident groups go first.

WRITING School concert

Use headings

Page 48

STAGE	TIME	FOCUS
GET STARTED		Ask and answer questions about an event.
READ		Read a flier and find specific information in the text. Learn how to use headings (writing subskill).
PRACTICE		Match headings to information in a flier.
DISCUSS		Talk about a fun museum exhibit you visited in preparation for writing a flier.
WRITE		Write a flier for the museum exhibit using headings.
SHARE		Exchange your flier with other students and decide which exhibit is the most interesting.

Get started

Exam-type task

Write the following question prompts on the board: *What? Where? When? What time / start? What time / finish? How much? Who for?*

Explain that you are thinking about an event, for example, a concert, and that students have to ask you questions and take notes to guess the event.

Refer students to the prompts and invite them to ask questions to find out information about the event.

Ask students to note the information you give them.

At the end of the task, have students compare their answers in pairs. Then choose students to share their answers. Write them on the board so that students can compare their answers with the answers on the board. Finally, tell them which event you were thinking of.

If there is time, students can repeat this activity in pairs and take turns either asking the questions and taking notes or thinking of the event and giving the answers.

READ

1

- Refer students to the picture and the text and ask them what they can see. Elicit that there is a photo of a school orchestra giving a concert and a flier with information about the concert.
- Ask students to read the flier and answer the questions. Set a time limit of two minutes for this.
- Stop students after two minutes and ask them to compare their answers in pairs.
- Choose students to share their answers with the class.

ANSWERS
1 The music room at the Hope Building 2 At 6:00 p.m.
3 The number 7 bus 4 Juice and cookies
5 Contact Mrs. Henderson

2

- Ask students to read the tips in the HOW TO box.
- Check students' understanding of the use of headings by asking them to identify the main heading and subheadings in the flier in Exercise 1.

PRACTICE

3

- Have students match the headings to the correct information.
- Ask students to compare their answers in pairs.
- Choose students to share their answers with the class.

ANSWERS
1 b 2 a 3 d 4 e 5 c

DISCUSS

4

- Tell students that they are going to write a flier for a museum exhibit.
- Ask the class to brainstorm different kinds of museums (e.g., *science museum, natural history museum, sports museum, transportation museum*). Write them on the board. Then ask students to think of types of exhibits the museums might have (e.g., *sports museum: sports clothes, famous athletes, Olympic events*).
- Elicit students' experiences with fun museum exhibits they have visited in the past. Ask them the following questions: *Why was it fun? Where was it? How did you get there? How much did it cost? When did you go?*

WRITE

5

- Go over the writing plan with students and refer them back to the information about headings in the HOW TO box.
- Ask them to think about the museum exhibit they discussed in Exercise 4 and then to write notes for each of the questions in the writing plan.
- Ask students to write their fliers. Tell them to write 50–60 words and remind them to refer to their notes. Set a time limit of 10 minutes for writing.
- Circulate and offer help as needed.
- When students have finished writing, ask them to check their fliers, referring to the points in the writing plan to make sure they have followed the steps and answered all the questions.

Extra activity
Having followed the steps above, you might want to make notes on errors and good use of language and have a class feedback session. You could then ask students to write the final draft of their flier for homework and illustrate it with photos or drawings. This encourages students to approach writing in various stages and to take pride in their written work.

SHARE

6

- Display the fliers around the classroom. Ask students to look at all the fliers and decide which exhibit looks the most interesting and which is the best flier. Take a class vote on the most interesting exhibit and the best flier.

Homework

Have students write a flier for a school club (e.g., a computer club, a dance club). Ask students to include the following points: a brief description of the club; where it is; days and times; who can join; where students can get more information.

Ask students to write 50–60 words and to refer to the points from the writing plan in Exercise 5.

At the beginning of the next class, ask students to display their fliers around the classroom. Have students go around and choose the most interesting clubs to join. A quick survey will give you a good picture of your students' common interests.

VOCABULARY Activity verbs

1

- Have students read the title and speech bubble.
- Ask students what the opposite of *past* is (*future*).
- Explain to students that they will write the opposites of the words 1–10. Tell them the first letter of each word and a line for each letter are given. Remind students that *get* has many meanings. If they have difficulty finding its opposite in number 6, you can help them by asking some concept-checking questions with *get* meaning "receive."
- Have students compare their answers in pairs and then check answers as a class.

ANSWERS
1 leave 2 go 3 cry 4 close 5 take off 6 send
7 sit 8 end 9 go out 10 listen to

Places in public buildings

2

- Read the instructions and ask students to complete the text with the words in the box.
- You could suggest that they read through the text quickly before completing it to get a general understanding.
- Have students compare their answers in pairs and then check answers as a class.

ANSWERS
1 ticket office 2 entrance 3 information desk
4 elevator 5 first floor 6 second floor 7 stairs
8 coffee shop 9 gift shop 10 restrooms

GRAMMAR Present progressive

3

- Read the instructions. Tell students they may need to use the question form and that they should use contractions when possible.
- Ask students to complete the sentences using the present progressive form of the verbs.
- Give students time to compare their answers in pairs before checking answers as a class.

ANSWERS
1 You're listening to 2 Are you having 3 we're sitting
4 is happening 5 is traveling 6 We're waiting

Present progressive and simple present

4

- Have students look at the picture and ask them what is happening. Tell students that the people talking on the phone are Zach and Molly.
- Explain that students will complete Zach and Molly's conversation by choosing between the present progressive and simple present forms of the verbs.
- Elicit the different uses of each form and remind students to use the time expressions to help them.
- Have students circle the correct form of the verbs.
- Give students time to compare their answers in pairs before checking answers as a class.

ANSWERS
1 You always arrive 2 We're waiting 3 We're standing
4 I know 5 You aren't waiting 6 we usually call
7 you're visiting 8 we call 9 do you call

Extra Resources

Go to the Teacher's Resource Center at mee2.macmillaneducation.com for:

- the Speaking section of Progress Check Units 3&4;
- a downloadable project linked to Units 3–4;
- videos, video worksheets, and video scripts;
- extra vocabulary at two levels of difficulty;
- extra grammar at two levels of difficulty;
- culture lessons, with full teacher's notes;
- life skills lessons, with full teacher's notes;
- Speaking Database materials;
- the *Move Beyond* Level 1 wordlist;
- downloadable PDF and Word tests for Unit 4;
- tips for using the Grammar Database;
- extra reading materials;
- and more!

Go to Workbook pages 120–131 for further practice material.

PROGRESS CHECK 3&4

Preparing for the Progress Check

Vocabulary review

- Draw a table on the board with the following headings: *School and school subjects*; *Clothes and accessories*; *Activities and hobbies*; *Public buildings*.
- Elicit one or two examples for each category and write them on the board.
- Divide the class into pairs or small groups. Ask them to look back through Units 3 and 4 and find more examples from each vocabulary category.
- After five minutes, encourage students to "rush" to the board and write their answers. Stop them when there are five or six words in each category.
- Finally, ask students to look at the Progress Check. Ask them to look quickly over the listening and writing sections and tell you which vocabulary they might need.

Grammar review

- Give students five minutes to read over the grammar covered on pages 33, 35, 43, and 45.
- Write three verbs on the board (e.g., *eat*, *go*, *play*) and ask students to write the first and third person (*he/she*) forms of all three verbs in the simple present. Then ask them to write them in the present progressive.
- Ask students when they could use each tense (*simple present for habits, routines, and things that are generally true*; *present progressive for actions happening now, around now, or in the near future*). Then ask students to complete the sentences with their own endings.
- Ask students to exchange their sentences with a partner and make them negative.
- Play a quick game to review possessives. Ask students to point to classmates and say what is on their desks (e.g., *Anna's book*, *Ben's pen*).

Optional warm-up activities

These activities are suitable when you are not using the Progress Check as part of a formal test.

READ Exercise 1

- Tell students that this type of exercise is a matching exercise and is common in standardized English exams.
- Elicit some information about signs and announcements from students by asking them how they go about trying to understand and interpret them, what types of signs they see most often, which ones they pay attention to, and which ones they ignore.
- Ask them to think about what colors and words they would expect to see on signs and how they could help them interpret a sign's meaning.
- Refer students to the signs and ask them to work in pairs to say where they might see these signs and who might have written them. Ask them not to do any matching yet.

LISTEN Exercise 2

- Refer students to the listening exercise. Ask them to look at the headings of the survey in pairs and discuss what types of words they will be listening for (e.g., *names*, *hobbies*).
- Ask them to write their own answers to the survey in their notebooks so they can familiarize themselves with what types of words and vocabulary they are listening for.
- Ask students to turn to a partner and discuss ways of expressing their likes and dislikes (*I like*, *I prefer*, etc.).
- Remind students that using their time to predict answers in a listening exam will help them focus better when they hear the audio.

WRITE Exercise 3

- Ask students to turn to page 48 in their books and take two minutes to look at the HOW TO box on headings.
- Refer students to the headings in the order form on page 51 and ask them to discuss in pairs what kind of information they need to write next to each one.
- Give students three minutes to read over the two texts. Then ask them to close their books and call out as many words as they can remember for types of clothes and then as many colors and adjectives as they can remember that were used to describe them.
- Remind students to be careful in the exercise and to notice the use of negatives.

Doing the Progress Check

READ Exercise 1

- Focus students' attention on the **Test-Taking Tips** and go through them as a class. Remind students that this type of task is very common in standardized English exams.
- Ask students to look at the example and say what words are similar and how the same thing is said in different ways.
- Ask students to take three minutes to read the sentences and think of any other possible ways to say the same thing.
- Ask students to do the exercise, reminding them that they won't need to use all the signs.

ANSWERS
1 E 2 A 3 B 4 D 5 G

LISTEN Exercise 2

▶63

- If you have decided not to do the full warm-up, refer students back to the techniques they studied on page 34.
- Then focus students' attention on the **Test-Taking Tips** and ask them to read through the tips and think about how they may be useful.
- Encourage students to spend a minute thinking about the types of information they need.
- Point out that they will hear the track twice. Remind them to use the second time to check their answers and fill in any answers they missed.

ANSWERS / AUDIO SCRIPT ▶63

1 Alexa 2 reading 3 history 4 classical 5 meet friends

Alexa: Hello?
Caller: Hi. I'm calling from *Teen Report*, the TV show. Do you know it?
Alexa: Yes, I do.
Caller: That's great. We're doing a survey about teenagers and free time. Are you a teenager?
Alexa: Yes, I am.
Caller: Good. Can I ask you some questions?
Alexa: Yes, of course.
Caller: Thanks. How old are you?
Alexa: I'm 13.
Caller: Perfect. And what's your name?
Alexa: Alexa.
Caller: Can you spell that, please?
Alexa: A-L-E-X-A.
Caller: The survey is about staying in and going out. We want to know what young people really like doing.
Alexa: OK.

Caller:	When you stay in, what's your favorite activity – watching TV, playing video games ... ?
Alexa:	I really like reading.
Caller:	OK. Are you reading a book right now?
Alexa:	Yes, I am.
Caller:	What kind of books do you like to read?
Alexa:	I like books about history.
Caller:	And do you listen to music?
Alexa:	Yes.
Caller:	What type of music do you prefer?
Alexa:	Classical music.
Caller:	That's interesting. Do you like pop music?
Alexa:	Yes, but I prefer classical.
Caller:	What do you usually do on the weekend?
Alexa:	I usually meet friends.
Caller:	Thank you very much, Alexa.
Alexa:	You're welcome.

WRITE Exercise 3

- Focus students' attention on the **Test-Taking Tips** and ask them to follow the tips as they do the exercise. Point out that this type of task is very common in standardized English exams.
- Have students read the texts and check that they understand where they are both from, who could have written them, and what they are for.
- Ask students to read the task and then to look at the headings in the order form.
- Remind students that they need to write the key information in note form in the order form, not in complete sentences.
- Have students do the task, reminding them to do a thorough check of spelling when they finish.

ANSWERS
1 sweater 2 gray 3 scarf 4 green 5 $27.99

After the Progress Check

Optional game

Ask students to think of a situation in which they would see a sign asking them not to do something. Give students five minutes to draw something to represent this. Then divide the class into pairs to guess the purpose of their partner's sign. Ask them to write instructions to go with their image.

Feedback and extension

After the Progress Check has been graded, provide feedback to the class as a whole and individually as much as possible. Ask students which parts they found the most difficult and how they think they could improve their grades next time.

READ Exercise 1

- Go through each of the signs, asking students where they might see these, whether they're written by one person or by an institution such as a school, and whether they're giving information or asking people to do something or not to do something.
- Look at the sentences and ask students how they decided on the correct answer. Help students break down each sentence and focus on key vocabulary (e.g., the use of *This person* in sentence 1 suggests they should look for a sign from an individual; the use of *afternoon* in sentence 2 suggests they should look for a sign with a time on it).
- Remind students that they should always look for synonyms (different words with the same meaning) in matching exercises, such as *door/entrance* and *show/play*.
- Divide the class into pairs and ask them to look at the signs that weren't matched in the exercise (signs C and F). Give them five minutes to come up with another way of saying the information on the signs. Then put the pairs with another pair and have one pair read a sentence while the other pair guesses which sign they are describing.

LISTEN Exercise 2

- Divide the class into pairs and hand out a copy of the audio script to each student.
- Ask them to act out the conversation in pairs and then work together to underline where each correct answer could be found. Remind them that answers are usually in the right order within the audio script. This may help them find the correct information.
- If necessary, ask students to highlight any parts that could have been misleading and discuss why these weren't correct.
- Have students rewrite the conversation using their own responses in place of Alexa's answers. Ask them to write a copy of the survey in their notebooks. Have pairs perform the conversation in front of another pair, who will fill out the form in their notebooks with the new answers. This will give students extended practice in listening and taking notes.

WRITE Exercise 3

- Students may have found this writing task difficult due to the use of negatives in Ron's note. Read the note again as a class and ask students to circle any negatives in the text.
- Then have students go back and highlight or check the things that Ron needs. Annotating a text will help them transfer information accurately without having to reread the whole text each time.
- Ask them which parts helped them eliminate incorrect answers.
- Make a note of any words that were commonly misspelled. Ask students to close their books and play a quick game of *Snowman* (see Games, page 29) to review these words.
- To extend the lesson, you could repeat the task with a different set of instructions (either written or spoken) to be used with the same information and order form. Vary the difficulty depending on the confidence of your class; include negatives to challenge students.

UNIT 5 IT'S GOOD FOR YOU!

IN THE PICTURE Food and drink

Talk about food and drink *Pages 52–53*

STAGE	TIME	FOCUS
GET STARTED		Brainstorm food and drink vocabulary and talk about what you eat at school.
WORK WITH WORDS		Review and learn food and drink vocabulary. Identify how many syllables a word has and which syllable is stressed. Watch a video and identify food.
SPEAK		Ask and answer "healthy and happy" survey questions.

Get started

Play a game in which students create an A–Z list of food and drink words.

Write the letters A–Z on the board with space to write a word after each. Have students stand up. Choose one student to select a letter and say a food or drink word. Add the word to the list and ask that student to choose another student. If a student can't add a word, he or she must choose another student and sit down. The game continues until the list is completed or until there's only one student left.

Then ask students to think about what they eat at school and elicit some ideas. Ask them to write as many sentences about what they eat as they can in two minutes. Encourage students to use the simple present and adverbs of frequency. After two minutes, have students compare their sentences in pairs. Monitor and note errors and good use of language to go over in a feedback session at the end of the activity. Choose students to share their answers with the class.

WORK WITH WORDS Food and drink

1 RECALL

- Read the instructions to the class and have students look at the example.
- Divide the class into pairs and give students one minute to do the task. When they finish, have them compare their answers in groups of four. Remind them to say why the word is different.
- Choose students from each group to share their answers with the class.
- Ask students to do the **Work with Words** task on page 73.

ANSWERS

2 egg (The other words are fruit.)
3 salad (The other words are things with bread or made with dough.)
4 rice (The other words are things with milk.)
5 pasta (The other words are meat or things with meat.)

Fast finishers

Encourage students to recycle any food and drink vocabulary they may already know by having them create their own lexical sets with a wrong word. Divide the class into pairs and ask them to make five lists using food and drink vocabulary. Remind them that four of the words in each list should be from the same category and one should be from a different catgegory. Set a time limit of two minutes and then have them work with another pair to read each other's lists and say which word is different in each list and why.

2a

- Ask students to look at the pictures and elicit that it is a food blog.
- Divide the class into pairs and ask them to say what food they can see in the pictures.
- Have students match the food and drink items to the words in the box. Ask them to write the words on the blank lines. Set a time limit of two minutes.
- Stop students and tell them not to worry if they haven't filled in all the words. Do not check answers yet.

2b 64

- Read the instructions aloud. Ask students to listen, check their answers, and fill in any missing words.
- Play the track for students to listen to Dan telling Myra about his blog.
- Choose students to share their answers to Exercise 2a with the class.

ANSWERS / AUDIO SCRIPT 64

1 butter 2 cake 3 soup 4 carrot 5 beef 6 potato
7 tomato 8 onion 9 yogurt 10 fries 11 soda
12 candy 13 chocolate 14 chips

Myra: Why is there so much food on your blog, Dan?
Dan: I like food! And I do a lot of sports ... soccer, running ... I'm just always hungry! ... This picture's a typical breakfast. I eat a lot of toast with butter!
Here I am at school. I usually eat fruit or some cake before homeroom.
This is lunch. Lunch at my school is usually fantastic. Not when it's soup – I don't like soup. My favorite meal is stew with beef, carrots, onions, tomatoes, and potatoes. We often have yogurt too. I always drink water with meals.
Myra: Mmm, those french fries in the next picture look good!
Dan: They *are* good! On the way home in the car, we sometimes buy snacks. My big sister's 17 – she drinks a lot of soda, and she loves fries. At night I sometimes eat chips, chocolate, or another kind of candy when I watch TV. I love chocolate!

2c 65

- Play the track for students to listen and repeat the food and drink words.

AUDIO SCRIPT 65

1 butter 2 cake 3 soup 4 carrot 5 beef
6 potato 7 tomato 8 onion 9 yogurt 10 fries
11 soda 12 candy 13 chocolate 14 chips

3a 66 PRONOUNCE

- Ask students to listen and say how many syllables each word has.
- Play the track and pause after each word. Choose students to say the answer and then have students repeat the word.
- Divide the class into pairs. Ask students to look at the words in the box, underline the stressed syllable in each word, and then decide which words have the same stress.
- Choose students to share their answers with the class.

ANSWERS / AUDIO SCRIPT 66

1 three
2 po<u>ta</u>to to<u>ma</u>to ba<u>na</u>na fan<u>tas</u>tic seven<u>teen</u>
The first four words have the same stress – on the second syllable.

3b 67

- Play the track. Ask students to listen and repeat the words. Encourage them to stress the correct syllable.

AUDIO SCRIPT 67

See Student's Book, page 52, for audio script.

Extra activity

Write the following stress patterns on the board as headings (without the words):

● (*toast, fruit, cake, soup, chips*)
●• (*<u>but</u>ter, <u>car</u>rot, <u>on</u>ion, <u>yo</u>gurt, <u>wa</u>ter, <u>sand</u>wich, <u>so</u>da, <u>can</u>dy, <u>cho</u>colate*)
•●• (*po<u>ta</u>to, to<u>ma</u>to, ba<u>na</u>na*)
••● (*seven<u>teen</u>*)

Invite students to say words from Dan and Myra's conversation for each of the patterns. Tell them to use food and drink words except for the last stress pattern. Elicit the number of syllables and invite students to the board to write the words next to the correct pattern. (See answers in parentheses.) Ask the class to say whether the number of syllables in each word is correct and then have them repeat the word. Elicit one or two words for each stress pattern. Then have students copy the table and add more words from the conversation to the first three stress patterns. Set a time limit of two minutes and then have students come to the board and add more words to the three stress patterns.

4

- Read the instructions aloud and elicit the word for the first definition.
- Set a time limit of three minutes and have students find the words.
- When they have finished, ask students to check their answers in pairs.
- Choose students to share their answers with the class.

ANSWERS

1 tomato 2 carrot, onion 3 cake
4 onion (when it's peeled), potato, yogurt (when it's plain)
5 soda 6 butter 7 soup 8 chocolate, candy, chips, soda

5

- Have a student read the instructions aloud. Check that students understand *healthy* and *unhealthy* by eliciting some examples of healthy and unhealthy food.
- Point out that a balanced diet is important for growing teenagers. A lot of unhealthy food and no exercise isn't good, but some fast food and high-fat food is OK if they also eat fruits, vegetables, fish, whole wheat bread, etc.
- Refer students to the PHRASE BYTES box and model an example; for example, *In picture 1 he's putting a lot of butter on some toast. It's OK to eat butter sometimes, but a lot is unhealthy.*
- Divide the class into pairs and have them do the activity. Encourage them to use the present progressive to describe what Dan is doing and to use complete sentences.
- Monitor and note errors and good use of language to go over in a feedback session at the end of the activity.
- Choose students to share their answers with the class. Ask them whether Dan is generally healthy or unhealthy.

6 THE MOVING PICTURE

- Explain that students are going to watch a video and that they should write down the foods they see.
- Show the video more than once if necessary. Then ask students to call out the foods they saw until they have listed all the foods.

ANSWERS / VIDEO SCRIPT

Lunch at home: sandwiches, salad
Lunch at school: sandwich, apple, orange juice, grapes, bread roll
Mmm, something sweet: ice cream, chocolate
A family picnic: bread, fruit, meat, carrots, tomatoes dip
A family barbecue: chicken, vegetables, fish
Dinner at home: meat, potatoes, onions, carrots
Dinner out: hamburger, french fries
Happy birthday, Myra: cupcakes, candy, cookies, yogurt, cheese, fruit, cake, ice cream, orange juice

There is no voiceover in this video.

SPEAK

7a

- Have students read the instructions and the survey.
- Divide the class into pairs and set a time limit of two minutes for them to ask and answer the questions.

7b

- Read the instructions aloud.
- Explain that students should add up how many As, Bs, and Cs they checked, and then refer to the notes on page 76.
- Have students read the appropriate comments to their partner and ask whether their partner agrees.
- Invite students to think about what the result was for them and whether they agreed with it, but avoid choosing students to answer, as this may be sensitive for some of them.

MOVE BEYOND

Ask students to do the **Words & Beyond** exercise on page 73.

Homework

Ask students to keep a food diary in English of everything they eat from now until the next class. At the beginning of the next class, ask students to compare their diaries in pairs and comment on the most interesting things; for example, *I ate a lot of meat and not many vegetables.* Be careful not to scrutinize students' eating habits in feedback, as this may be a sensitive issue for some students, and eating diaries are sometimes associated with dieting.

READING What's for lunch?

Identify who a text is for *Page 54*

STAGE	TIME	FOCUS
GET STARTED		Talk about typical dishes in different countries.
SPEAK AND READ		Describe photos of different school lunches. Read blog posts that describe school meals in different countries. Discuss tips on how to identify who a text is for (reading subskill).
REACT		Talk to a partner about your typical lunch and describe your dream lunch.

MOVE BEYOND FOR TEACHERS

Meals

There are three main meals of the day: *breakfast*, *lunch*, and *dinner*. Mealtimes vary widely around the world, but breakfast is eaten in the morning, lunch is usually eaten around midday, and dinner is eaten in the evening. In the USA, dinner is usually the main meal of the day. Some other times for food you might like to tell students about are a midmorning snack or an afternoon snack.

It is always interesting to have students compare mealtimes in their country with those in other countries because of differences in times and the kinds of meals people eat in different places.

Get started

These warm-up activities will recycle the names of countries and introduce students to some typical dishes in those countries.

Play *Snowman* (see Games, page 33) with the following countries: *Italy*, *Spain*, *India*, *China*, *Peru*, *Korea*, *Senegal*, *Poland*.

Write each of the countries on the side of the board and check that students know where the countries are.

Write the following foods on the board without writing the country: *bibimbap* (Korea), *biryani* (India); *ceviche* (Peru); *chow mein* (China); *gazpacho* (Spain); *pierogi* (Poland); *risotto* (Italy); *yassa chicken* (Senegal).

Explain that they are typical dishes of the countries on the board. Divide the class into pairs and have students match the foods to the countries. Choose students to share their answers with the class.

SPEAK AND READ

1a

- Explain that students are going to look at a food blog about school lunches in different countries.
- Divide the class into pairs and have students describe what they can see in the photos. Refer them to the useful phrases in the **PHRASE BYTES** box.
- Choose students to share their answers with the class. Use the photos to pre-teach the words *mussels* and *tacos*.

ANSWERS

Mikkel: sandwich (made with wheat bread, cheese, and salad), vegetables (carrots and cucumber), apple
Jalissa: taco, rice, lettuce, milk, apple
Dae-Ho: soup, vegetables, rice, salad
Mathilde: mussels, fries
Camila: soup, banana, vegetables, rice, egg, sausage

1b

- Ask students to discuss the questions as a class. Have them raise their hands if they'd like to eat each of the lunches. Choose students to say why.

MOVE BEYOND FOR TEACHERS

School lunches

Many countries started to offer free or subsidized school lunches in the middle of the 20th century as an attempt to promote better child nutrition. They were often offered to poorer families. They are now offered in many countries around the world. In some countries, students can have lunch either at school or at home, while in other countries, students may bring a packed lunch with them or choose to have a school lunch. In some countries, such as Ecuador, where the school day finishes at lunchtime, children go home for lunch.

2a

- Have a student read the tips in the **HOW TO** box aloud.
- Refer students back to page 10 to review the tips.

2b 68

- Ask students to read the text and identify who it is for. Don't play the audio at this point. It is an extra feature, and a suggestion for using it in class is included at the end of the lesson.
- Check the answer with the class.

ANSWER
B

3

- Ask students to check the tips in the HOW TO box that they used to help them with Exercise 2b and to compare their answers with a partner.
- Go through the tips in the HOW TO box and ask students to raise their hands to find out how many checked each tip.

4

- Have students answer the questions and then compare their answers with a partner.
- Check answers as a class.

ANSWERS
Mikkel's lunch has no meat. Dae-Ho's lunch has no or not much meat. Mathilde's lunch has dessert.

REACT

5

- Explain that a "dream lunch" is your idea of a perfect lunch. Give an example of your own dream lunch; for example, *My dream lunch is fried fish, lobster stew, and tiramisu.*
- Encourage students to use adverbs of frequency and/or days of the week when they are talking about their typical lunches; for example, *On Mondays we usually have soup and meat and rice, but sometimes we have omelettes.*
- Divide the class into pairs to talk about typical lunches and their dream lunches.
- Invite volunteers to give feedback on their partners' responses.

MOVE BEYOND

Refer students to the Move Beyond task.

Ask them to write a lunch menu for two days. Give them five minutes to do this. Then divide the class into small groups and have them vote on whose menu is the best.

Recorded reading text 68

Use the audio as an alternative lead-in to the lesson. With books closed, play the introduction and the first two sections of the audio (about Mikkel's and Jalissa's lunches) and ask students what they think the main idea of the text will be and what photos they think will be used.

Homework

Ask students to write a post for the blog about lunches in their country. Ask them to mention whether they have their lunch at school or at home and what they eat and drink for lunch on a typical school day (50–60 words). Encourage them to illustrate the blog post with pictures of their typical lunch. At the beginning of the next class, have students compare their lunches in small groups and discuss any differences.

GRAMMAR *A lot of*, *much*, *many*, *some*, and *any*

Describe how much there is of something *Page 55*

STAGE	TIME	FOCUS
GET STARTED		Talk about what you have for dinner. Play a game using food vocabulary and find similarities in pictures.
READ AND LISTEN		Read and listen to a conversation between a boy and his mom about what to have for dinner.
STUDY		Complete explanations and examples of countable and uncountable nouns and the quantifiers *a lot of*, *much*, *many*, *some*, and *any*.
PRACTICE		Choose the correct options to describe a menu. Use the quantifiers *a lot of*, *much*, *many*, *some*, and *any* in a written exercise.
SPEAK		Talk about what you want or don't want to eat.

Get started

Dictate the following questions and have students write them down (see Teaching Tips, *Dictation*, page 27): *Who usually prepares dinner at your house? What do you usually have for dinner? What do you have for "special" dinners such as birthdays or holidays?*

Divide the class into pairs and have students compare the questions they wrote down and then discuss the answers. Invite students to share their answers with the class.

Ask students to draw a refrigerator in their notebooks and put 10 food items in it.

Explain that students are going to describe their refrigerators in pairs to try to find out foods that they both have. Encourage them to use phrases such as *I have ...* ; *There's/There are ...* ; *Me too!*; *I don't have ...* .

Model the task with a student and then have students do the task with a partner.

READ AND LISTEN Grammar in context

1 ▶69

- Ask students to read and listen to the conversation and say what's for dinner.

ANSWER / AUDIO SCRIPT ▶69
Spaghetti with tomato sauce and salad See Student's Book, page 57, for audio script.

STUDY

2

- Have students find words for food in the text to complete the grammar examples. (See Teaching Tips, *Countable and uncountable nouns*, page 29.)
- Allow students to compare their answers in pairs before you choose students to read the explanations and examples aloud.

ANSWERS
tomatoes pasta

Extra activity

If students need further practice in differentiating between countable and uncountable nouns, have them draw two columns in their notebooks and label them *Countable* and *Uncountable*. Then dictate 15–20 food and drink words (singular, plural, and uncountable) and have students write them in the correct column. Let students compare their answers in pairs before you check them as a class.

3

- Have students complete the grammar explanations individually. Remind them to look at Exercise 2 to help them.
- Check answers as a class and then refer students to the Grammar Database on page 68.

ANSWERS
uncountable uncountable countable uncountable countable; uncountable countable; uncountable

PRACTICE

4

- Ask students to look at the menu and choose the correct options.
- Let students compare their answers in pairs before you check them as a class.

ANSWERS
1 B 2 B 3 A 4 B

Extra activity

Divide the class into pairs. Have students cover the menu and then ask each other questions using *Are there … ?* and *Do they have much/many … ?* For example:

A: Do they have many sandwiches?

B: Yes, they do. They have cheese and avocado, egg salad, … .

Monitor and note errors and good use of language to go over in a feedback session at the end of the activity.

5

- Ask students to choose the correct words to complete the conversation.
- Let students compare their answers in pairs before you check them as a class.

ANSWERS
1 a 2 many 3 some 4 much/a lot of 5 a 6 any 7 some 8 a lot of 9 any 10 some

Fast finishers

Ask fast finishers to find examples of countable and uncountable nouns in the text on page 56. When they have made their lists, they can compare them with a partner.

SPEAK

6

- Have students read the instructions and look at the examples. Remind them to use the quantifiers from Exercise 3. You may want to ask two confident students to read the examples aloud.
- Monitor and note errors and good use of language to go over in a feedback session at the end of the activity.
- Invite students to share their answers with the class.

Alternative procedure

On the board, make a simple drawing of two stick figures looking at a menu in a café. Elicit or explain that they are two friends looking at the menu and they are trying to decide what to have. Ask students to imagine that they are those people and to think of three things they'd like to have that aren't on the menu. Explain that they are going to role-play the conversation. During the role-play, they should tell their partner what they'd like that isn't on the menu, and the partner should suggest alternatives from the menu. Encourage students to use expressions from the lesson, as well as the quantifiers from Exercise 3. For example:
I'd like … ; I want … / I don't want … ; They don't have any/many/much … ; What about … ?

Homework

Ask students to write a blog post (50–60 words) called "What I like to order from the menu at my favorite restaurant." Ask them to write about what they usually have when they eat at a restaurant. Encourage students to use a range of countable and uncountable nouns and the quantifiers from the lesson. At the beginning of the next class, you could collect the texts, read some aloud, and have students guess whose blog post each one is.

LISTENING AND VOCABULARY Food for the brain

Identify the speaker

Page 56

STAGE	TIME	FOCUS
GET STARTED		Talk about what is good and bad for the brain.
SPEAK AND LISTEN		Take a class survey about how many hours you sleep. Listen to a radio report about sleep. Learn how to identify the speaker in a listening task (listening subskill).
REACT		Discuss questions about sleep.
WORK WITH WORDS		Listen and match words to different quotes. Learn adjectives to describe lifestyle. Discuss questions about your lifestyle.

Get started

In this activity, students will think about what the title of the lesson, *Food for the brain*, means and discuss things that are good and bad for the brain. Write *Food for the brain* on the board and elicit the meaning of *brain*. Divide the class into pairs and ask students to discuss what they think the title means. Invite students to share their ideas with the class. Ask students to draw two columns in their notebooks and label them *Good for the brain* and *Bad for the brain*. Explain that you are going to say some activities/situations and you want students to write them in one of the columns.

Dictate the following list: *reading*, *listening to music*, *being stressed*, *going out with friends*, *working a lot*, *doing exercise*, *sleeping*, *doing crosswords*, *learning languages*.

Ask students to compare their ideas in pairs. You might want to put the following useful phrases on the board to help students with their answers: *I think doing exercise is good for your brain*; *I agree*; *I disagree*; *I'm not sure*; *It depends.*

Invite students to share their ideas with the class and suggest other things that are good for your brain.

SPEAK AND LISTEN

1

- Have students look at the photo and elicit what is happening in it.
- Explain that they are going to do a class survey to find out how much people sleep.
- Read the instructions aloud and choose one student to ask the questions and another to write the results on the board.
- Ask students how many hours of sleep they think teenagers need, but don't confirm the answer at this point.
- Leave the survey results on the board for students to refer to in Exercise 5.

2a

- Choose students to read the tips in the HOW TO box aloud.

2b 70

- Ask students to listen to the four speakers and decide who each speaker is.
- Elicit answers from the class.

ANSWERS / AUDIO SCRIPT 70

Speaker 2: a student/teenager
Speaker 3: a father/the father of the student
Speaker 4: a doctor

Teacher: A lot of my students find it difficult to stay awake in class because they don't sleep enough at night. They're tired when they come to school, so they can't learn. They need more sleep.

Teenager: My school starts at 7:45. I take the bus, so I get up at 6:15. I go to bed late, and it's hard to get up in the morning. But I hate going to bed early. I don't feel tired then.

Dad: My son goes to bed really late. He's always busy with things. I tell him that he doesn't sleep enough. I tell him all the time: "When you don't sleep enough, you eat more, you don't feel well, and you feel unhappy and stressed." But he doesn't listen to me.

Doctor: Your body and your sleeping times change when you're a teenager. This means teenagers prefer going to bed much later, usually after 11 p.m. Then they're tired because most schools start early. But teenagers need eight and a half to nine hours of sleep every night or they can't lead a healthy life. As I tell my patients: sleep is food for the brain.

3

- Ask students to check the tips in the HOW TO box that they used to help them with Exercise 2b.
- Invite students to share their answers with the class.

4 70

Exam type task

- Play the track again. Ask students to listen to the four speakers and choose the correct option for each one.
- Let students compare and justify their answers in pairs before you check them as a class.

ANSWERS / AUDIO SCRIPT 70

1 C 2 A 3 C 4 B
See Exercise 2b for audio script.

Alternative procedure: less confident classes
Hand out copies of the audio script and have students read through it and check their answers. Then ask them to circle any expressions they don't understand (e.g., *they can't lead a healthy life*). Divide the class into pairs and ask students to compare their expressions and see if their partner knows the meanings. Invite students to discuss their expressions with the class.

REACT

5

- Read the questions aloud and focus students' attention on the word *enough*. Explain that here it means "sufficiently" or "the correct amount."
- Have students discuss the questions in pairs.
- Choose students to share their answers with the class.

WORK WITH WORDS Lifestyle adjectives

6a ▶71

- Have students match the words to the quotations. Then play the track for them to listen and check their answers.
- Ask students to compare their answers with a partner. Then choose students to share their answers with the class.

ANSWERS / AUDIO SCRIPT ▶71

1 d 2 e 3 a 4 c 5 b 6 i 7 h 8 j
9 f 10 g
1 d, active 2 e, healthy 3 a, tired 4 c, busy 5 b, lucky
6 i, unhappy 7 h, stressed 8 j, well 9 f, sick 10 g, lazy

6b ▶72

- Play the track and do a choral drill of the words. Pay particular attention to the pronunciation of *tired*, *busy*, *stressed*, and *lazy*.

AUDIO SCRIPT ▶72

active healthy tired busy lucky unhappy stressed
well sick lazy

Extra activity
Divide the class into pairs and have students mime words from Exercise 6a for their partner to guess. Set a time limit of two minutes.

7

- Divide the class into pairs to discuss the questions. Encourage them to justify their answers.
- Invite students to share their answers with the class.

MOVE BEYOND

Ask students to do the **Words & Beyond** exercise on page 73.

You may want to ask students if they know opposites for the other adjectives on the list.

Homework

Have students write a set of tips for a website called *Food for the Brain*. Ask students to choose four things that are good for the brain and say why they are good. Encourage them to use the lifestyle adjectives from Exercise 6a. At the beginning of the next class, you could ask students to read their tips aloud and then put the best ones together for an information poster to display on the classroom wall.

GRAMMAR *Like + -ing*

Talk about your likes and dislikes *Page 57*

STAGE	TIME	FOCUS
GET STARTED		Play a game to find classmates who like the same things as you.
READ		Read an internet thread on a teen forum about likes and dislikes.
STUDY		Identify verbs to express likes and dislikes in the text. Focus on verb (*like*, *love*, *hate*, etc.) + noun/*-ing* and spelling of *-ing* forms.
PRACTICE		Practice the target language in written exercises.
SPEAK		Ask and answer questions to find out about likes and dislikes.

Get started

Have students think about things they like. Draw a 4x4 grid on the board and ask students to copy it and write something they like in each square. Elicit some examples (e.g., *chocolate*, *swimming in the ocean*, *playing sports*). Have students play a variation of *Bingo* in which they move around, asking different students about their likes; for example, *Do you like running?* If they find a student who likes one of the things on the card, they can mark that square with the name of the student. The objective is to get four different names in a row. When students achieve this, they call out *Bingo!* This game can be extended by asking students to complete the whole grid before saying *Bingo!*

READ Grammar in context

1

- Ask students to look at the text and elicit what type of text it is and where you find it (*an internet forum thread*).
- Ask students to read the text and answer the question.
- Divide the class into pairs and have students compare their answers. Encourage them to give reasons.
- Invite students to share their answers with the class.

STUDY

2

- Ask students to complete the grammar explanations with words from Exercise 1.
- Let students compare their answers in pairs before you check them as a class.

ANSWERS

like don't like don't like like cleaning

Extra activity

In order for students to understand how the verbs relate to each other, have students put them on a scale. Draw a diagram on the board like the one below and invite students to come to the board and write the verbs in the correct places.

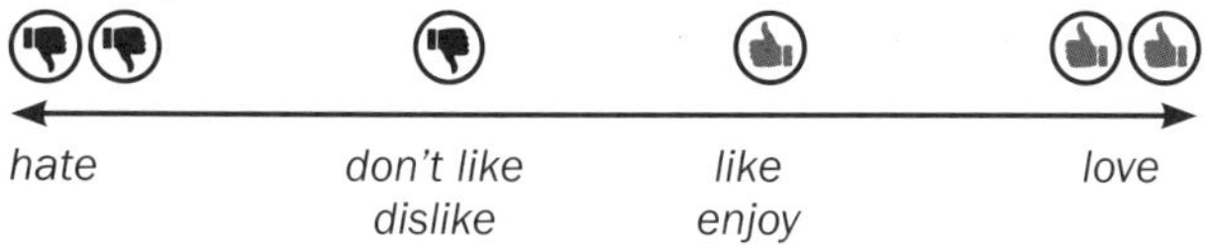

3

- Ask students to refer to Exercise 1 and write the *-ing* forms.
- Have students compare their answers in pairs. Then choose different students to spell the verbs aloud.

ANSWERS
1 being 2 studying 3 riding 4 writing 5 running
6 swimming

PRACTICE

4a

- Read the instructions aloud and have students write the *-ing* forms of the verbs in parentheses.
- Have them compare their answers in pairs before checking answers as a class.

ANSWERS
1 playing 2 traveling 3 visiting 4 dancing 5 getting
6 waiting 7 keeping 8 making

4b

- Ask students to find the things that Susie13 and Marc both like and dislike.
- Have them compare their answers in pairs. Then choose students to share their answers with the class.

ANSWERS
They both like being with friends.
They both dislike cleaning their rooms / keeping their rooms neat.

Extra activity

Ask students to compare their own likes and dislikes with those of Susie13 and Marc in groups of three or four.

5

- Ask students to complete the sentences so that they are true for them and then to compare them in pairs.
- Invite students to share their answers with the class.

6a

- Ask students to write the questions. Refer them to the example.
- Circulate and monitor as students work, helping them with any difficulties.
- Choose students to read the answers aloud. Pay attention to students' word stress in the questions.

ANSWERS
2 Do you enjoy speaking English?
3 Do you like using social networking sites?
4 Do you enjoy meeting new people?
5 Do you like cooking?
6 Do you like shopping for clothes?

6b

- Ask students to write another question to ask a partner. Encourage them to think of an interesting question.
- Monitor students and help them as needed.

Fast finishers

If students finish Exercise 6a quickly, ask them to write three questions instead of one for Exercise 6b.

SPEAK

7

- Divide the class into pairs and have students ask and answer a question from Exercise 6. Encourage students to ask their partner to explain his or her answer.
- Invite students to tell the class what they found out about their partner.

Homework

Ask students to think of a celebrity and imagine his or her likes and dislikes. Have them write a list of the celebrity's top three likes and dislikes for a social media page. Instruct students to use the different verbs in Exercise 2 and to illustrate the text with pictures. At the beginning of the next class, have students compare their pages in pairs.

LANGUAGE & BEYOND *RESPECT OTHERS*

Follow the rules in electronic communication *Page 58*

STAGE	TIME	FOCUS
GET STARTED		Think about rules. Make a list of the rules you have to follow at school and talk about why we need rules.
SPEAK AND READ		Talk about the different forms of electronic communication you use. Read about certain situations and talk about how you feel if they happen to you.
DO		Discuss rules for good use of electronic communication.
REFLECT		Reflect on ways in which you use electronic communication and problems you may have.
EXTEND		Think of more rules for electronic communication.

LIFE SKILLS

RESPECT OTHERS: FOLLOW THE RULES IN ELECTRONIC COMMUNICATION

This life-skills lesson focuses on netiquette, or rules for electronic communication on the internet. It also indirectly touches on cyberbullying, which is a growing problem in many countries. Netiquette is essentially a set of moral standards that has evolved in response to the emergence of new forms of electronic communication. For example, it is very easy to take a photo of someone and upload it to a social networking site without the subject's permission. However, as this may cause distress, netiquette would suggest that you ask permission before doing so. Cyberbullying is closely associated with this, as it involves breaking those standards, intentionally or unintentionally, in order to cause some degree of distress. In this lesson, students will think about how online actions can affect the lives of others and what "rules" of netiquette can be applied.

Get started

Write *School rules* on the board and elicit some examples (e.g., *Don't run in the hallways*, *Be polite*). Write them on the board in the imperative, as the form is easy to use and it won't be necessary to explain it at this stage.

Ask students to think of other school rules. Divide the class into pairs and have students compare their rules. If they have the same rules, ask them to think of more. Invite students to come to the board and add their rules. Write the following questions on the board: *Are these rules useful? Why or why not? What rules would you like to change? Why do we need rules? Where else do we have rules?*

Have students discuss the questions in pairs. Then invite students to share their ideas with the class. Explain that they are going to read and think about rules for electronic communication.

SPEAK AND READ

1

- Refer students to the photos and ask them what they can see. Try to elicit some of the expressions that will come up in the lesson (e.g., *on the computer* or *a website*, *talking on the phone*, *sending a text message*).
- Divide the class into pairs to discuss the question. Remind them to ask complete questions and to use adverbs of frequency.
- Choose students to share their answers with the class.

2

- Read the instructions aloud and go through the situations one by one as a class. You could choose students to do this or read them yourself.
- Pre-teach the meaning of new vocabulary (e.g., *by mistake*, *silly*, *delete*) in the text.
- Refer students to the PHRASE BYTES box to help them structure their answers. Check that students understand *rude*.
- Divide the class into pairs to discuss the situations.
- Invite students to share their ideas with the class.

DO

3

- Read the instructions aloud and model an example by having students suggest the situation that matches the first rule.
- Divide the class into pairs and ask them to discuss the rules.
- Encourage students to use expressions for agreeing and disagreeing. (See Teaching Tips, *Encouraging extended answers*, page 27.)
- Choose a student from each group to share the group's answers with the class.

ANSWERS

a 2 b 1 c 3 d 2 e All

REFLECT

4

- Ask students to read and discuss the questions in pairs or small groups. Then invite students to share their answers with the class.
- Choose a student to read the REFLECTION POINT and check any new vocabulary (e.g., *polite*, *hate messages*).
- Invite students to tell the class whether they agree.

EXTEND

5

- Read the instructions aloud and then elicit one or two examples.
- Divide the class into small groups and have them think of more rules.
- Invite a student from each group to share the group's rules with the class.
- Ask students to say which rules they think are most useful.

Extra activity

Have students design a questionnaire with the title "Are You a Cyber Star?"

Explain that the questionnaire should have 6–10 questions with multiple-choice answers. There should also be a key to interpret the answers. For example, 5–6 points = Cyber Star, 3–4 points = Cyber Citizen, etc.

Elicit some examples of questions and multiple-choice answers. For example:

You want to put a friend's photo on Facebook. Do you ask for permission?

A Yes, always B Sometimes C Never

Divide the class into small groups and set a time limit of 10 minutes for them to prepare the questionnaire. Explain that everyone in the group should write down the questions and answer options.

Circulate and help students as necessary.

Stop the activity after 10 minutes and divide the class so that students are working with students from a different group.

Have students ask and answer the questions from each other's questionnaires.

Ask students to tell the class whether they found any Cyber Stars.

Homework

Ask students to create a poster with the rules that they thought of in Exercise 5. Ask them to try to add one or two more and to illustrate their posters. At the beginning of the next class, display the posters around the classroom and vote on which is the most eye-catching.

SPEAKING I don't believe it!

React to news

Page 59

STAGE	TIME	FOCUS
GET STARTED		Write sentences about good and bad news.
SPEAK		Look at photos and talk about whether the people are giving good news, bad news, or surprising news.
LISTEN		Listen to conversations in which people are giving good, bad, and surprising news. Focus on expressions for reacting to good, bad, and surprising news (speaking subskill).
ACT		Practice reacting to good, bad, and surprising news.

Get started

Write the following pieces of news on the board: *Your mother wins the lottery*; *Your dog runs away*; *Your local café is closed*; *Your favorite band is giving a concert next month*; *Your local soccer team loses a game*; *You lose your house keys.*

Ask students whether they think each example is good news or bad news. Have them compare their ideas in pairs and then share their ideas with the class.

Explain that you now want them to make the good news bad and the bad news good; for example, *Your mother wins the lottery, but it's only $5*; *… but your neighbors find him in the park*; *… but it is reopening as a cybercafe*; *… but tickets cost $100*; *… but they ask you to play for them next season*; *… but your brother has a second set of keys for you.*

Elicit an example and have students do the activity in pairs.

Invite students to share their sentences with the class.

SPEAK

1

- Ask students to look at the photos and decide who is receiving the different types of news.
- Ask students to compare their ideas in pairs. Encourage them to justify their answers; for example, *I think she's receiving good news because she looks happy.*
- Choose students to share their answers with the class, but don't confirm answers at this point.

Extra activity

Ask students to say what they think the news is in each situation without reading the conversations. They can then listen, read, and check their ideas in Exercise 2.

LISTEN

2 73

- Play the audio track for students to listen and check their answers to Exercise 1.
- Check answers as a class and elicit from the class what the news is in each case.
- You might also want to check students' understanding of some of the words and expressions (e.g., *fast food*, *sugar*).

ANSWERS / AUDIO SCRIPT 73

1 Beth says they put sugar on fries.
2 Elaine says her grandmother is in the hospital.
3 Sam says they don't have a math test tomorrow.

1
Beth: No more fries from fast food places for me!
Kevin: Really? I don't believe it!
Beth: Do you know that they put sugar on fries?
Kevin: Seriously?! That's amazing!

2
Elaine: My grandma's in the hospital.
Paula: Oh, I'm sorry, Elaine. That's terrible.
Elaine: Yeah, she's really sick.
Paula: That's so sad!

3
Sam: Guess what! Tomorrow we have two extra PE classes. No math test!
Liz: Really? Wow! Great!
Sam: I know – no math test!
Liz: That's fantastic!

3a 73

- Read the instructions to the class and focus students' attention on the words in the box.
- You may want to check that students understand the words by asking them which words have a positive meaning and which words have a negative meaning.
- Play the track again for students to listen and complete the conversations with words from the box.

ANSWERS / AUDIO SCRIPT 73

See underlining in audio script in Exercise 2.

Alternative procedure: more confident classes

Have students complete the conversations with the words in the box before they listen to check their ideas. This way they will have to rely on their memory of what they heard and their understanding of the text and the vocabulary.

3b 74

- Play the track for students to listen and check their answers.

AUDIO SCRIPT 74

1 Really? I don't believe it! 2 That's amazing!
3 I'm sorry, Elaine. 4 That's so sad! 5 Great!
6 That's fantastic!

4 ▶75
- Refer students to the useful phrases in the PHRASEBOOK.
- Play the track for students to listen and repeat the phrases. Encourage students to use appropriate intonation.

AUDIO SCRIPT ▶75

See Student's Book, page 59, for audio script.

ACT

5a ▶76
- Read the instructions aloud and check that students understand all of the situations. You might want to elicit which situations are good news and which are bad news.
- Divide the class into pairs and have students do the task. Remind them to use the expressions from the PHRASEBOOK and encourage them to stand up and act out the parts. Also remind them to take turns giving and reacting to news.

5b
- Have students think of two different pieces of news.
- Divide the class into pairs and ask students to give their news and reactions.
- Invite different students around the class to give and react to news.

Alternative procedure: less confident classes
Rather than have students think of the news on their own, have them do it in pairs and then work with a different partner for the second part of the activity.

Homework

Ask students to write mini-conversations for the new situations they thought of in Exercise 5b. Explain that the conversations should have a maximum of four lines and that they should use language from the PHRASEBOOK. At the beginning of the next class, have students compare and practice their conversations in pairs.

WRITING My favorite meal

Use *because* Page 60

STAGE	TIME	FOCUS
GET STARTED		Play a game to review countable and uncountable nouns.
SPEAK AND READ		Talk about favorite food and drinks. Read a description of a meal and find specific information in the text. Learn how to use *because* (writing subskill).
PRACTICE		Match sentence halves linked by *because*.
DISCUSS		Talk about your favorite meal, dessert, and drink. Say why they are your favorites.
WRITE		Write a description of your favorite meal and check that you have followed the writing plan.
SHARE		Read your description to other students and decide which meals, desserts, and drinks are the class favorites.

Get started

Recycle food and drink vocabulary and countable and uncountable nouns by playing an alphabet game of *I went to the market ...* . Start the game off by saying *I went to the market and bought apples.* Choose a student to continue; the student repeats your sentence and adds a food item that begins with the next letter of the alphabet. That student then chooses another student to continue the game. Try to continue all the way through the alphabet!

SPEAK AND READ

1
- Choose a student to read the instructions aloud. Then divide the class into pairs and have students tell their partner about their favorite food and drinks.
- Remind students to use *some* and *any* where appropriate; for example, *I don't like any vegetables.*
- Choose students to tell the class what food and drinks they and their partner both like.

Alternative procedure: less confident classes
Have students write a list of their favorite food and drinks before they talk to their partner. This will provide support to students who may lack confidence in speaking.

2
- Ask students to look at the text and establish that it's a website where people can ask questions, similar to Yahoo Answers or Ask.com.
- Read the instructions aloud. Have students read the text and find out what Alejandro's favorite meal, dessert, and drink are.
- Have students compare their answers in pairs. Then choose students to share their answers with the class.

ANSWERS

Favorite meal: tacos
Favorite dessert: chocolate ice cream with a lot of chocolate sauce
Favorite drink: water

3a
- Choose a student to read aloud the tips in the HOW TO box.

3b
- Ask students to find the answers to the questions in the text and underline them.
- Have students compare their answers in pairs. Then choose students to share their answers with the class.

ANSWERS
1 Because his mom makes them at home
2 Because soda is really bad for your teeth and he doesn't like it

PRACTICE

4

- Explain that students have to match the sentence halves. Elicit an example.
- Have students do the exercise and then compare their answers in pairs.
- Choose students to share their answers with the class.

ANSWERS
1 e 2 d 3 a 4 c 5 b

Fast finishers
Ask fast finishers to write more endings for the phrases 1–5 in Exercise 4 (e.g., *I don't like grapes because they taste terrible*).

DISCUSS

5

- Explain to students that they are going to write a description of their favorite meal for an internet site. Divide the class into pairs to talk about their favorite meals, desserts, and drinks. Tell them to give reasons for why the food or drink is especially good.
- Set a time limit of five minutes for students to talk to their partners. While they are doing this, circulate and help them generate ideas.

WRITE

6

- Tell students that they are now going to write their descriptions and that they should write 50–60 words.
- Go through the steps in the writing plan one at a time and make sure students understand what they have to include in their descriptions. Refer them back to the HOW TO box and remind them to use *because* for giving reasons.
- Set a time limit of 10 minutes for writing. Circulate and offer help as necessary.
- When students have finished writing, ask them to check their descriptions against the writing plan to make sure they have followed the steps and included all of the necessary information.

SHARE

7

- Divide the class into groups. Tell each group to select one student to write three headings on a piece of paper: *Meal*, *Dessert*, and *Drink*.
- Ask students to read their descriptions aloud. As they read, the student keeping the list should write each student's favorite meal, dessert, and drink in the correct column.
- When they have finished reading their descriptions, make a class list on the board. Ask a student from each group to write that group's favorite meals, desserts, and drinks on the board.
- Count the results for each category to find out what the favorite meal, dessert, and drink are for the whole class.

Alternative procedure
You could have students work in groups to prepare posters of their favorite meals using their descriptions. Ask them to find photos to include on their posters and have them finish them in the next class. Display them around the classroom and ask students to decide which is their favorite poster.

Homework

Explain to students that they are having a meal with their favorite celebrity. Ask them to think of a celebrity and the food they think that celebrity likes. Ask them to write a description in 50–60 words and to refer to the points from the writing plan to help them. At the beginning of the next class, read some of their descriptions aloud and ask students to guess who each celebrity is.

VOCABULARY Food and drink

MOVE BEYOND FOR TEACHERS

"Rewards for Schools" websites

In the USA, and increasingly in the UK, schools work with companies to get extra money for their school. One way many schools do this is to ask parents to buy their groceries from a particular website and put in a code for the school. The school then gets a percentage of all the profits from the food bought by parents.

1

- Ask students to look at the pictures and explain that this is a website. Read the text from the website aloud. Ask students if they know any websites like this.
- Tell students that they will write the correct food and drink words from the box under the pictures.
- Have students compare their answers in pairs. Then choose students to share their answers with the class.

ANSWERS
1 onion 2 carrots 3 tomatoes 4 butter
5 potatoes 6 yogurt 7 soda 8 fries 9 cake
10 soup 11 candy 12 chocolate

Lifestyle adjectives

2

- Ask students to complete the text by completing the adjectives.
- You may want to suggest that they read through the text quickly before completing it to get a general understanding.
- Have students compare their answers in pairs. Then choose students to share their answers with the class.

ANSWERS
1 busy 2 active 3 tired 4 stressed 5 unhappy
6 sick 7 lazy 8 lucky 9 healthy 10 well

GRAMMAR *A lot of*, *much*, *many*, *some*, and *any*

3

- Ask students to choose the correct options to complete the text.
- You might want to elicit the rules for countable and uncountable nouns and the quantifiers before students do the exercise.
- Give students time to compare their answers in pairs before choosing students to share their answers with the class.

ANSWERS
1 much 2 any 3 a lot of 4 some 5 many 6 a
7 any 8 a lot of

Like + -ing

4

- Ask students to look at the text and elicit that it is the comments section of the website.
- Read the instructions aloud and elicit possible answers for the first item.
- Have students do the exercise.
- Give students time to compare their answers in pairs before choosing students to share their answers with the class.

ANSWERS
1 like/enjoy helping 2 like/enjoy eating
3 don't like / dislike trying 4 like/enjoy choosing
5 hate shopping 6 love buying

Extra Resources

Go to the Teacher's Resource Center at mee2.macmillaneducation.com for:

- videos, video worksheets, and video scripts;
- extra vocabulary at two levels of difficulty;
- extra grammar at two levels of difficulty;
- culture lessons, with full teacher's notes;
- life skills lessons, with full teacher's notes;
- Speaking Database materials;
- the *Move Beyond* Level 1 wordlist;
- downloadable PDF and Word tests for Unit 5;
- the *Move Beyond Level 1* Midterm Test (all skills);
- tips for using the Grammar Database;
- extra reading materials;
- and more!

Go to Workbook pages 132–143 for further practice material.

PROGRESS CHECK 5

Preparing for the Progress Check

Vocabulary review

- Divide the class into two groups and give each group a vocabulary category (*Food and drink* or *Lifestyle adjectives*).
- Explain that students have to find the vocabulary and write eight clues for words in their categories. (They should also write down the answers so they don't forget them.) Students can split the writing among themselves or appoint one team member to do the writing. Provide an example for each category and write the examples on the board, eliciting the answers.
- When each team has eight "clues," they then test the other team by reading them aloud. Anyone can answer, but the team member must raise his or her hand. The first person to raise his or her hand gives the answer. Teams score one point for each correct answer but lose a point if they get it wrong. If a team member makes a mistake, his or her team is not allowed to try again for that question.
- For more difficult words, explain to students that they have to spell the word correctly before they get the point. Keep score on the board.

Grammar review

- Give students 10 minutes to look over the grammar points they have covered in Unit 5 on pages 55 and 57.
- Ask students to close their books and work with a partner to come up with a list of five countable and five uncountable nouns. Write some of their suggestions on the board in two columns.
- Then write *a lot*, *much*, *many*, *some*, and *any* on the board.
- Ask students to give you example sentences using each of these along with a noun from the correct column.
- To review *like* + *-ing*, ask students to give you example sentences of things they like doing.

Optional warm-up activities

These activities are suitable when you are not using the Progress Check as part of a formal test.

READ Exercise 1

- Predicting the content in multiple-choice activities can help students focus on what the correct answer could be and eliminate possible incorrect answers.
- Ask students to cover up the answer options in the text and focus only on the sentences on the left. Give them two minutes to read through the sentences.
- Go through each item with the class, drawing students' attention to the language used; for example, *Is this a question? Is it affirmative or negative? Is it a statement you can agree or disagree with?*
- Then ask students to think in general terms about language they could use to respond. Refer them back to the **PHRASEBOOKS** on page 59 if they need to remind themselves of phrases and expressions they can use.
- Ask students to write their own answers and responses to 1–5 in their notebooks. Then divide the class into pairs to discuss their responses.
- Remind students that thinking of some possible responses before looking at the options will help them focus on the correct answer.

LISTEN Exercise 2

- If you haven't done the vocabulary review with your class, refer students back to page 61 to review words for food and drink.
- Ask them to think about what reasons people might have for liking or disliking a particular food or drink (*it tastes good, it's delicious, it's too salty, it looks funny*, etc.). Having a reminder of positive and negative vocabulary will help them make the connections and eliminate wrong answers during the listening.

WRITE Exercise 3

- Ask students to read the text quickly. Give them 30 seconds to do this and then ask them to close their books.
- Ask students to name as many foods that are mentioned in the profile as they can (*burgers, French fries, pickles, ketchup, tomatoes, lettuce, cheese*).
- Write the words *like* and *don't like* on the board and ask students to write their own sentences using the foods from the text.
- Refer students to page 57 and ask them to check the grammar of their sentences. Ask them to pay particular attention to the endings of verbs and whether the word *to* is used before the verb. Focusing students on the structures of sentences and the words that come before and after the blanks will help them select the correct words to fill in the blanks.
- Ask students to open their books again and look at the words that come before and after each blank. Encourage them to guess which words could possibly fit, but don't confirm answers at this point.

Doing the Progress Check

READ Exercise 1

- Focus students' attention on the **Test-Taking Tips**. Remind students that this type of task is very common in standardized English exams and review some of the multiple-choice techniques they have used in other exercises (such as in Progress Check Units 1&2).
- Ask students to look at the example and to discuss in pairs why answers A and C are wrong. (*Neither is a food.*)
- Encourage students to try to eliminate one wrong answer where they can, reminding them to look at both grammar and vocabulary.

ANSWERS
1 C 2 B 3 A 4 B 5 A

LISTEN Exercise 2

▶77

- Focus students' attention on the **Test-Taking Tips**. Make sure they understand that they must use only five of the eight food and drink options (A–H) in their answers.
- Remind students that they will hear the track twice. Encourage them to use the short amount of time between the first and second listening to refocus on what they need to listen for the final time. If they have completed their answers, they should use the second listening as an opportunity for checking.

ANSWERS / AUDIO SCRIPT ▶77
1 B 2 B, F 3 G 4 C, A 5 A

Aaron: Hi, Angela. That milkshake sure looks good.
Angela: It isn't mine. It's my sister's. She'll be back in a minute.
Aaron: I thought your brother was meeting you for lunch today.
Angela: No. He decided to go out to get pizza with his friends.
Aaron: Why would he go out for pizza? Don't your parents make the best pizza in town?
Angela: Yes, they do. Well, actually Dad is the pizza chef, and he loves to make pasta, too. Mom makes an amazing cheesecake. It tastes so good.
Aaron: Mmmm, I've never had her cheesecake. But I have had your grandma's cookies.
Angela: Yes, Grandma makes delicious chocolate chip cookies. In fact, she and my aunt are making cookies together today.
Aaron: What kind?
Angela: Peanut butter. That's my aunt's favorite kind. Mine too.
Aaron: Yum! I may be following you home from the mall today.

WRITE Exercise 3

- Focus students' attention on the **Test-Taking Tips** and ask them to follow the tips as they do the exercise. Point out that this type of task is very common in standardized English exams.
- Remind students to look at the words before and after the blanks to help them arrive at the correct answers.
- Ask students to complete the text with only one word in each blank. Encourage them to go back and check the words, paying particular attention to the ends and forms of verbs used, as accuracy is vital in this kind of exercise.

ANSWERS
1 food 2 fries 3 you 4 on 5 many 6 like
7 What 8 of 9 are [also possible: *taste*] 10 favorite

After the Progress Check

Optional game

To give students a chance to relax a little after the test, play a game of *Snowman* to follow up on the theme from the listening section (see Games, page 29).

- Ask students to look back at the vocabulary for food and drinks in the vocabulary lessons and **Words & Beyond** section. Ask them to memorize as many words as possible in three minutes.
- Have students play the game with those words. Invite different students to the front to lead the game each time. If possible, continue until all students have had a turn.

Feedback and extension

After the Progress Check has been graded, provide feedback to the class as a whole and individually as much as possible. Ask students which parts they found the most difficult and how they think they could improve their grades next time.

READ Exercise 1

- Review the items one at a time and tell students they are going to focus on the wrong answers.
- Divide the class into pairs and ask them to find reasons why each of the wrong answers is incorrect. For example, number 1 is a question that would elicit a specific individual response. The two wrong answers do not do this.
- After a few minutes, conduct a class discussion about what students have found.
- Students may find items for which they have to notice things such as tone and register, which is more difficult than recognizing correct or incorrect grammatical responses.
- Practice responding to news by giving students some examples of situations (e.g., *I failed my English test*; *I'm going on vacation*). Prepare a long list of these to give students a lot of practice.
- For the first few items, ask students to tell you if they should give a positive or negative response.
- Then ask them to call out any appropriate responses they can think of as quickly as possible, encouraging them to be spontaneous if they can.
- Let them know if any responses are not correct or appropriate before moving on to the next one. Students will start to become more confident at responding correctly and will be more likely to choose the correct answer on tests.

LISTEN Exercise 2

- Divide the class into pairs. Hand out photocopies of the audio script – one for each pair – and ask students to practice the conversation, switching roles to practice both parts.
- Ask pairs to underline the sections of the conversation where the answers can be found.

WRITE Exercise 3

- This writing task was relatively straightforward, but it is likely that students will have lost points for mistakes in verb forms used or spelling.
- Go over each answer as a class and ask students to volunteer any answers that they got wrong. If students are reluctant to volunteer, use examples of common mistakes from the class.
- Ask students to work in pairs to find reasons why each wrong answer is not possible.
- If you have time, ask students to write a short paragraph on foods they like or dislike.

WORKBOOK AUDIO SCRIPT

Unit 1

Track 78

Page 88, Exercise 2

John: Yeah, I love my brother. He's the only one I have, and he's important to me. We have our problems, but all families are like that. I don't have a sister or cousins my age, so Matt and I have to get along.

Sam: You know, it's good to be by yourself sometimes. I need to get away from the noise and not talk to other people. I turn off my phone and computer and go inline skating in the park. It gives me time to think about things. When I come back, I always feel much better.

Eva: With my mom, dad, grandpa, and two brothers in my house, I never feel lonely. But on weekends, I prefer to go to my cousins' house. You know why? Because they're girl cousins! We talk and laugh all day. We're almost like sisters.

Track 79

Page 88, Exercise 3

John: Yeah, I love my brother. He's the only one I have, and he's important to me. We have our problems, but all families are like that. I don't have a sister or cousins my age, so Matt and I have to get along.

Track 80

Page 88, Exercise 4

Sam: You know, it's good to be by yourself sometimes. I need to get away from the noise and not talk to other people. I turn off my phone and computer and go inline skating in the park. It gives me time to think about things. When I come back, I always feel much better.

Track 81

Page 88, Exercise 5

Eva: With my mom, dad, grandpa, and two brothers in my house, I never feel lonely. But on weekends I prefer to go to my cousins' house. You know why? Because they're girl cousins! We talk and laugh all day. We're almost like sisters.

Track 82

Page 91, Exercise 3

Ask for directions

Excuse me, ...
How do I get to ... ?
Can you tell me the way to ... , please?
I think I'm lost.

Give directions

Go straight ahead.
Turn left.
Turn right.
Take the first left.
Take the first right.
Take the second left.
Take the second right.
It's on the left.
It's on the right.
It's just around the corner.
You can't miss it.

Track 83

Page 91, Exercise 4 and Exercise 6

Conversation 1

Lee: Excuse me, can you tell me the way to the station?
Kim: The bus station or the train station?
Lee: The bus station, please.
Kim: OK. Take the first right and go straight ahead for about 200 meters. You can't miss it.
Lee: Thanks a lot.

Conversation 2

Mark: How do I get to the main square, please?
Will: It's just around the corner after the movie theater, on the left.
Mark: Thanks.

Conversation 3

Eva: Excuse me, I think I'm lost.
Dave: Well, where do you want to go?
Eva: Can you tell me how to get to the art museum, please?
Dave: I'm not sure, but I think it's next to the bus station. Turn left at the next big street and go about half a kilometer.
Eva: Thank you.

Track 84

Page 91, Exercise 7

1
Lee: Excuse me, can you tell me the way to the station?
2
Lee: The bus station, please.
3
Lee: Thanks a lot.
4
Mark: How do I get to the main square, please?
5
Mark: Thanks.
6
Eva: Excuse me, I think I'm lost.
7
Eva: Can you tell me how to get to the art museum, please?
8
Eva: Thank you.

Unit 2

Track 85

Page 99, Exercise 6

goes
plays
does
finishes
washes
brushes
buys
meets
wants
chooses

Track 86

Page 100, Exercise 3

1
The sound of someone snoring, rolls over in bed, and then an alarm clock.
2
The sound of a dishwasher and food processor and someone chopping food.
3
The sound of a TV show.
4
The sound of a shower and someone opening and closing a shampoo bottle.

Track 87

Page 100, Exercise 4 and Exercise 5

Conversation 1

Susan: Come on! You need to get up.
Kim: Huh? Uh? Go away ...
Susan: School starts at a quarter after 8! You have 30 minutes. Get up now!
Kim: In a minute.
Susan: No, now! I won't tell you again.

Conversation 2

Harry: What's for dinner?
Tom: Soup.
Harry: Just soup?
Tom: Yes, why?
Harry: I'm really hungry!
Tom: Well, there's some fish.
Harry: But I don't like fish!

Conversation 3

Jasmine: Is there anything better on?
Dad: I'm happy watching the news.
Jasmine: Why can't I have a TV in my bedroom?
Dad: You're too young. When you're 14, you can.
Jasmine: That's so unfair!

Conversation 4

Hurry up ... I have to take a shower.
Pete: I'm getting into the shower.
Sarah: But I'm going out. Get out now!
Pete: No.
Sarah: Mom, Pete won't get out of the bathroom!

Track 88

Page 103, Exercise 2

1
9:00
2
7:30
3
11:15
4
2:45

5
8:20
6
9:50

Track ▶89

Page 103, Exercise 3

Lily: When's the next train to Washington?
Gina: The schedule says there's one at 2:25.
Lily: When does it get to Washington?
Gina: It arrives at 4:05.
Lily: Is there an earlier train?
Gina: There is one, but it leaves in a few minutes.
Lily: How long do we have until it leaves?
Gina: It leaves at 2:05, so 10 minutes. It arrives in Washington at 3:20.
Lily: Let's buy tickets for that train.
Gina: OK.

Track ▶90

Page 103, Exercise 5 and Exercise 6

Ask for and tell the time
What time is it?
What time's the next ... ?
When's the next ... ?
There's one at ...
(I think) it's at ...
"thirteen oh five" is the same as "five after one"
"seventeen forty-five" is the same as "a quarter to six"
How long do we have until it leaves?
Make time to think
Well, ...
Um ...
Let me see ...

Unit 3

Track ▶91

Page 112, Exercise 2 and Exercise 4

Philip: I'm Philip, from the United States, and we don't wear uniforms at my school. Kids usually wear casual clothes like jeans and T-shirts. But some schools in the States have rules about uniforms. At my cousin's school, the students wear white shirts and blue pants.
All the schools in Mexico have uniforms. It's the same in Brazil. They often wear shorts because it's hot. In schools in high altitudes in Peru, a hat is sometimes part of the uniform.
In most European countries, like Spain, Germany, and Italy, students in public schools don't wear uniforms. But in England, students in all schools, public and private, wear uniforms.
Students in Japan and China wear uniforms. They often have a different uniform for summer and winter.
I don't know what's best. What are the rules about school clothes in your country?

Track ▶92

Page 115, Exercise 2

Describe appearance
What does he look like?
What does she look like?
She's average height.
She's tall.
She's old.
She's young.
He wears glasses.
She wears glasses.
Describe hair and eyes
He has blond hair.
He has gray hair.
He has dark hair.
He has black hair.
He has brown hair.
She has short hair.
She has long hair.
She has straight hair.
She has wavy hair.
He has blue eyes.
He has brown eyes.
He has green eyes.
Describe habits and activities
She wears a lot of jewelry.
She wears black clothes.
He plays the guitar.

Track ▶93

Page 115, Exercise 3

Paula: So, what's Rafael like?
Beth: Well, he's tall and he has brown, wavy hair. He plays basketball every day. He's on the school team. He tells a lot of jokes, and he's a lot of fun. He has a twin brother, Tony, but they're very different.
Paula: Do they look the same?
Beth: No, they don't. Tony is tall too, but he has short, straight blond hair. He always wears black clothes. They also like different things. Tony doesn't like sports. He wears glasses, and he plays the piano really well.
Paula: They both sound interesting.

Unit 4

Track ▶94

Page 124, Exercise 3

1
Announcer: The 9:20 train for Oceanside is now leaving from platform four, stops at Kearney, Mesa, La Jolla, and Del Mar.
2
Tour Guide: The Great Room has life-size models of some of the biggest animals in the world. You can see how big a whale is just by looking at it next to an elephant.
3
Lisa: So, I usually come here after school on Fridays.
Tim: Great place. And this burger's good.
4
Speaker: Today I'm talking to you about the history of Chicago. Chicago is a big city with over nine million people. It has an interesting history.

Track ▶95

Page 124, Exercise 4 and Exercise 5

1
Waiter: Are you ready to order?
Matt: Can I have a glass of milk and a muffin, please?
Jessica: And can I have orange juice and a cookie, please?
Waiter: Of course.
2
Announcer: Attention shoppers. The store is closing in fifteen minutes. Please take your items to the cashier. And thank you for shopping with us.
3
Teacher: OK everyone, quiet please. I have an important announcement about the exam this afternoon. All students, please arrive at least 10 minutes before it starts so we can check your identification.
4
Tour Guide: In this room are the paintings of Picasso from the last years of his life. And if you follow me into the next room, we can see a number of paintings by other artists of the 20th century. As you can see ...

Track ▶96

Page 127, Exercise 2

Robert: Excuse me, do you speak English?
Assistant: Yes, of course. Can I help you?
Robert: Yes, I want to buy presents for my family, but I need some information about the mall.
Assistant: What information do you need?
Robert: Do you have a list of all of the stores?
Assistant: Yes, here's a map of the mall. All the stores are listed in alphabetical order.
Robert: Thanks. Can I ask something else?
Assistant: Of course. Go ahead.
Robert: Where is the restroom, please?
Assistant: There are restrooms on every floor next to the elevators.
Robert: Thanks. Sorry, I have another question. Is there a café so I can have lunch?

Assistant: Yes, there are a lot of places to eat in the food court.
Robert: How do I get there?
Assistant: Take the elevator to the second floor.
Robert: Great. One final question: What time does the mall close?
Assistant: We close at nine o'clock. Have a good day.
Robert: Thank you for your help.
Assistant: You're welcome.

Track 97

Page 127, Exercise 4 and Exercise 5

Information questions
Where's the museum?
Where's the stadium?
How much does it cost?
When does it open?
When does it close?
What time does it open?
What time does it close?
How do we get there?
Polite requests and answers
Excuse me. Do you speak english?
Can I ask a question?
Yes, of course.
Sorry, I have another question.
Can I ask something else?
Of course.
Thank you for your help.
You're welcome.

Unit 5

Track 98

Page 136, Exercise 2, Exercise 3, and Exercise 4

Elizabeth: Welcome to our program on dreams. I'm Elizabeth Black. Our first question is from a young listener. Here's Katie.
Katie: I want to know, do some animals dream?
Elizabeth: Well, Katie, let's ask Doctor Michael Kent from International University. Doctor...?
Michael: Katie, that's an interesting question. Well, there are two types of sleep. There's sleep with dreams and sleep with no dreams. Now, we know that cows and horses can sleep when they stand up and when they lie down, but they only dream in their sleep when they lie down.

Track 99

Page 136, Exercise 5

Speaker 1
Scientist: I'm under this big tree, and there are hundreds of bats here. They're all sleeping upside down. They sleep like this because bats start to fly from an upside-down position.
Speaker 2
Vampire: I sleep in the day. I go out at night. My eyes are red, and my face is white.
Speaker 3
Mother: Sshh ... sleep. Yes. You're going to sleep. Oh, yes you are. Good night. Sleep tight, my little girl. See you in the morning light.
Speaker 4
Songwriter: My songs often come to me in dreams when I'm asleep. Not the words, but the music. I always write down my dreams when I wake up.

Track 100

Page 136, Exercise 7

Speaker 1
Grandfather: I have a lot of free time these days because I don't work anymore. It's great. I don't have any stress, and I feel lucky because I get to spend more time with Nick.
Speaker 2
Nick: I always have a lot of homework to do. I'm very busy, and sometimes I don't have any free time on weekdays. But my grandfather always helps me, so I usually do well in school.
Speaker 3
Teacher: Now, class, listen, please ... I have your homework here. Jackie: Great work. You have a very active and busy imagination! You get an A. And Nick: Your grandfather sounds like a very nice man. Wonderful story!

Track 101

Page 139, Exercise 2

React to good news
Great!
That's fantastic!
Wow!
React to bad news
I'm sorry.
That's so sad.
That's terrible.
React to surprising news
Really?
Seriously?
I don't believe it!
That's amazing!

Track 102

Page 139, Exercise 3

Conversation 1
Gina: What's wrong, Tim? You don't look very happy.
Tim: We can't find Romeo, our dog. We've looked everywhere, but he's been missing for two days now.
Gina: I'm sorry, Tim. That's terrible news. I know how much you love him. I'm sure he's just playing somewhere.

Track 103

Page 139, Exercise 4

Conversation 2
Tim: Guess what, Gina! Romeo is back home!
Gina: Wow, great! That's fantastic! How is he?
Tim: He's fine. Really good. And he has a girlfriend.
Gina: Really?
Tim: It's true. He meets her in the park. And her name is Juliet.
Gina: Romeo and Juliet? Really? I don't believe it! That's amazing!

Track 104

Page 139, Exercise 5

1
Gina: I'm sorry, Tim. That's terrible news.
2
Gina: Wow, great! That's fantastic!
3
Gina: Really? I don't believe it! That's amazing!

WORKBOOK ANSWER KEY

Starter Unit

VOCABULARY
Page 80

1 30 days: April, June, September, November; 31 days: *January*, March, May, July, August, October, December
2 February
3 **1** *American* **2** Mexican **3** Italian **4** Japanese **5** German **6** Colombian **7** Spanish
4a **1** *first* **2** fourth **3** second **4** sixth **5** seventh **6** third **7** fifth
4c **1** Monday **2** Tuesday **3** Wednesday **4** Thursday **5** Friday **6** Saturday
5 **1** *c* **2** d **3** e **4** b **5** a

GRAMMAR
Page 81

1 **1** *am* **2** is **3** are
2 **1** *I'm a student.* **2** My grandmother is from the USA. **3** He's my brother. **4** My friends are from Lima. **5** We're from Japan. **6** I'm from Germany. **7** She's Mexican.
3 **1** *How old is Paula?* **2** Where are they from? **3** What's your name? **4** How old are you? **5** When's your birthday? **6** How old is your sister?
4 **1** *'s* **2** 'm **3** 'm **4** Where **5** from **6** 'm **7** How **8** are **9** When **10** 's

VOCABULARY
Page 82

1a **1** *red* **2** orange **3** blue **4** brown **5** yellow **6** green **7** white **8** black; **a** 3 **b** *1* **c** 7 **d** 5 **e** 6 **f** 4 **g** 2 **h** 8

2a

B	O	R	A	N	G	E	N	A
L	R	E	R	B	R	O	W	N
A	T	D	E	L	E	N	H	T
C	N	B	L	U	E	F	I	R
K	G	E	P	I	N	L	T	Y
Y	E	L	L	O	W	T	E	O

2b **1** purple **2** pink
3 **1** *clock* **2** door **3** window **4** wall **5** floor **6** board **7** chair **8** desk

GRAMMAR
Page 83

1 **1** *this* **2** that **3** those **4** these
2 **1** *sandwiches* **2** bags **3** fish **4** women **5** boxes **6** tomatoes **7** days **8** cities
3 **1** *me* **2** him **3** her **4** it **5** us **6** you **7** them
4a **1** *We* **2** them **3** they **4** us **5** Her **6** He **7** He **8** him
4b **1** These **2** her **3** that's **4** They **5** That's **6** those are

Unit 1

VOCABULARY 1
Page 84

1 **1** *apartment* **2** museum **3** stadium **4** airport **5** station **6** café **7** library **8** store **9** theater **10** tower **11** zoo

Z	M	S	T	A	D	I	U	M	M
S	O	W	T	H	E	A	N	W	U
Y	I	O	Y	A	E	O	F	C	S
F	D	R	X	U	T	A	X	A	E
G	A	E	V	W	O	I	T	F	U
I	T	M	A	G	W	V	O	E	M
P	S	T	O	R	E	S	A	N	R
M	S	L	I	B	R	A	R	Y	B
A	P	A	R	T	M	E	N	T	Q
K	T	R	A	I	R	P	O	R	T

2 **1** *airport* **2** zoo **3** square **4** shopping mall **5** park **6** house
3 **1** *park* **2** park **3** station **4** station **5** pool
4 **1** *school* **2** Street **3** park **4** apartment **5** restaurant **6** stadium
5 **1** *station* **2** park **3** museum **4** square **5** theater **6** café

READING
Page 85

1 **1** *titles* **2** text **3** schedule **4** article **5** pictures
2 **1** *d* **2** e **3** a **4** c **5** b
3 b
4 c
5 **1** d **2** f **3** a **4** c **5** b **6** g **7** e

GRAMMAR 1
Page 86

1 **1** is **2** are **3** isn't **4** aren't **5** Is **6** is **7** isn't **8** Are **9** are **10** aren't
2 **1** *There's* **2** isn't **3** There are **4** aren't **5** There are **6** There's **7** There are **8** isn't
3a **1** *any* **2** any **3** a **4** a **5** any **6** any
b **1** *there aren't* **2** there are **3** there is **4** there isn't **5** there aren't **6** there are
4 **1** *any* **2** some **3** some **4** some **5** any **6** any
5 **1** aren't **2** is/'s **3** isn't **4** is **5** are

Page 87

6 **1** *between* **2** behind **3** next to **4** in front of **5** near **6** across from
7 **1** *on* **2** in **3** behind **4** between **5** near **6** under
8 **1** *are* **2** in **3** aren't **4** is **5** above **6** isn't **7** is **8** across from
9 **1** *Is there anything to do tonight?*
2 Yes, there is. There's a good movie at the mall.
3 Great! Is there a restaurant in the mall?
4 No, there isn't, but there's a café with food.
5 Let's go. Are there any night buses to get back?
6 Yes, there's the number 12.
7 There's one problem. I don't have any money.

LISTENING
Page 88

1 **1** *understand* **2** word **3** Listen **4** know **5** Use **6** understand **7** ideas
2 **a** Eva **b** John **c** Sam
3 b
4 c
5 a
6 With my mom, dad, grandpa, and four brothers in my house, I never feel lonely. But on weekends I prefer to go to my cousins' house. You know why? Because they're girl cousins! We talk and laugh all day. We're almost like sisters.

VOCABULARY 2
Page 89

1 male: *dad*, brother, husband, son, uncle;
female: aunt, daughter, mom, sister, wife;
both: cousin, parent
2 **1** ✗ *one sister* **2** ✓ **3** ✗ three cousins **4** ✗ two cousins **5** ✓ **6** ✗ Ben's wife **7** ✗ Lily's husband **8** ✓
3 **1** *aunt* **2** sister **3** uncle **4** cousin **5** grandfather **6** mom **7** sister **8** husband **9** grandson
4 **1** *aunt* **2** husband **3** uncle **4** sons **5** sister **6** parents **7** cousins

Words & Beyond

5 **1** *f* **2** a **3** c **4** g **5** e **6** d **7** b **8** h
6 **a** *guidebook* **b** weekend **c** website (any order)
7 **1** *quiet* **2** boring **3** small **4** lonely **5** happy **6** big **7** nice
8 **1** *Chinese* **2** Mexican **3** Colombian **4** Japanese **5** American **6** Italian **7** Spanish **8** German **9** Brazilian **10** French

GRAMMAR 2
Page 90

1 **1** have **2** has **3** don't have **4** doesn't have **5** Do **6** Does **7** do **8** doesn't
2 **1** *don't* **2** don't **3** don't **4** has **5** doesn't **6** don't **7** have
3a **1** *Does Karen have a brother?* **2** Does Karen have a sister? **3** Does Lucy have a brother? **4** Does Lucy have a sister? **5** Do they have any cousins? **6** Do they have long hair? **7** Does Lucy have a pet?
3b **1** *No, she doesn't.* **2** Yes, she does. **3** Yes, she does. **4** No, she doesn't. **5** No, they don't. **6** Yes, they do. **7** Yes, she does.
4 **1** *Do you have any cousins?* **2** I don't have any here, but I have a lot in America. **3** How many do you have?

4 I don't have any boy cousins. **5** I don't have any family in America, but I have a cousin in Australia. **6** They all have computers.

SPEAKING
Page 91
1 1 *tell* **2** Take **3** ahead **4** miss **5** How **6** around **7** on **8** left
2 1 *Excuse* **2** get **3** way **4** lost **5** straight **6** Turn **7** Take **8** on **9** corner **10** miss
4 1 e **2** a **3** d
5 1 *Excuse me* **2** please **3** Thanks **4** please **5** Thanks **6** Excuse me **7** please **8** Thank you

WRITING
Page 92
1 1 *capital* **2** nationalities **3** periods **4** commas **5** ideas **6** apostrophes **7** verbs **8** question marks **9** questions **10** exclamation points
2a
1 *Hi Roman* (,)
2 Best wishes, Raul
3 It's near a park, a castle, and the Prado museum.
4 Why don't you visit?
5 My dad has an apartment here.
6 There's also Real Madrid's stadium to see.
7 How are you?
8 I'm in Madrid now.
2b Hi Roman,
How are you? I'm in Madrid now. My dad has an apartment here. It's near a park, a castle, and the Prado museum. There's also Real Madrid's stadium to see. Why don't you visit?
Best wishes,
Raul
3 Hi Toby,
I love Belmont Park in San Diego. There are so many things to do there for young people. The best thing is the Ferris wheel. You can see the city from above. There's also a cool café, two ice-cream places, and a great pizza restaurant. Why don't you visit some time?
Love,
Gina

LIFE SKILLS
Page 93
1 1 Good morning. **2** Good morning. **3** Hello, Charles. How are you? **4** Fine, thank you, George. How are you?
2 1 *F* **2** F **3** F **4** T **5** F **6** T **7** T
3 1 *meet* **2** it **3** morning **4** you **5** Paula **6** you **7** Jack
4 1 *b* **2** c **3** a **4** b **5** a **6** c

VOCABULARY REVIEW 1
Page 94
1 1 *green* **2** red **3** yellow **4** white **5** orange **6** blue
2a 1 *wall* **2** light **3** pictures **4** clock **5** door **6** window **7** desk **8** table **9** chair **10** floor
2b 1 *clock*, pictures **2** desk, chair, table **3** window, door, (possibly: desk)
3 1 *roof* **2** apartment **3** tower **4** building **5** café **6** station **7** street

GRAMMAR REVIEW 1
Page 95
1 1 *them* **2** They **3** they **4** us **5** her **6** she **7** we **8** her **9** He **10** me
2a 1 *Where* **2** Who **3** How **4** Where **5** What **6** When **7** How
2b a *1* **b** 5 **c** 7 **d** 3 **e** 2 **f** 4 **g** 6
3a 1 *Is this your pen?* **2** Do you have my book? **3** Is she looking at me? **4** Is there a problem? **5** Is that the new teacher? **6** Do you have the right answer?
3b 1 *b* **2** c **3** b **4** a **5** b **6** c

Unit 2

VOCABULARY 1
Page 96
1 1 *seven twenty* **2** six o'clock or six **3** quarter to nine or eight forty-five **4** one thirty **5** ten after four or ten minutes after four or four ten **6** ten to two or one fifty **7** twenty five to three or two thirty-five **8** five minutes after ten or five after ten or ten oh five
2 1 c **2** f **3** a **4** e **5** d **6** g **7** b
3 1 *get up* **2** *seven fifteen* / (a) quarter after seven **3** get to school **4** eight fifteen / (a) quarter after eight **5** have/ eat lunch **6** twelve thirty **7** go home **8** three thirty **9** go to bed **10** nine thirty
4 1 *take a shower* **2** get home / leave home **3** brush my teeth **4** get dressed **5** pack my school bag **6** brush my hair
5 1 *T* **2** T **3** F **4** T

READING
Page 97
1 1 *a* **2** c **3** d **4** b
2 c
3 1 How many <u>people</u> live there? **2** <u>How many</u> of the residents are <u>students</u>? **3** What can you do on the <u>river</u>? **4** <u>Where</u> can you <u>ride</u> a bike, <u>run</u>, or go for <u>walks</u>? **5** Does Boston have any <u>historical sites</u>? **6** Are there a lot of <u>aquariums</u> in Boston?
4 1 About 600,000 **2** 40 percent **3** fish, sail, and enjoy water sports **4** on the paths **5** many **6** one

GRAMMAR 1
Page 98
1 1 generally true **2** habits and routines **3** *I, you, we, they* **4** *he, she, it* **5** *-ch/-s/-sh/-x/-o* **6** consonant-*y*
2 1 days, dates, *the weekend* **2** months, years, seasons, *the morning* **3** *midnight, night, lunchtime, six o'clock*
3 1 *plays* **2** ✓ **3** offers **4** ✓ **5** flies **6** ✓ **7** brushes **8** ✓
4a 1 *celebrate* **2** has **3** snows **4** stay **5** goes **6** watch **7** finishes **8** sees
4b Generally true: *1*, 3, 4, 7
Habits or routines: 2, 5, 6, 8

Page 99
5 1 *in* **2** on **3** at **4** in **5** in **6** in **7** at **8** on
6 /ɪz/ brushes, chooses, finishes, washes
/z/ goes, buys, does, plays
/s/ meets, wants
7 1 *see* **2** on **3** go **4** at **5** In **6** play **7** go **8** play **9** at **10** In **11** visit/see **12** sleep/stay

LISTENING
Page 100
1 1 *hear* **2** decide **3** help
2 1 *bedroom* **2** bathroom **3** kitchen **4** living room
3 1 *bedroom* **2** kitchen **3** living room **4** bathroom
5 1 c **2** b **3** b **4** c

VOCABULARY 2
Page 101
1a 1 *armchair* **2** bookshelf **3** carpets **4** stove **5** cabinet **6** curtains **7** refrigerator **8** lamp **9** shelf **10** sofa **11** closet **12** dishwasher
1b 1 c **2** d **3** b **4** e **5** a

Words & Beyond
2 1 *equator* **2** seasons **3** rain **4** winter **5** shines **6** warm **7** windy **8** midnight **9** snows
3 1 *lunchtime* **2** hungry **3** bored **4** quiet **5** schedule **6** school year

GRAMMAR 2
Page 102
1 1 sometimes **2** often **3** usually **4** adverb
2 1 *never* **2** hardly ever **3** usually **4** always **5** often **6** sometimes
3 1 *He often listens to the radio.* **2** They sometimes read books. **3** I always get up at 7:00 a.m. **4** Ruth and Frank are often hungry. **5** My grandmother normally goes for a walk in the evening. **6** Jack usually helps his father in the kitchen. **7** They never watch TV in the afternoon. **8** Christine never answers her phone.

4 **1** *Bertha's always late.* **2** Jack is hardly ever here. **3** When he's late, Jack often forgets to call. **4** Bertha usually does her homework in her bedroom. **5** Jack never replies to my emails. **6** Bertha is always on the phone. **7** Jack sometimes watches movies on my computer. **8** Bertha is normally busy in the evening.

SPEAKING
Page 103
1 **1** *9:00* **2** 7:30 **3** 11:15 **4** 2:45 **5** 8:20 **6** 9:50
3 c ✓
4 **1** *time* **2** next **3** one **4** long **5** until **6** Um …
7 **1** 1:10 **2** 11:35 **3** 4:15

WRITING
Page 104
1 **1** *add* **2** before **3** end
2 **1** *Marina* **2** Marina **3** Yes
3 **1** *also* **2** too **3** also
4 **1** *also* **2** too **3** also **4** too **5** also **6** also

LIFE SKILLS
Page 105
1 **1** *c* **2** a **3** b
2 Suggested answer: Alice is not very good at organizing her time or keeping her room organized.
3 Suggested answers:
She can put her books on the shelf.
She can organize her desk.
She can make a plan or schedule.

VOCABULARY REVIEW 1 & 2
Page 106
1 **Across:** **4** cabinet **5** shelf **6** lamp **7** stove **8** curtains
Down: **1** sofa **2** armchair **3** dishwasher **4** carpet
2 **1** *zoo* **2** theater **3** sports center **4** swimming pool **5** store **6** restaurant
3 **1** *library* **2** square **3** airport **4** station **5** bridge **6** museum **7** mall **8** theme park
4 **1** *guidebook* **2** guide **3** directions **4** turn **5** straight ahead **6** corner **7** bridge **8** miss

GRAMMAR REVIEW 1 & 2
Page 107
1 **1** *under* **2** over **3** in front **4** behind **5** in **6** on **7** next to **8** near **9** across from **10** between
2 **1** *are* **2** are **3** is **4** Is **5** Are **6** aren't **7** isn't **8** are
3 **1** ✗ *Do you have any pets?* **2** ✓ **3** ✓ **4** ✗ Do you have a big family? **5** ✗ We don't always have a lot to talk about. **6** ✓ **7** ✗ She has a new car. **8** ✗ My grandparents have a house in the country.

4 In: April, winter, the afternoon, the morning, 2015
At: lunchtime, six o'clock
On: April 23, Sunday, weekends

Unit 3

VOCABULARY 1
Page 108
1 **1** ✓ **2** ✓ **3** ✓ **4** ✓ **5** ✗ **6** ✓ **7** ✓ **8** ✗ **9** ✗
2 **1** *a* **2** h **3** g **4** e **5** c **6** d **7** f **8** b
3 **1** *b* **2** c **3** f **4** e **5** d **6** a
4a **1** *languages* **2** PE **3** history **4** math **5** science **6** music
4b Students' own answers.

READING
Page 109
1 **1** *quickly* **2** Don't try **3** general topic
2 b
3 c
4 **1** c **2** a **3** c
5 **A** 1 **B** 4 **C** 2 **D** 3

GRAMMAR 1
Page 110
1 **1** don't **2** doesn't **3** do **4** don't/do not **5** Does **6** doesn't/does not **7** do **8** does
2 **1** *a* **2** a **3** b **4** a **5** c **6** c
3 **1** *Do* **2** do **3** do you **4** doesn't **5** Do **6** don't
4a **1** *Where* **2** What **3** When **4** How **5** What **6** Who **7** Where **8** Which **9** Why

Page 111
4b **a** *1* **b** 2 **c** 7 **d** 6 **e** 9 **f** 3 **g** 8 **h** 4 **i** 5
5a **1** *Do they often go to the movies?* **2** Where does she usually spend her vacation? **3** Does it rain a lot in your country? **4** When does he have free time? **5** Does she go to restaurants? **6** What do they like to eat? **7** Do you drink soda? **8** Why do I sometimes make mistakes?
5b **a** *7* **b** 3 **c** 1 **d** 5
6 **1** *doesn't send* **2** don't have **3** does your family love you **4** Yes, all of them do **5** Why don't you **6** doesn't want **7** Why doesn't it **8** Do you know
7 **1** *Does John like math? Yes, he does.* **2** Do Kate and Mary go to the same school? Yes, they do. **3** Does Anna study science? Yes, she does. **4** Do you go to museums? No, I don't. **5** Do your parents help you with your homework? No, they don't. **6** Do I have the correct answers? Yes, you do. **7** Does Paul read a lot? No, he doesn't.

LISTENING
Page 112
1 **1** *task* **2** important **3** information
2 United States, Mexico, Brazil, Peru, Spain, Germany, Italy, England, Japan, China
3 **1** Which countries have school uniforms? **2** Which countries do not have school uniforms? **3** In which countries is a hat part of the uniform? **4** In which countries do the uniforms change from winter to summer?
4 **1** *N* **2** A **3** A **4** N **5** N **6** A **7** A **8** S **9** A
5 **3** Peru **4** China, Japan

VOCABULARY 2
Page 113
1 **1** *belt; a* **2** tie; c **3** sweater; h **4** skirt; d **5** jeans; g **6** shirt; b **7** coat; e **8** gloves; f **9** jacket; i

B	E	L	T	W	S	L	U	G	N
J	E	A	N	S	S	K	S	H	A
T	J	H	V	A	Z	E	I	H	E
I	A	W	Q	T	V	T	L	R	J
E	C	G	O	O	C	D	Q	T	T
L	K	F	L	R	C	O	R	J	A
T	E	G	C	A	J	I	A	Z	U
F	T	Y	Z	W	H	K	M	T	W
T	E	A	X	S	Z	S	E	U	T
S	W	E	A	T	E	R	E	U	T

2 **1** *B* **2** T **3** T **4** TB **5** B **6** T **7** B
3 **1** *bag* **2** Earrings **3** gloves **4** sneakers **5** dress

Words & Beyond
4 **1** *typical* **2** uniform **3** stripes **4** earrings **5** rules **6** track **7** breaks **8** amazing **9** stuff

GRAMMAR 2
Page 114
1 **1** Bill's **2** Jones's **3** students'
2 **1** is this **2** are these
3 **1** mine **2** yours **3** his **4** hers **5** ours **6** theirs
4a **1** *Whose books are these?* **2** Whose backpack is this? **3** Whose scarf is this? **4** Whose hat is this? **5** Whose sneakers are these? **6** Whose earrings are these? **7** Whose tie is this? **8** Whose gloves are these?
4b **1** *They're Matt's.* **2** It's Mary's. **3** It's Matt's. **4** It's Mary's. **5** They're Matt's. **6** They're Mary's. **7** It's Matt's. **8** They're Mary's.
5 **1** *b parents'* **2** b sisters' **3** a cousin's **4** a neighbor's/neighbors' **5** a team's **6** b students'
6 **1** *mine* **2** sister's **3** mom's **4** hers **5** dad's **6** people's **7** parents'
7 **1** *Whose earrings are these? They're Juanita's.* **2** Whose shorts are these? They're mine. **3** Whose hoodie is this? It's Mario's. **4** Whose top is this? It's hers. **5** Whose cat is this? It's theirs. **6** Whose sneakers are these? They're Kim's.

SPEAKING

Page 115

1 **1** *average height* **2** wears **3** blond **4** wavy **5** green **6** a lot of jewelry **7** guitar

3	**Rafael**	**Tony**
tall	✓	✓
blond hair		✓
brown hair	✓	
basketball	✓	
piano		✓
jokes	✓	
black clothes		✓
glasses		✓

4a **1** *tall* **2** has **3** plays **4** tells **5** brother's **6** has **7** wears

4b He's tall. He has blond hair. He plays the piano. He wears glasses. He wears black clothes.

5 **1** *She has* **2** She **3** She's **4** She **5** has **6** She's

WRITING

Page 116

1 **1** *and* **2** or **3** but **4** or

2 **1** *but* **2** or **3** and **4** and **5** or **6** but

3 B

4 **1** *or* **2** and **3** or **4** or **5** but **6** or/and **7** but/and **8** or

LIFE SKILLS

Page 117

1 **1** *V* **2** K **3** A **4** V **5** A **6** K

3 Suggested answer: The teacher can show videos about history, take the class on field trips to historical sites, and use visual materials.

VOCABULARY REVIEW 1–3

Page 118

1 **1** *d* **2** f **3** b **4** c **5** a **6** e

2 **1** *hat* **2** gloves **3** socks **4** scarf **5** sunglasses **6** belt **7** jacket **8** skirt

3 **1** *up* **2** up **3** take **4** get **5** have **6** brush **7** pack **8** take **9** do

4 **1** *sister* **2** uncle **3** children **4** wife **5** cousins **6** married **7** son **8** grandfather

5 **1** *b* **2** f **3** a **4** e **5** c **6** d

6 **1** *library* **2** stadium **3** airport **4** bridge **5** school **6** station **7** museum

GRAMMAR REVIEW 1–3

Page 119

1a **1** *Whose* **2** Who is **3** Who has **4** Whose **5** Who is **6** Whose **7** Who has **8** Whose

b **1** *Adam's* **2** *Adam* **3** Adam **4** Adam's **5** Adam **6** Adam's **7** Adam **8** Adam's

2 **1** *a* **2** d **3** b **4** e **5** c **6** g **7** f

3 **1** *your* **2** don't **3** my **4** at **5** has **6** do **7** her **8** ask **9** What is **10** sister's

4 **1** *plays* **2** likes **3** doesn't **4** are **5** wears **6** they

Unit 4

VOCABULARY 1

Page 120

1 **1** *listen to music* **2** go shopping **3** watch television **4** play the piano **5** play video games **6** meet friends **7** go on the internet **8** ride a bike

2 **1** *listen to music* **2** ride a bike **3** watch television **4** go shopping **5** play the piano **6** go on the internet **7** meet friends **8** play video games

3 (word snake reads: close, come, cry, end, *go out*, arrive, get, stand, take off, talk to)

1 *go out* **2** end **3** cry **4** come **5** close **6** talk to **7** take off **8** stand **9** get **10** arrive

4 **1** *talk to; listen to* **2** arrive; leave **3** stay in; go out **4** get; send **5** take off; take off **6** sit; stand

READING

Page 121

1 **1** *top* **2** message **3** dates **4** correct

2 **1** *blogs* ✓ **6** text messages ✓ **7** internet forums ✓

3 a ✓

4 2, 5, 4, 3, 1, 6

5 **1** Sophie (C/Carter) **2** 3 **3** Because she loves movies. **4** He thinks the love story is boring. **5** He's not interested in vampires or love stories. **6** He thinks there are great actors in it.

GRAMMAR 1

Page 122

1 **1** am ('m) **2** are ('re) **3** are not (aren't) **4** she (note: can also be *he*, but *she* is best option since related short answer also uses *she*) **5** is

2 **1** *a* **2** b **3** b **4** a **5** b

3 **1** 's walking/is walking **2** 's reading/is reading **3** 're playing/are playing **4** 're riding/are riding

Page 123

4 **1** *am/'m getting out of* **2** is/'s watching **3** isn't / is not / 's not working **4** is/'s sitting **5** am/'m not feeling **6** are/'re going **7** Is (Matt) going **8** Am (I) sitting

5 **1** *now* **2** studying **3** not studying **4** are you going **5** I'm meeting **6** are **7** 're **8** I'm leaving

6 **1** *Why's Jill smiling?* **2** Are you leaving tomorrow? **3** Are you going anywhere? **4** The children are laughing. **5** Matt is reading the newspaper. **6** When is your mother coming home? **7** Who is going to the party tomorrow? **8** Are you waiting for me?

7 **1** + *We're going to the movies later.*
– *We aren't going to the movies later.*
? *Are we going to the movies later?*

2 + He's / He is going to the party.
– He isn't / is not going to the party.
? Is he going to the party?

3 + She's / She is crying.
– She isn't / is not crying.
? Is she crying?

4 + They're / They are playing computer games.
– They aren't / are not playing computer games.
? Are they playing computer games?

5 + You're / You are listening to music.
– You aren't / are not listening to music.
? Are you listening to music?

LISTENING

Page 124

1 **1** *speaking* **2** information **3** sounds

2 **1** *announcement* **2** conversation **3** audio tour **4** lesson

3 **1** *announcement* **2** audio tour **3** conversation **4** lesson

4 **1** *café* **2** store **3** school **4** museum

5 **1** *milk and orange juice* **2** The store is closing. **3** 10 minutes before the exam starts (or similar) **4** Picasso

VOCABULARY 2

Page 125

1 **1** *café* **2** entrance **3** first **4** information **5** elevator **6** second **7** restrooms **8** gift **9** ticket **10** stairs

E	R	P	A	K	T	S	E	G	R	Z	D
I	A	E	S	C	T	T	E	E	I	R	D
S	N	F	S	E	R	T	T	C	Q	F	H
T	K	F	K	T	T	L	S	Z	O	E	T
A	M	C	O	I	R	T	A	W	F	N	T
I	I	J	Y	R	E	O	N	W	B	T	D
R	R	O	O	L	M	Z	O	B	J	R	C
S	G	G	I	Y	E	A	E	M	U	A	A
K	C	A	F	E	T	E	T	L	S	N	R
G	T	F	I	R	S	T	W	I	F	C	O
E	L	E	V	A	T	O	R	F	O	E	V
Y	J	D	T	I	C	K	E	T	S	N	F

2 **1** *gift shop* **2** first **3** café **4** second **5** elevator **6** stairs **7** entrance **8** ticket office **9** restrooms **10** information desk

Words & Beyond

3 **1** *truth* **2** announcement **3** exhibition **4** event **5** park **6** umbrella **7** playground **8** tour

4 **1** *looking forward to* **2** festival **3** social networking **4** performer **5** hip hop

GRAMMAR 2
Page 126

1 **1** is studying **2** now **3** always **4** plays **5** every day

2 Simple present: always, hardly ever, most of the time, never, often, sometimes, usually
Present progressive: *at the moment*, later, now, this week, today

3 **1** *b* **2** e **3** a **4** c **5** d **6** f

4 **1** *Are they coming* **2** Ana doing **3** Do they have **4** are you doing **5** 're studying **6** Do you drink **5a** **a** *Are you coming* **b** am/'m walking **c** goes **d** eat **e** Do (they usually) study **f** don't drink **g** is/'s sleeping **h** are not / aren't coming

5b **1** *f* **2** e **3** b **4** a **5** c **6** d

SPEAKING
Page 127

1 Suggested answers: Where is the museum? How much does it cost? When does it open/close?

2 restrooms 1 closing times 3 a café 2

3 **1** *Where's* **2** cost **3** time **4** get **5** question **6** ask **7** help **8** welcome

WRITING
Page 128

1 **1** a main heading **2** other headings

2 **1** *winter fair* **2** Sunday **3** homemade food **4** free for children, $6 for over 16 on site, or $5 online in advance

3 **1** *a* **2** d **3** c **4** f **5** e **6** b

LIFE SKILLS
Page 129

1 Suggested answer: Andrea needs to take some Colombian students on a shopping trip around New York City. She doesn't know where to take them.

2 Suggested answer: friends, family, the internet, "What's Happening" pages in magazines/newspapers, guidebook

3 Suggested answer:
Hi, Andrea.
Don't panic! There are a lot of really good websites that tell you where to go in New York City. You can also borrow a guidebook from a library. Or you could try asking your friends for ideas.

VOCABULARY REVIEW 1–4
Page 130

1 **1** *square* **2** library **3** stadium **4** station **5** mall **6** museum **7** building **8** airport **9** elevator **10** café

2 **1** *vacuum cleaner* **2** cabinet **3** toys **4** sofa **5** armchair **6** refrigerator **7** bookshelf **8** carpet **9** closet **10** dishwasher

3 **1** *g* **2** f **3** b **4** d **5** e **6** a **7** c **8** h

4 **1** *start school* **2** get up **3** have my breakfast **4** take a shower **5** get dressed **6** brush my hair **7** ride my bike **8** have lunch **9** get home **10** do my homework **11** go swimming

GRAMMAR REVIEW 1–4
Page 131

1 **1** *in*, on **2** between **3** in front of **4** on, on **5** near / next to, at **6** next to / near **7** near / next to, on **8** in, next to / near

2 **1** *sometimes* **2** always **3** rarely **4** often **5** never **6** later **7** at six o'clock **8** next weekend

3 **1** *think* **2** 's jumping **3** 's shopping **4** 'm living **5** live **6** have **7** 's raining **8** rains

Unit 5

VOCABULARY 1
Page 132

1 **1** *fish* **2** tea; juice **3** steak; burger **4** soup **5** egg 6 yogurt; cheese **7** pasta **8** grape **9** rice

S	Z	N	I	J	W	R	K
A	Y	P	J	U	I	C	E
G	O	A	F	I	S	H	R
R	G	S	O	U	P	E	I
A	U	T	O	M	E	E	C
P	R	A	D	E	G	S	E
E	T	B	U	R	G	E	R
S	T	E	A	K	T	E	A
E	W	G	E	R	Z	Y	S

2 **1** *potatoes* **2** vegetable **3** butter **4** green **5** sugar **6** yellow **7** cookie **8** bread **9** meat

3 **1** ✓ **2** ✗ **3** ✓ **4** ✗ **5** ✓ **6** ✗ **7** ✗ **8** ✓

4 **1** *cake* **2** candy **3** soda **4** juice **5** carrot

5a **1** *tomato* **2** milk **3** meat **4** onions **5** chocolate **6** rice **7** pasta

5b **a** 3 **b** 4 **c** 6 **d** 1 **e** 2 **f** 7 **g** 5

READING
Page 133

1 **1** *Identify* **2** Look **3** underline **4** Decide

2 **1** *anybody* (cook, rice) **2** parents (child, lunch) **3** students (can't eat in class) **4** students (talk to a partner) **5** teachers (tell your class) **6** students (check) **7** anybody (vegetable soup)

3 **1** *c* **2** b **3** a

4 **1** *d* **2** b **3** a

GRAMMAR 1
Page 134

1 **1** singular **2** plural **3** affirmative **4** many **5** negative **6** countable **7** offers

2 Much: *cheese*, bread, food, meat, pasta, rice
Many: *bananas*, carrots, oranges, eggs, potatoes, sandwiches

3 **1** *much* **2** many **3** many **4** much **5** many **6** much

4 **1** *any* **2** some **3** a **4** a **5** some **6** many **7** any/some **8** any **9** some

Page 135

5 **1** *b* **2** c **3** a **4** a **5** b **6** c **7** a **8** a **9** c

6 **1** *much* **2** many **3** any **4** some **5** any **6** some **7** any/some **8** some

7 **1** *We don't have much food.* **2** I have a pen and some paper. **3** We don't have any meat. **4** Do we have any vegetables? **5** Let's buy a bag of carrots and some broccoli. **6** I hope you have a lot of money.

LISTENING
Page 136

1 **1** *voice* **2** old **3** topic **4** people

2 three

3 **1** *c* **2** a **3** b

4 b

5 Speaker 1 *d* Speaker 2 c Speaker 3 a Speaker 4 b

7 Speaker 1: a Speaker 2: c Speaker 3: b

VOCABULARY 2
Page 137

1 **1** *tired* **2** stressed **3** unhappy **4** sick **5** lucky **6** well **7** healthy **8** lazy **9** busy

2 **Positive meaning:** *busy*, healthy, well, active, lucky **Negative meaning:** sick, stressed, lazy, unhappy, tired

S	L	O	E	S	I	C	K	L	D
N	T	V	S	X	F	D	R	A	Q
U	L	R	T	I	R	E	D	Z	N
N	L	P	E	W	Q	B	V	Y	H
H	Q	U	E	S	I	W	I	L	E
A	T	L	C	H	S	L	G	V	A
P	L	K	W	K	J	E	I	K	L
P	G	C	E	A	Y	T	D	K	T
Y	Y	A	R	B	C	M	H	P	H
O	Y	A	G	A	B	U	S	Y	Y

Words & Beyond

3 **1** *menu* **2** dish **3** onions **4** sauce **5** dessert **6** lemon

4 **1** *a* **2** b **3** c **4** a **5** b **6** c

GRAMMAR 2
Page 138

1 **1** enjoy **2** hate **3** noun/verb **4** verb/noun

2 **1** *driving* **2** running **3** swimming **4** using **5** writing **6** riding **7** traveling **8** visiting

3 **1** ✗ *I love eating fries.* **2** ✗ I enjoy cooking. **3** ✓ **4** ✗ I hate being late **5** ✗ Javier likes playing tennis. **6** ✗ Hannah doesn't like getting up early. **7** ✓

4 **1** *Where do you like going out for dinner?* **2** Why don't you like parties? **3** Which subject do you enjoy studying? **4** Why don't you like fish? **5** Do you dislike cooking? **6** What's your favorite meal?

5 **a** 2 **b** 4 **c** 6 **d** 1 **e** 3 **f** 5

6 **1** *Felipe loves riding his new bike.* **2** He likes/enjoys going to school on the bike. **3** He doesn't like / dislikes taking tests. **4** He hates shopping with his little brother. **5** He likes/enjoys studying art. **6** He doesn't like / dislikes eating meat. **7** He loves meeting new people.

SPEAKING

Page 139

1 **1** *fantastic* **2** sorry **3** terrible **4** believe **5** amazing

3 The dog's missing. / Romeo's missing. (or similar)

4 **1** The dog's back home. / Romeo is back home. **2** He has a girlfriend, and her name's Juliet.

WRITING

Page 140

1 **1** *reasons* **2** Why **3** verb **4** Don't use

2 **1** ✓ **2** ✗ **3** ✓ **4** ✗ **5** ✓ **6** ✗ **7** ✗

3 **1** e **2** a **3** f **4** c **5** d **6** b

LIFE SKILLS

Page 141

1 **1** *say* **2** Ask **3** share **4** Don't write **5** Think **6** Be polite **7** block **8** tell

VOCABULARY REVIEW 1–5

Page 142

1 **1** *b* **2** c **3** a **4** d **5** e

2 **1** *seasons* **2** lunchtime **3** Northern Lights **4** shines **5** mess **6** windy

3 **1** *café* **2** floor **3** elevator **4** office **5** first **6** desk

4 **1** *bridge* **2** tower **3** sports center **4** park **5** airport **6** station **7** square

5 **1** *get up* **2** take **3** get **4** eat **5** do **6** brush **7** pack **8** go

GRAMMAR REVIEW 1–5

Page 143

1 **1** *any* **2** don't **3** any **4** some **5** want **6** us **7** My **8** yours

2 **1** *Are* **2** am **3** 'm/am **4** Do **5** 's/is **6** don't **7** are **8** Do

3 **1** Where, friend's **2** What, I'm waiting **3** How, never go **4** When, At **5** Who, do **6** Which, Italy **7** How, use **8** Who, isn't **9** What, like **10** Why, It's

4 **1** *a* **2** c **3** c **4** b **5** c **6** a **7** c

Macmillan Education
4 Crinan Street
London N1 9XW
A division of Macmillan Publishers Limited

Companies and representatives throughout the world

ISBN 978-1-380-00778-0

Written by Anna Cole, David Corp, and Alexandra Hearn

Go Beyond First published 2015
First edition entitled *Beyond* published 2015

Designed by EMC Design Ltd.

Cover design by EMC Design Ltd.

On-body design by Dynamo Studio, Co.

Full acknowledgements for illustrations and photographs in the facsimile pages can be found in the *Move Beyond* combined Student's Book/Workbook.

Printed and bound in China

2021 2020 2019 2018 2017
10 9 8 7 6 5 4 3 2 1